Building an Intranet

M000159875

Network Security Tips

- ✔ Choose a proper password for all accounts with administrative privileges.
- ✔ Use a secure file system, and make sure that you have secured any important files.
- ✔ Use and examine auditing provided by your operating system and web servers.
- ✔ Make backups! Have a backup of the state your system was in before it was brought up online. Perform backups in a regularly scheduled manner.
- ✔ Have a disaster recovery plan in place. Know how to contact the proper authorities to report any network compromises.
- ✔ Use a virus scanner on your network clients and web servers.

Quick List of Abbreviations

CGI (Common Gateway Interface): Common Gateway Interface (CGI) is a way to write programs that run on your web server. You can use CGI programs to process form information, perform searches of your intranet web site, and other neat things. CGI programs are mostly written by serious programmers.

HTML (HyperText Markup Language): HyperText Markup Language is the language you use to create Web pages. HTML tells the web browser how every piece of text and image needs to appear.

HTTP (HyperText Transfer Protocol): HTTP is the language web browsers and web servers when they talk to each other.

LDAP (Lightweight Directory Access Protocol): LDAP is a way to communicate that's used by directory/ user locator servers. Many virtual meeting applications use this standard to provide access to the list of users that are currently available to conference with.

MIME (Multimedia Internet Mail Extensions): MIME is a way to encode normal text mail messages so that you can include attachments such as pictures, formatted text, and sound files.

PDF (Portable Document Format): PDF is the format used by Adobe Acrobat to save your documents for the Acrobat Reader.

POP (Post Office Protocol): POP is a way for e-mail clients such as Eudora and Netscape mail to read e-mail messages from a mail server.

SMTP (Simple Mail Transfer Protocol): SMTP is a way for a mail client to send mail to a mail server.

TCP/IP (Transmission Control Protocol/Internet Protocol): TCP/IP is the networking protocol used on the Internet and intranets that allows all computers on these networks to talk to each other.

URL (Uniform Resource Locator): URL is the address of a web page. Much like your home address tells someone where you live, a URL tells your web browser where the web page can be found. The most typical URLs you will see look something like `http://website`. The `http://` part just means that you're looking for a document that's written using HTML standards, and the `website` is where you can find that document. Most browsers let you just enter the stuff after `http://` and still get you to the web site.

IDG BOOKS WORLDWIDE

...For Dummies: #1 Computer Book Series for Beginners

Building an Intranet For Dummies®

Cheat Sheet

Assembling Your Intranet Management Team

The key members of your intranet management team include:

- **Management:** Direct support from your corporate management for your intranet certainly enhances your chances of success. However, you also need to realize that management support isn't an absolute necessity. Blasphemy, you say? Well, perhaps, but many intranets begin as pet projects of specific departments and slowly grow into an organizational project — which can be a good thing. To move your intranet into a role as a resource for your entire organization, however, you absolutely need the support of corporate management. Corporate management can be a big asset in setting the overall goals and tone of your intranet — they undoubtedly have certain goals to meet with an intranet.

- **Webmaster:** The director of the show is the webmaster. The webmaster is charged with keeping the overall continuity for your intranet web site. While intranets can truly become an organization-wide collaborative effort, someone needs to have the task of keeping a common look and feel. The major benefit of an intranet comes from its ease of use, and your intranet web site needs to provide web pages that are consistent to realize this benefit.

- **Department Heads — Content Creators:** As with a good show, someone needs to create a script, or in the case of an intranet, a plan. A good plan specifies where you want to go with your intranet and how you're going to get there. Department and division heads are the best people for gathering together the information relevant to their areas of responsibility. They may also consider gathering suggestions for web pages and intranet-based applications that they and their employees would like to see deployed. These department and division heads can then relay their suggestions to the webmaster for implementation.

- **Special Effects Crew:** If your company is big enough, you may have an art department where you can offload the development of your intranet web site graphics. If you're working for a smaller company, you may need to be your own special effects department. While the graphically based special effects are not at all critical to the success of your intranet, they can bring a level of sophistication and polish to your intranet.

- **IS Support Staff:** While the IS support staff can sometimes be hidden behind the scenes, they are the individuals charged with keeping your intranet running and answering user questions. If your users can't access or don't understand how to use your intranet, it won't be useful to your organization. Support staff needs to be easily available and willing to help users work out their difficulties.

Important Intranet Related Web Sites

- Microsoft Intranet Solutions Center: www.microsoft.com/intranet
- Building an Intranet from Fortune Magazine: pathfinder.com/fortune/specials/intranets/index.html
- Intranet Solutions: home.netscape.com/comprod/at_work/index.html
- The Intranet Resource Center: www.cio.com/WebMaster/wm_irc.html
- Intranut: www.intranut.com
- Intranet Journal: www.intranetjournal.com
- Intranet Design Magazine: www.innergy.com
- A Guide to Intraprise-Wide Computing: www.process.com/news/intrawp.com
- The Intranet Information Page: www.strom.com/pubwork/intranet.html
- The Complete Intranet Resource: www.intrack.com/intranet

...For Dummies: #1 Computer Book Series for Beginners

®

References for the Rest of Us!®

COMPUTER BOOK SERIES FROM IDG

Are you intimidated and confused by computers? Do you find that traditional manuals are overloaded with technical details you'll never use? Do your friends and family always call you to fix simple problems on their PCs? Then the *...For Dummies®* computer book series from IDG Books Worldwide is for you.

...For Dummies books are written for those frustrated computer users who know they aren't really dumb but find that PC hardware, software, and indeed the unique vocabulary of computing make them feel helpless. *...For Dummies* books use a lighthearted approach, a down-to-earth style, and even cartoons and humorous icons to diffuse computer novices' fears and build their confidence. Lighthearted but not lightweight, these books are a perfect survival guide for anyone forced to use a computer.

Already, millions of satisfied readers agree. They have made *...For Dummies* books the #1 introductory level computer book series and have written asking for more. So, if you're looking for the most fun and easy way to learn about computers, look to *...For Dummies* books to give you a helping hand.

BUILDING AN INTRANET FOR DUMMIES®

BUILDING AN INTRANET FOR DUMMIES®

by John Fronckowiak

Foreword by Louis J. F. Boyle
VP and Chief Information Officer (CIO)
Computer Task Group

IDG BOOKS
WORLDWIDE

IDG Books Worldwide, Inc.
An International Data Group Company

Foster City, CA ♦ Chicago, IL ♦ Indianapolis, IN ♦ Southlake, TX

Building an Intranet For Dummies®

Published by
IDG Books Worldwide, Inc.
An International Data Group Company
919 E. Hillsdale Blvd.
Suite 400
Foster City, CA 94404
www.idgbooks.com (IDG Books Worldwide Web site)
www.dummies.com (Dummies Press Web site)

Library of Congress Catalog Card No.: 97-80307

ISBN: 0-7645-0276-X

Printed in the United States of America

10 9 8 7 6 5 4 3 2 1

1DD/SS/QZ/ZX/IN

Distributed in the United States by IDG Books Worldwide, Inc.

Distributed by Macmillan Canada for Canada; by Transworld Publishers Limited in the United Kingdom; by IDG Norge Books for Norway; by IDG Sweden Books for Sweden; by Woodslane Pty. Ltd. for Australia; by Woodslane Enterprises Ltd. for New Zealand; by Longman Singapore Publishers Ltd. for Singapore, Malaysia, Thailand, and Indonesia; by Simron Pty. Ltd. for South Africa; by Toppan Company Ltd. for Japan; by Distribuidora Cuspide for Argentina; by Livraria Cultura for Brazil; by Ediciencia S.A. for Ecuador; by Addison-Wesley Publishing Company for Korea; by Ediciones ZETA S.C.R. Ltda. for Peru; by WS Computer Publishing Corporation, Inc., for the Philippines; by Unalis Corporation for Taiwan; by Contemporanea de Ediciones for Venezuela; by Computer Book & Magazine Store for Puerto Rico; by Express Computer Distributors for the Caribbean and West Indies. Authorized Sales Agent: Anthony Rudkin Associates for the Middle East and North Africa.

For general information on IDG Books Worldwide's books in the U.S., please call our Consumer Customer Service department at 800-762-2974. For reseller information, including discounts and premium sales, please call our Reseller Customer Service department at 800-434-3422.

For information on where to purchase IDG Books Worldwide's books outside the U.S., please contact our International Sales department at 415-655-3200 or fax 415-655-3295.

For information on foreign language translations, please contact our Foreign & Subsidiary Rights department at 415-655-3021 or fax 415-655-3281.

For sales inquiries and special prices for bulk quantities, please contact our Sales department at 415-655-3200 or write to the address above.

For information on using IDG Books Worldwide's books in the classroom or for ordering examination copies, please contact our Educational Sales department at 800-434-2086 or fax 817-251-8174.

For press review copies, author interviews, or other publicity information, please contact our Public Relations department at 415-655-3000 or fax 415-655-3299.

For authorization to photocopy items for corporate, personal, or educational use, please contact Copyright Clearance Center, 222 Rosewood Drive, Danvers, MA 01923, or fax 508-750-4470.

About the Author

John W. Fronckowiak is president and founder of IDC Consulting, Inc., a company that specializes in Internet/intranet consulting, application development, and network consulting. He has extensive experience with database application development, client server networking, Internet and intranet presence development, application development, and project management.

John currently holds degrees in Computer Science and Management Information Systems. He has performed a number of research projects using Artificial Intelligence and Expert Systems. He has also worked on projects that have involved creating large database data repositories, and data mining of these repositories using neural networks.

John has actively been on the Internet since the early eighties. He has helped a number of corporations develop a Web presence, including assisting businesses in developing their own internal intranets.

John lives in East Amherst, New York with his wife Diane and their cat Eiffel. He is a part time Computer Science graduate student at the State University of New York at Buffalo, a member of Mensa, and listed in Who's Who In Media and Communications.

John's previous writing experience includes *Microsoft BackOffice 2 Unleashed* and *Microsoft BackOffice 2.5 Unleashed, Teach Yourself Database Programming With Visual J++ In 21 Days,* and *Teach Yourself OLE DB and ADO In 21 Days.* John also a writes the *Visual J++ Corner* column for *Java Developers Journal.*

John can be reached at `john@buffnet.net`.

ABOUT IDG BOOKS WORLDWIDE

Welcome to the world of IDG Books Worldwide.

IDG Books Worldwide, Inc., is a subsidiary of International Data Group, the world's largest publisher of computer-related information and the leading global provider of information services on information technology. IDG was founded more than 25 years ago and now employs more than 8,500 people worldwide. IDG publishes more than 275 computer publications in over 75 countries (see listing below). More than 60 million people read one or more IDG publications each month.

Launched in 1990, IDG Books Worldwide is today the #1 publisher of best-selling computer books in the United States. We are proud to have received eight awards from the Computer Press Association in recognition of editorial excellence and three from *Computer Currents'* First Annual Readers' Choice Awards. Our best-selling *...For Dummies®* series has more than 30 million copies in print with translations in 30 languages. IDG Books Worldwide, through a joint venture with IDG's Hi-Tech Beijing, became the first U.S. publisher to publish a computer book in the People's Republic of China. In record time, IDG Books Worldwide has become the first choice for millions of readers around the world who want to learn how to better manage their businesses.

Our mission is simple: Every one of our books is designed to bring extra value and skill-building instructions to the reader. Our books are written by experts who understand and care about our readers. The knowledge base of our editorial staff comes from years of experience in publishing, education, and journalism — experience we use to produce books for the '90s. In short, we care about books, so we attract the best people. We devote special attention to details such as audience, interior design, use of icons, and illustrations. And because we use an efficient process of authoring, editing, and desktop publishing our books electronically, we can spend more time ensuring superior content and spend less time on the technicalities of making books.

You can count on our commitment to deliver high-quality books at competitive prices on topics you want to read about. At IDG Books Worldwide, we continue in the IDG tradition of delivering quality for more than 25 years. You'll find no better book on a subject than one from IDG Books Worldwide.

John Kilcullen
CEO
IDG Books Worldwide, Inc.

Steven Berkowitz
President and Publisher
IDG Books Worldwide, Inc.

VIII
WINNER
*Eighth Annual
Computer Press
Awards ≥1992*

IX
WINNER
*Ninth Annual
Computer Press
Awards ≥1993*

X
WINNER
*Tenth Annual
Computer Press
Awards ≥1994*

XI
WINNER
*Eleventh Annual
Computer Press
Awards ≥1995*

IDG Books Worldwide, Inc., is a subsidiary of International Data Group, the world's largest publisher of computer-related information and the leading global provider of information services on information technology. International Data Group publishes over 275 computer publications in over 75 countries. Sixty million people read one or more International Data Group publications each month. International Data Group's publications include: **ARGENTINA:** Buyer's Guide, Computerworld Argentina, PC World Argentina; **AUSTRALIA:** Australian Macworld, Australian PC World, Australian Reseller News, Computerworld, IT Casebook, Network World, Publish, Webmaster; **AUSTRIA:** Computerwelt Osterreich, Networks Austria, PC Tip Austria; **BANGLADESH:** PC World Bangladesh; **BELARUS:** PC World Belarus; **BELGIUM:** Data News; **BRAZIL:** Annuário de Informática, Computerworld, Connections, Macworld, PC Player, PC World, Publish, Reseller News, Supergamepower; **BULGARIA:** Computerworld Bulgaria, Network World Bulgaria, PC & MacWorld Bulgaria; **CANADA:** CIO Canada, Client/Server World, ComputerWorld Canada, InfoWorld Canada, NetworkWorld Canada, WebWorld; **CHILE:** Computerworld Chile, PC World Chile; **COLOMBIA:** Computerworld Colombia, PC World Colombia; **COSTA RICA:** PC World Centro America; **THE CZECH AND SLOVAK REPUBLICS:** Computerworld Czechoslovakia, Macworld Czech Republic, PC World Czechoslovakia; **DENMARK:** Communications World Danmark, Computerworld Danmark, Macworld Danmark, PC World Danmark, Techworld Denmark; **DOMINICAN REPUBLIC:** PC World Republica Dominicana; **ECUADOR:** PC World Ecuador; **EGYPT:** Computerworld Middle East, PC World Middle East; **EL SALVADOR:** PC World Centro America; **FINLAND:** MikroPC, Tietoverkko, Tietoviikko; **FRANCE:** Distributique, Hebdo, Info PC, Le Monde Informatique, Macworld, Reseaux & Telecoms, WebMaster France; **GERMANY:** Computer Partner, Computerwoche, Computerwoche Extra, Computerwoche FOCUS, Global Online, Macwelt, PC Welt; **GREECE:** Amiga Computing, GamePro Greece, Multimedia World; **GUATEMALA:** PC World Centro America; **HONDURAS:** PC World Centro America; **HONG KONG:** Computerworld Hong Kong, PC World Hong Kong, Publish in Asia; **HUNGARY:** ABCD CD-ROM, Computerworld Szamitastechnika, Internetto online Magazine, PC World Hungary, PC-X Magazin Hungary; **ICELAND:** Tolvuheimur PC World Island; **INDIA:** Information Communications World, Information Systems Computerworld, PC World India, Publish in Asia; **INDONESIA:** InfoKomputer PC World, Komputek Computerworld, Publish in Asia; **IRELAND:** ComputerScope, PC Live!; **ISRAEL:** Macworld Israel, People & Computers/Computerworld; **ITALY:** Computerworld Italia, Macworld Italia, Networking Italia, PC World Italia; **JAPAN:** DTP World, Macworld Japan, Nikkei Personal Computing, OS/2 World Japan, SunWorld Japan, Windows NT World, Windows World Japan; **KENYA:** PC World East African; **KOREA:** Hi-Tech Information, Macworld Korea, PC World Korea; **MACEDONIA:** PC World Macedonia; **MALAYSIA:** Computerworld Malaysia, PC World Malaysia, Publish in Asia; **MALTA:** PC World Malta; **MEXICO:** Computerworld Mexico, PC World Mexico; **MYANMAR:** PC World Myanmar; **NETHERLANDS:** Computer! Totaal, LAN Internetworking Magazine, LAN World Buyers Guide, Macworld Netherlands, Net, WebWereld; **NEW ZEALAND:** Absolute Beginners Guide and Plain & Simple Series, Computer Buyer, Computer Industry Directory, Computerworld New Zealand, MTB, Network World, PC World New Zealand; **NICARAGUA:** PC World Centro America; **NORWAY:** Computerworld Norge, CW Rapport, Datamagasinet, Financial Rapport, Kursguide Norge, Macworld Norge, Multimediaworld Norge, PC World Ekspress Norge, PC World Nettverk, PC World Norge, PC World ProduktGuide Norge; **PAKISTAN:** Computerworld Pakistan; **PANAMA:** PC World Panama; **PEOPLE'S REPUBLIC OF CHINA:** China Computer Users, China Computerworld, China InfoWorld, China Telecom World Weekly, Computer & Communication, Electronic Design China, Electronics Today, Electronics Weekly, Game Software, PC World China, Popular Computer Week, Software Weekly, Software World, Telecom World; **PERU:** Computerworld Peru, PC World Profesional Peru, PC World SoHo Peru; **PHILIPPINES:** Click!, Computerworld Philippines, PC World Philippines, Publish in Asia; **POLAND:** Computerworld Poland, Computerworld Special Report Poland, Cyber, Macworld Poland, Networld Poland, PC World Komputer; **PORTUGAL:** Cerebro/PC World, Computerworld/Correio Informático, Dealer World Portugal, Mac*In/PC*In Portugal, Multimedia World; **PUERTO RICO:** PC World Puerto Rico; **ROMANIA:** Computerworld Romania, PC World Romania, Telecom Romania; **RUSSIA:** Computerworld Russia, Mir PK, Publish, Seti; **SINGAPORE:** Computerworld Singapore, PC World Singapore, Publish in Asia; **SLOVENIA:** Monitor; **SOUTH AFRICA:** Computing SA, Network World SA, Software World SA; **SPAIN:** Communicaciones World España, Computerworld España, Dealer World España, Macworld España, PC World España; **SRI LANKA:** Infolink PC World; **SWEDEN:** CAP&Design, Computer Sweden, Corporate Computing Sweden, Internetworld Sweden, it.branschen, Macworld Sweden, MaxiData Sweden, MikroDatorn, Nätverk & Kommunikation, PC World Sweden, PCaktiv, Windows World Sweden; **SWITZERLAND:** Computerworld Schweiz, Macworld Schweiz, PCtip; **TAIWAN:** Computerworld Taiwan, Macworld Taiwan, NEW ViSiON/Publish, PC World Taiwan; **THAILAND:** Publish in Asia, Thai Computerworld; **TURKEY:** Computerworld Turkiye, Macworld Turkiye, Network World Turkiye, PC World Turkiye; **UKRAINE:** Computerworld Kiev, Multimedia World Ukraine, PC World Ukraine; **UNITED KINGDOM:** Acorn User UK, Amiga Action UK, Amiga Computing UK, Apple Talk UK, Computing, Macworld, Parents and Computers UK, PC Advisor, PC Home, PSX Pro, The WEB; **UNITED STATES:** Cable in the Classroom, CIO Magazine, Computerworld, DOS World, Federal Computer Week, GamePro Magazine, InfoWorld, I-Way, Macworld, Network World, PC Games, PC World, Publish, Video Event, THE WEB Magazine, and WebMaster; online webzines: JavaWorld, NetscapeWorld, and SunWorld Online; **URUGUAY:** InfoWorld Uruguay; **VENEZUELA:** Computerworld Venezuela, PC World Venezuela; and **VIETNAM:** PC World Vietnam.   3/24/97

Dedication

In memory of my grandmother, Helen, and my godfather, Don.

Author's Acknowledgments

I would like to thank everyone that helped make this book possible. My wife Diane for helping me work through the day to day ups and downs while helping to keep me focused on my larger goals. My family — Mom, Dad, Kim, Mike, Marie, Mom S, Alicia, and Becky — for understanding and supporting my desire to write. I'd like to send special thanks to Studio B Productions, Inc. for presenting me with the opportunity to work on this project. David Rogelberg who believed in me and my abilities, and thought I would be a good fit for this project. And especially Brian Gill who has provided an immeasurable amount of assistance in working through the many details of this project I could never handle on my own. Thanks also goes to Gareth Hancock for giving me the opportunity to write this book, to Clark Scheffy who really helped to turn this book into the polished book you see before you, David Helda for working through the technical details, and all the unseen individuals who helped turn this book into reality. Finally thanks to my cat, Eiffel, for providing companionship and all those loud meows on weekend mornings to make sure I'd get up and get to work.

Publisher's Acknowledgments

We're proud of this book; please send us your comments about it by using the IDG Books Worldwide Registration Card at the back of the book or by e-mailing us at feedback/dummies@idgbooks.com. Some of the people who helped bring this book to market include the following:

Acquisitions, Development, and Editorial

Project Editor: Clark Scheffy

Acquisitions Editor: Gareth Hancock

Media Development Manager: Joyce Pepple

Associate Permissions Editor:
Heather H. Dismore

Copy Editors: William Barton, Elizabeth Kuball, Linda Stark, Suzanne Thomas

Technical Editor: David Helda

Editorial Manager: Mary C. Corder

Editorial Assistant: Michael Sullivan

Production

Project Coordinator: Valery Bourke

Layout and Graphics: Lou Boudreau, Angela Bush-Sisson, Maridee V. Ennis, Anna Rohrer, Brent Savage, Kathie Schutte M. Anne Sipahimalani, Deirdre Smith, Kate Snell

Proofreaders: Betty Kish, Carrie Voorhis, Kelli Botta, Rachel Garvey, Nancy Price, Rebecca Senninger, Robert Springer, Janet Withers, Karen York

Indexer: David Heiret

Special Help

Michael De Oliveira, IDG Books Worldwide, Indianapolis LAN site manager; Nancy DelFavero, Project Editor; Kevin Spencer, Associate Technical Editor; Karen York, Associate Project Coordinator

---

General and Administrative

IDG Books Worldwide, Inc.: John Kilcullen, CEO; Steven Berkowitz, President and Publisher

IDG Books Technology Publishing: Brenda McLaughlin, Senior Vice President and Group Publisher

Dummies Technology Press and Dummies Editorial: Diane Graves Steele, Vice President and Associate Publisher; Kristin A. Cocks, Editorial Director; Mary Bednarek, Acquisitions and Product Development Director

Dummies Trade Press: Kathleen A. Welton, Vice President and Publisher

IDG Books Production for Dummies Press: Beth Jenkins, Production Director; Cindy L. Phipps, Manager of Project Coordination, Production Proofreading, and Indexing; Kathie S. Schutte, Supervisor of Page Layout; Shelley Lea, Supervisor of Graphics and Design; Debbie J. Gates, Production Systems Specialist; Robert Springer, Supervisor of Proofreading; Debbie Stailey, Special Projects Coordinator; Tony Augsburger, Supervisor of Reprints and Bluelines; Leslie Popplewell, Media Archive Coordinator

Dummies Packaging and Book Design: Patti Sandez, Packaging Specialist; Lance Kayser, Packaging Assistant; Kavish + Kavish, Cover Design

♦

The publisher would like to give special thanks to Patrick J. McGovern, without whom this book would not have been possible.

♦

Contents at a Glance

Cartoons at a Glance

By Rich Tennant

page 295

page 275

page 81

page 311

page 247

page 7

Fax: 508-546-7747 • **E-mail:** the5wave@tiac.net

Table of Contents

Foreword

● ●

A mere three years ago, I was an intranet and Internet dummy, and now I am the Chief Information Officer of CTG (Computer Task Group), one of the country's leading information technology service providers. Back then, as I became CTG's first CIO, my job was to get the right information to the right people at the right time and I was looking for the best ideas and tools to get it done.

A company with 5,000 employees in 55 locations worldwide, CTG was fast becoming a leader in the information technology services marketplace, and we had to move fast to keep our position. We didn't take long to realize that in order to continue our growth, we had to connect: with investors, vendors, clients, the outside world, and most importantly, each other.

I hasten to add that the word *intranet* didn't even exist back then! I also say, a bit immodestly, that CTG eventually became one of the pioneers in implementing intranet and Internet technology — "bleeding edge" doesn't begin to describe our adventure into this uncharted territory, but my CTG colleagues and I persevered. Now we can boast state-of-the-art intranet and Internet sites, and we continue to push the envelope when it comes to using new technologies. However, looking back, all I can say is getting here wasn't easy.

In my job before CTG, I'd worked with several Internet technologies that seemed promising for what we were trying to do at CTG. So, we used what we knew from the Internet and created an "internal web site" (the term *intranet* hadn't even been coined yet). We lovingly dubbed it *CTG-Net,* and its goal was to give our colleagues access to the best practices and intellectual capital within our organization (other than Minesweeper and Solitaire, that is). Soon, we were exchanging information, sharing documents and using e-mail, all of which added value not only to our company, but also to our clients.

We thought we had it made! We were UNIX gurus, using the tools of the time, and the Internet infrastructure was mostly — and still is — UNIX based! What could be simpler than just extending this expertise to serve our internal needs, right? Not so fast. Things changed faster than we anticipated. When we started this process in 1993, the Internet/intranet world was pre-Graphical User Interface (GUI), pre-Java, pre-almost everything! We had a few neat tools like *gopher* (a way to get documents that predates web browsers), *Hytelnet* (a simple way to view text documents with hyperlinks that predates web pages), and something new a guy named Tim created — the World Wide Web. Now we were in mid-storm, but we had no how-to manual, no *Building an Intranet For Dummies.*

Intranets are powerful tools, especially in the way that they allow employees to communicate — regardless of time, location, or the size of the group. Recognizing this, CTG is still extending our intranet capabilities, using many of the tools John discusses in this book. With them, we've created a world-class, first-of-its-kind interactive knowledge application that's clearly driving our growth as a market leader. We can see it happening, and with this book, so can you.

John's comprehensive reference information will help you, shortly and simply, set up, manage, and run a really cool intranet. You, too, can join the ranks of the reformed intranet dummies gone intranet pros!

Louis J.F. Boyle

VP & Chief Information Officer (CIO)

Computer Task Group

Introduction

· ·

*W*elcome to *Building an Intranet For Dummies!* In this book, I walk you through the process of planning, building, and deploying your corporate intranet. I introduce you to all the cool new ways intranets are changing the way organizations share information, how to convince your boss that a corporate intranet is a good idea, and how to stay on top of the latest intranet developments. With this book, you get step-by-step instructions for getting your intranet up and running, concepts and terms explained in plain language, and tips on using all the cool tools out there to create your intranet and make it great. By the time you finish with any chapter, you have a new understanding of a key intranet concept and can get a new component of your intranet up and running on your own — don't worry, advice on how to wear a pocket protector isn't part of the deal. The goal here is to demystify the technology behind Intranets, and to get the nerd factor out of the equation.

About This Book

Maybe you got to this book because of a situation similar to the following:

You see the looming figure walking down the hall to your cubicle, your heart starts to pound faster and a little bead of sweat appears on your brow. Great, it's your boss! What now? The boss comes over to you and tells you about the big division head meeting next week — all of the division heads have been complaining about the computer network. It's not like it doesn't work, but isn't all this stuff supposed to help everyone communicate *better?* Seems like the network is just another daily roadblock to the constructive use of time, not a time-saver. Sales is complaining that it never has the most recent prices from Marketing; Marketing never knows what those guys in Research are working on and when it's going to be released; no one can ever find any of the information they need; and getting everyone away from their desk long enough to have a meaningful meeting is darn near impossible.

Oh, and by the way, you need to give a presentation with a plan to solve the computer network problems at the meeting next week.

You may as well have been asked to coach your office employee pool to the Super Bowl. That would have been easier. Oh well, you want to keep your job, you've only got a week, and you really don't want to walk into this meeting without an answer, so you grudgingly trudge on over to the book store to see if you can find any information on intranets.

You walk into the book store to see what's there, only to find that all the books on the shelf are about 900 pages. You don't have time for *War and Peace and Intranets* for crying out loud! You need a book that can explain Intranets and tell you about the latest technologies out there. You need a plan! And by next week!

You see it out of the corner of your eye, that comforting yellow glow of a ...*For Dummies* book! You pause, and yes! There it is, *Building an Intranet For Dummies*. You quickly thumb through it (cool! I can do this!). It shows you how to integrate a database, find things on the network, and broadcast information to the rest of the company! And a bunch of the stuff you need to get started is on the CD-ROM! You think, I can blow them away at this meeting! I can do better than just a plan — I can show everyone how this stuff works! Maybe a raise is in your future. . . . You rush to the cashier and buy the book, and then head back to the cubicle to get things rolling — so what if you've only got a week? No sweat.

How This Book Is Organized

I organize this book into six parts, each with a different main focus. In each part, you find a few chapters covering a specific topic in detail, including your options, the technobabble you may run into, and things to look out for. In chapters where I discuss a specific piece of technology, I even include numbered steps so that you can get your own version up and running today.

Part I: Creating an Intranet

With no time to waste, you roll up your sleeves and get right to work. While I begin with a brief overview of intranets, I jump into the process of selecting and configuring your web server almost immediately. I show you how to select the web server that's appropriate for your needs, and proceed right to installing and configuring a couple of examples so that you can have a web server working on your intranet by the end of work today! I know you can't do anything without a good plan, so I also include a chapter on putting together a plan for your intranet project. I wrap up this first part with a review of the client side and how to pick the browser that's right for your organization, and make sure that your client workstations are up to the task of participating in your fledgling intranet.

Part II: Using Your Intranet to Achieve World Domination

This part takes on the key hot intranet technologies and tackles them one at a time. Each technology is covered independently so you can select the one that's right for you at the moment and jump right in! To begin the discussion of each key technology, I review what it's all about, who can benefit from it, why you want it, where to find it, what you need to get it running (on both the client and server side). I also take the time to demystify the techno-babble that the nerds secretly use to try and make intranets difficult.

Part III: Intranet Administration

In this part, I review the important intranet security issues, and show you how to keep nasty people from mucking around with your intranet. I cover how to plan for disasters, implement virus scanners, and create backups so that in the event of a disaster, you can recover quickly. I end this section with a discussion of how to feed and care for your intranet over the long haul — how to monitor intranet activity, plan for problems, and manage future upgrades.

Part IV: Intranet Groundwork

For those that still need to convince their boss that this intranet stuff is a good idea, I show you how — I give you an arsenal of answers to all of your boss' key questions about the intranet, and show how to make the argument for an intranet without dropping to your knees and begging. In addition, to help keep your intranet up and running smoothly, I discuss how to build your intranet management team, and give you an overview of the roles everyone must play.

Part V: The Part of Tens

The traditional *...For Dummies* Part of Tens is not forgotten in *my* book! I answer the top ten frequently asked questions about intranets, show you the ten ways your intranet is different from the Internet, and ten ways to utilize your intranet in new and exciting ways.

Part VI: Appendixes

I wrap up with a reference guide covering the future of intranet technologies looming on the near horizon, and a guide to where you can find out more about intranets. Finally, I give you a reference of free (yes, FREE!) intranet tools, and intranet-related web sites and magazines worth checking out.

Who Are You?

I wrote this book with motivated employees, middle managers, and Information Systems (IS) department workers in mind. Whether you have been charged with the task, or just want to find out more about setting up a corporate intranet, you can find all you need to know inside these hallowed pages. I want to help you understand what an intranet is and how to get one working inside your company.

You can benefit from this book if you are someone who doesn't know (and doesn't want to know) all the boring technical details, and you just need to get the job done quickly and easily. I expect that you are someone who is a doer, not a person who sits and thinks about doing all day — you want to *build* an intranet, not read about intranets for the next five weeks. I mean, sure, I give you an overview of intranets technology and terms, but more importantly, I show you how to set one up on your own without a lot of silly jargon.

What You Need

Much of this book focuses on developing your intranet using a PC-based network running Microsoft-specific technologies. The reason I focus on Microsoft technology is because almost every one of the products I mention is available as a free download from the Internet — 0 dollars, tons of fun. Keep in mind that many of these downloads are full featured (do all that the store-bought versions do), but are *time-limited demos,* meaning that they stop working after a prescribed amount of time.

These Microsoft products are certainly not the only way to get the job done. I review the pros and cons of your technological alternatives — listing the alternative products that are available and how to go about obtaining them for free whenever possible. I do get down and dirty too — showing you how to get up and running with each different technology. While I focus on specific products as I go through these reviews — many of the concepts can be generally applied if you choose a different product. I've tried to focus on specific products that I personally have used and relied on to deploy intranets in various companies. To obtain the most from this book, you will find it useful to you have the following:

- ✔ **A computer that you can configure as your intranet web server.** Ideally, this is a machine running the latest version of Windows NT, but I also show you how to set up a smaller scale intranet using Windows 95-based web servers.

- ✔ **A local area network (LAN) using the TCP/IP-based protocol (Transfer Control Protocol/Internet Protocol).** If you have no familiarity at all with the TCP/IP networking protocol and you want more in-depth information about it, *TCP/IP For Dummies* by Marshal Wilensky and Candice Leiden (IDG Books Worldwide, Inc.) is a great introductory reference.

- ✔ **A connection to the Internet.** Many of the excellent tools and utilities you can use to create your intranet are available as free, free, FREE! downloads from the Internet. Along with my introduction and discussion of any freely available intranet tools, I include the Web addresses you need to pick them up or get more info on them.

A Field Guide to the Funny Icons

As you read through this book, you are likely to come across any of a variety of icon species. The following sections explain each icon's special niche and function in the vast field of intranet knowledge you are about to experience.

 Alerts you to a heavy dose of the nerd factor. You can skip these sections if you want — nobody cares, not even me. The nerd police don't have your home address and they won't quiz you on anything with the Technical Stuff icon. However, if you would like to understand the technical side, or pick up the latest cool tidbit to share at the next pocket protector party, jump right in!

 Indicates a note to the current discussion — I use this icon to point out an important fact or a reference to where material is covered in more depth elsewhere in the book.

 A Tip is just that — a nifty time saver or shortcut to help you use the information in this book even more effectively. I think of the tips as really helpful bits of information, almost the opposite of the technical stuff icons.

 This icon points to another *...For Dummies* book that covers a topic in much more depth than I can do in the space of this book.

The Remember icon highlights a juicey tidbit of information that is worth committing to your long-term memory.

Oooops! You want to watch out for these. I use the warning icon to alert you to potential pitfalls and even more importantly, how to steer clear of them. All I can say is pay careful attention to the warnings, and you should have no problem at all.

Navigate icons show you where you can go on the Internet or in this book to find additional information on a particular subject.

I include this icon to point out a piece of software that is included on the CD-ROM at the back of this book.

Jump In!

Different people come to this book with different needs and expectations. If you feel that you know enough about the concept of the intranet and you are ready to put yours together, go forward to Part I and jump right into the process of setting up and configuring your intranet. If you want a review of intranet background information, including assembling your intranet development team and planning the course of your intranet as it grows, you may want to jump ahead to Parts III and IV first. If you already have an intranet up and running and you want to explore what you can do with it, jump right in to Part II where I review all the key and hot intranet technologies in detail.

Keep in Touch!

I love to hear from readers! Please let me know what you like, dislike, or would like to see more of in this book. You can contact me care of:

IDG Books Worldwide, Inc.
7260 Shadeland Station, Suite 100
Indianapolis, IN 46256

You can also contact me directly though electronic mail at john@buffnet.net. Be sure to also visit the Dummies web site at www.dummies.com for more information on this book and other intranet related ...*For Dummies* titles. Finally, you can contact the publisher or other Dummies authors at info@idgbooks.com.

Part I
Creating an Intranet

The 5th Wave   By Rich Tennant

"For us it was total intranet integration or nothing. For instance, at this terminal alone I can access departmental data, printer and storage resources, ESPN, Home Shopping and the Sci-Fi channel."

In this part . . .

With no time to waste, this part is where you roll up your sleeves and start building your intranet. While I begin with a brief overview of intranets, I go pretty quickly into the process of selecting and configuring your web server. I show you how to select the web server that's appropriate for your needs, and proceed right to installation and configuration. I know you can't do anything without a good plan, so I continue by helping you get together a plan for your intranet. I wrap up this first part with a review of the client side — how to pick the browser that's right for you, and how to make sure that your client workstations are up to the task.

Chapter 1

You Can Pick Your Friends, You Can Pick Your Server, But . . .

In This Chapter

▶ Getting to know the differences between the Internet and an intranet

▶ What you need to get your own intranet up and running

▶ Selecting the intranet web server that's right for you and your company

▶ Getting the heart of your intranet pumping — how to get your intranet web server working

▶ Freaking out if things go wrong with your web server (and then fixing the problem)

*B*uilding an intranet, in the simplest sense, is just networking a bunch of computers together. Hang on — I don't get all technical here and expect you to understand the difference between NetBEUI, TCP/IP, and IPX (pronounced "netbeeyooEE, tissIPipp, and Ipcks — bless you!). If you have some familiarity with networking computers or working with computers on a network, you're already ahead of the game. For everyone else in the crowd, a network is a lot like a telephone system. You have a whole bunch of telephones in the world, and to talk to someone on another phone, all you need to do is pick up your handset and dial a number. Basically, all the telephones are wired to each other so that you can reach any other telephone from the one you have — the path that your phone call takes may go all over the place, but eventually, it gets to the phone with the number you dialed. Computer networking is pretty much the same: Instead of telephones, imagine computers. All the computers that are on the same network can talk to each other and share information, such as files, or other stuff that's connected to them, such as printers.

Now that you understand a little bit about networking computers, the next logical question is "What's an intranet? And what can I do with it?" Well, buckle your seat belt and strap yourself in, because you've just gotten on the latest, hottest, and coolest techno-thrill ride around — hang on, enjoy the ride, and have some fun!

Intra-what??

I'm sure you've heard of the *INTERnet* — how can you escape the buzz and excitement it's created in the past few years? You may not be so familiar, however, with the Internet's little cousin, the *INTRAnet*. Well, I do my best in this book to take you to new levels of enlightenment — at least as far as intranets are concerned. (If you're here looking for the meaning-of-life-type of enlightenment, I've been told the answer is 42.) So what's the difference between the INTRAnet and the INTERnet?

To understand what an intranet (I'm going to stop using capitals to distinguish INTER- from INTRA- — I think you get the point) is, you need to understand what the Internet is first. The Internet is a whole bunch of computers, all around the world, that can all talk to each other using the same language. (This language is called *TCP/IP*, which stands for Transmission Control Protocol/Internet Protocol.) From any computer that's on the Internet, you can pretty much talk to any other one as long as the owner allows you.

An intranet is pretty much the same thing as the Internet, just a lot smaller — instead of being a big, open, campus-wide, BYOCM (Bring Your Own Chocolate Milk) bash like the Internet, an intranet's more like an exclusive little party that requires you to present your invitation at the door before you can join in the festivities. The key to the success of this private party is that an intranet and the Internet both use the same popular and proven language (TCP/IP). And because just about every computer in the world needs to connect to the Internet and use this language, just about any type of computer in the world can also be a part of your intranet (including those Macintosh diehards in your Art department).

The history of intranets

Back in the late 1960s, the U.S. government created a computer experiment to test the idea of computer networking and to link together Department of Defense research contractors. This experiment was called the *ARPANET* (Advanced Research Project Administration Network). Many people who are often skeptical of the success of government projects may be surprised to learn that this little experiment slowly grew over the years into the unqualified success that today we call the *Internet.*

Corporations have been networking personal computers since the mid-1980s. As the Internet grew in popularity with the advent of the World Wide Web, it quickly became evident that this stuff was easy to use. People started thinking how cool things could be if they could bring together the connectivity of corporate networks with the ease of use of the Internet. Voilá — intranets were born. The *intra* part of the intranet name comes from the fact that these networks are primarily used internally by businesses.

Honey, I shrunk the Internet!

A useful old computer axiom that also applies to intranets says that *smaller means faster.* Generally, because they're smaller and private, intranets are much faster than the Internet, meaning that you can do everything you can do on the Internet as well as many of the things that may take too long, or are inappropriate to do on the Internet, like:

- ✔ **Publish corporate information** — for example, the latest product information, human resource handbooks, reports, marketing information, and even corporate telephone directories.

- ✔ **Provide access to electronic mail** — electronic mail provides a fast and easy way to distribute short messages and documents throughout your organization.

- ✔ **Conduct virtual meetings** — run advanced video conferencing applications on your intranet.

- ✔ **Provide an easy way to access centralized databases** — including asking questions of the database and displaying the answers in nicely formatted web pages.

- ✔ **Broadcast the latest corporate news and information to all computers at the same time.**

Remember that an intranet is more than any one of these applications — it's the sum of these applications working together to help your organization communicate more effectively and efficiently. You need to share information quickly within your organization, and a corporate intranet provides a cost-effective way to do that using technologies and applications that are already proven to work on the Internet.

Before you go out and create an intranet, you need to take into account many important business, management, and business culture considerations. If you haven't considered these issues yet, I discuss them in Chapters 2, 12, and 15.

What Do You Need?

Before you begin, you need to make sure that you've got the right stuff — not that you need the latest Super Computer to get your intranet off the ground, but you do need to have a few things in place before you begin. The discussion gets a little technical here, but don't worry — I walk you through things. If you don't know the answers to the questions that I ask, you may need to check with your Information Systems department or your resident computer guru.

You need two primary things to start building your intranet — think of these items as the foundation of your intranet:

- ✓ **A network that links together the computers you have in your company.** A LAN (Local Area Network) is what I'm talkin' about here.

- ✓ **A fast computer with a bunch of free disk space.** (Who doesn't want one?) This computer is where you store the files that you make available on your intranet. This computer doesn't need to be dedicated to storing intranet files — however, if it isn't, you find that as your intranet usership increases, this computer begins to slow down.

Do you have a Local Area Network (LAN)?

You need the answer to the following two all-important questions before you get started:

- ✓ **Does your company have a Local Area Network in place?** If you're not sure, an easy way to tell is if you have a place where you store files (on a shared central computer, called a *server*) that other people you work with can access. Another way to tell is if you have access to the Internet from your desktop (without using a modem) — if you do, you also have a Local Area Network in place. If you're not sure, you may need to ask your resident computer expert. (Go ahead — he's *probably* not going to *byte* you!)

- ✓ **What's the *networking protocol* that your Local Area Network uses?** A *protocol* is just a fancy way of saying what language the computers on your network use to talk to each other. If you want to impress your resident computer nerd, ask whether your network is running the TCP/IP protocol. TCP/IP (Transmission Control Protocol/Internet Protocol) is the language of the Internet and the language your intranet needs to speak to use the really cool applications (some of which are included on the CD at the back of this book).

You need to begin with the answer to the first question: Does your company have a Local Area Network in place? If it does, proceed with the section under the "Yep! We've got a LAN" heading that follows. Oh, and congratulations! You're a step ahead of the game! If it doesn't, proceed to the section after that one, under the "Nope! Don't have a LAN" heading — you don't need to feel left out, but you have a little more work cut out for you.

Need to beef up your networking and TCP/IP networking protocol knowledge? *Networking For Dummies,* 2nd Edition by Doug Lowe, and *TCP/IP For Dummies* by Marshall Wilensky and Candace Leiden, both published by IDG Books Worldwide, Inc., offer a great introduction.

Yep! We've got a LAN!

Cool! Now you need to know whether your network is running the TCP/IP networking protocol — this point is very important because you need that protocol to run most intranet applications. If you're running Windows 95, here's a quick and easy way to check. (If you're running Windows NT Version 4.0, this same basic procedure applies.) Just follow these steps:

1. **Click Start⇨Settings⇨Control Panel.**

   The Windows 95 Control Panel appears.

2. **Double-click the Network icon in the Control Panel window.**

   The Network Configuration dialog box appears. If you're running Windows 95, the dialog box shown in Figure 1-1 is what you see; continue with Step 3. If you're running Windows NT Version 4.0, the dialog box in Figure 1-2 appears; skip to Step 4.

TCP/IP protocols are installed ⌐

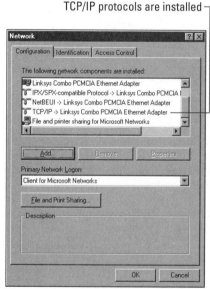

Figure 1-1:
The
Windows 95
Network
configuration
dialog box.

3. **If you're running Windows 95, click the Configuration tab and look in the list box at the top of the dialog box that reads** The following network components are installed.

   If the words TCP/IP appear on the same line as Ethernet Adapter, you're good to go! Your Local Area Network has no problem supporting your intranet. If you can't find the TCP/IP option or are unsure, you need to check with your resident computer guru. You need to have the TCP/IP protocol up and running before you can continue.

TCP/IP protocols are installed

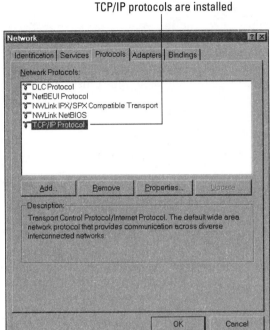

Figure 1-2:
The
Windows
NT Version
4.0 Network
configuration
dialog box.

4. If you're running Windows NT Version 4.0, click the Protocols tab.

If TCP/IP Protocol appears in the Network Protocols list box, you're all set! Again, if you can't find the TCP/IP option or you're unsure, you need to check with your resident computer guru. You need to have the TCP/IP protocol up and running before you can continue.

5. Click the OK button to close the Network configuration dialog box.

Nope! Don't have a LAN

You need to have a network in place to get a corporate intranet up and running — after all the *net* in intranet does stand for *network!* So where do you begin? You have a bunch of things to consider as you put together a network, but you need to be concerned with only a couple for your intranet:

✔ **You need network adapters in each computer.** These adapters enable your computer to talk to other computers — kind of like a modem but for a local network. Typically, if you set up a network for an intranet, you need to use *Ethernet* network adapters. Ethernet adapters aren't anything magical; they just happen to be capable of running the necessary TCP/IP networking protocol.

✔ **You need to choose the type of wires to use as you hook your computers together.** You basically have two choices: *twisted pair wires* (which look like modular telephone wires on steroids) or *coaxial cable* (which looks like the cable for cable television). Your choice depends on a number of factors — including the distance of the computers linked together and the physical restraints on wiring the computers together. With either type, your network can run the TCP/IP networking protocol.

If you're unsure how to get your company's computers networked together, consult one of your company's computer experts. Undoubtedly, you need to work with them to get things off the ground.

Do you have a server?

The second question that you need to answer is: Do you have a *server?* A server is a computer that's hooked into your Local Area Network, runs reasonably fast, and has a bunch of disk space where you can store your intranet files. If you have a dedicated server computer running Windows NT, it can enable you to do more with your intranet than if you don't have a dedicated server. You can also set up your intranet by using a PC running Windows 95 that you also use to do other work. If you're going to support just a few people on your intranet, not having a dedicated server doesn't present too many problems.

Each time a user accesses a file stored on your intranet server, the computer takes a quick moment to answer the request. If you also do your own non-intranet work on the same computer where you store your intranet files, you may notice these periodic slowdowns.

Consider the following two important points as you select a computer to be your intranet server:

✔ The computer needs to be on all the time to answer requests.

✔ If you don't plan to use a dedicated computer as your server, you need to realize that every time you shut off or reboot your computer — poof! — your intranet goes with it and can't answer requests until it's running again. This situation can frustrate users who are requesting files and can ultimately doom your project. If you have any possible way to get a dedicated server, do it! A dedicated server makes your entire intranet experience much more positive.

Yep! Got a dedicated server

Great! You should be all set to get a web server up and running. You need to determine one final thing about your server — its name:

1. **Click Start⇨Settings⇨Control Panel.**

   The Control Panel window appears.

2. **Double-click the Network icon.**

   The Network configuration dialog box appears.

3. **Click the Identification tab.**

   Figure 1-3 shows the Network dialog box in Windows 95; Figure 1-4 shows the same dialog box in Windows NT. The Computer name text box tells you the name of your computer. In Figure 1-3, it's something boring: IDC_LAPTOP. In Figure 1-4 it's another boring name: IDCNTSERVER.

4. **Click the OK button to close the Network configuration dialog box.**

Unless you have a photographic memory, write this name down — you need to remember it later, after you install your web server.

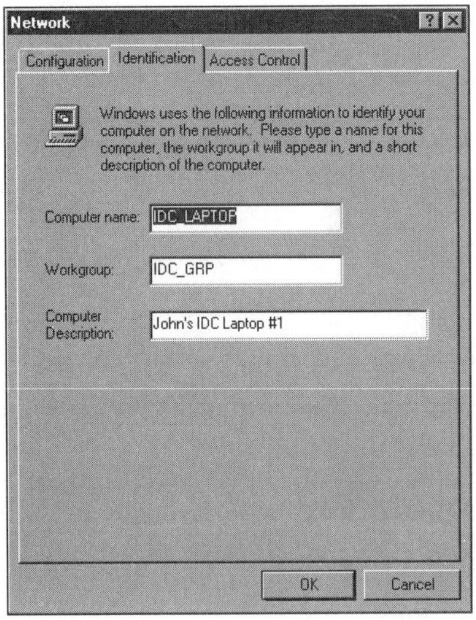

Figure 1-3:
The Identification tab of the Windows 95 Network dialog box.

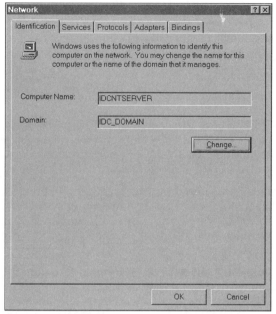

Figure 1-4:
The
Identification
tab of the
Windows
NT Network
dialog box.

Nope! No dedicated server available

You really need to consider getting a computer that you can use as your intranet server. If you can afford it, a dedicated machine makes the most sense. You probably want to know what kind to machine to get. Well, in the ever-changing, fast-paced world of computers, any specific configuration I give you today is going to be quickly eclipsed by something new and better tomorrow. My recommendation, therefore, is based more on price.

Personal computers are amazing things. In the 15 years since they were first introduced, the price point for getting the fastest machines available has been relatively stable at somewhere around $3,000. Your best long-term strategy (if you can even think long-term about computers) therefore, is to review machines with prices around $3,000. Because your server needs to run all the time, answering user requests for files, you want to have the fastest machine you can get. If you can't afford a $3,000 computer, however, that's okay, too. But I do recommend that you spend as much as you can afford — skimping on the server only makes things run slowly and lessens your overall experience. With all that said, following are a few specific things that you need to make sure of if you get a new server:

✔ **Make sure that the computer includes a network card and is ready to hook up to your network.** The network card needs to be compatible with the type of network cabling used in your organization.

✔ **Make sure that you have plenty of disk space on the computer to store your intranet files.** Disk space is relatively cheap and gets used quickly — get as much as you can early on.

✔ **Make sure that you get a computer with plenty of RAM (Random Access Memory).** The computer uses its RAM to save frequently accessed files, so getting one with lots of RAM makes your response time even faster.

✔ **If you're not going to use the computer for purposes other than as a server, don't worry about all the bells and whistles such as big monitors and sound cards.** These peripherals just increase the cost, and you can better use the money for more disk space or memory.

✔ **If you're really serious about putting together a dedicated server, make sure that it includes a high-end operating system such as Windows NT or UNIX.** Windows NT or UNIX can provide a faster and more secure intranet, than Windows 95, especially if you expect to have hundreds of users.

✔ **Because the computer needs to be running all the time to process requests, you may want to include a UPS.** No, you're not going to use big brown trucks to deliver your files around your office — a *UPS* is an *Uninterruptable Power Supply*. That way, if the electric company turns off your power because you didn't pay the bill (or you have a blackout), you have at least 20 or 30 minutes more to use your computer and shut it down correctly.

Configuring your server

As I describe earlier in this chapter, the primary role for your server is answering requests for files. If you're running Windows 95 or Windows NT, you can control how much time your computer spends answering file requests (however, it needs to be connected to a network first). To tell your computer how much time to spend, you need to get back to the Control Panel — just follow these steps:

1. **Click Start⇨Settings⇨Control Panel.**

   The Control Panel appears.

2. **Double-click the System icon.**

   The System Properties dialog box appears.

3. **Click the Performance tab.**

4. **Click the File System button to open the File System Properties dialog box and then click the Hard Disk tab to display the version of this shown in Figure 1-5.**

   Boy, this stuff is really buried in here, isn't it?

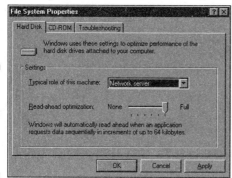

Figure 1-5:
The
Windows 95
File System
Properties
dialog box.

5. **Now you set how your computer should respond to requests in the** **Typical role of this machine drop down list box: Change the setting** **to Network server.**

   This setting makes your Windows 95 system answer file requests more quickly.

6. **Click the OK button in the File System Properties dialog box, and** **then click the OK button in the System Properties dialog box to save** **your changes.**

You want to change the typical role of your computer only if you're going to be using it as an intranet server. Don't make this change for a computer that you don't use as a server — this setting only makes it run slower, causes you to get frustrated, and maybe, in a fit of rage, causes you to throw this book at your boss. You don't want to do that now, do you?

If you're running Windows NT, controlling the time your computer spends answering file requests is much easier. I think the fact that changing this feature under Windows NT is easier than in Windows 95 is kind of odd, considering that Windows NT is a more complex operating system. Windows NT, however, makes your life easier in this one case. Just follow these steps:

1. **Click Start⇨Settings⇨Control Panel.**

   The Control Panel pops up.

2. **Double-click the System icon to open the System Properties dialog box.**

3. **Click the Performance tab to display the version of the dialog box** **shown in Figure 1-6.**

4. **Move the Boost slider to None to set your system to answer file** **requests more quickly.**

5. **Click the OK button to close the System Properties dialog box.**

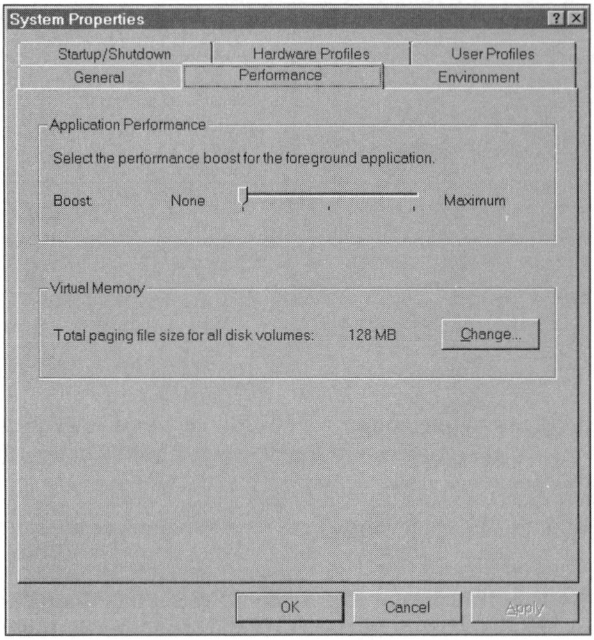

Figure 1-6:
The
Windows
NT System
Properties
dialog box,
which you
use to make
your system
respond
to file
requests
more
quickly.

Now that you now how to configure your server system, you're ready to set up your *web server.* (Yep — they're two different beasts.)

Checking Out Web Servers

Web servers are applications that answer requests made by *web browsers,* such as Microsoft Internet Explorer and Netscape Navigator, for web pages (HTML files). Having a web server on your company intranet enables you to create your own mini-version of the World Wide Web, just for use by your company. The World Wide Web — with its document, graphics, animation, and sound capabilities — is what most people identify with the Internet. Although the Web is a very important piece of the Internet, and an intranet web is likely to be a very important part of your company intranet, it's only one aspect of what you can do.

The only way to support a web on your intranet is to be running a web server application. Just as in choosing to use Word or WordPerfect as your word processor, you must also choose a particular web server application. Your choice of web servers first depends on the operating system that you're running. Table 1-1 lists operating systems and some of the web servers they support. Keep in mind that this list is of only the more popular web servers available and isn't meant to be complete.

Table 1-1	The Short List of Web Servers Available by Operating System
Operating System	*Web Servers Supported*
Windows 95	Microsoft Personal Web Server
	O'Reilly WebSite Server
Windows NT Server	Microsoft Internet Information Server
	Netscape Enterprise Server
Macintosh	Microsoft Personal Web Server
	MacHTTP/WebStar
UNIX	Apache Web Server
	Netscape Enterprise Server
	CERN Web Server
	NCSA Web Server

In this book, I focus on how to set up and configure Microsoft Personal Web Server under Windows 95 and Microsoft Internet Information Server under Windows NT Server 4.0. Both of these web servers come at the right price — they're FREE! FREE! FREE! Internet Information Server comes with Windows NT Server Version 4.0, and Personal Web Server is a free download from the Microsoft Internet Explorer Web site at the following Web address:

```
www.microsoft.com/ie
```

Many of the applications that I discuss in this book are also included on the accompanying CD-ROM — pretty cool, huh? Appendix C, "What's on the CD?," contains more information about the applications on the CD-ROM and how to access them.

While I focus primarily on using Microsoft Windows 95 and NT as the platform for your web server, you need to understand that UNIX-based systems still are the most popular out there. If you're interested in finding out more about these other web servers, I suggest that you visit their corresponding Internet Web sites:

  ✔ **Apache Web Server:** www.apache.org

  ✔ **O'Reilly Web Server:** www.oreilly.com

  ✔ **Netscape Web Server:** www.netscape.com

  ✔ **HTTPd Web Server:** hoohoo.ncsa.uiuc.edu

  ✔ **CERN Web Server:** www.w3.org/hypertext/WWW/Daemon

How do they spin the web?

You may be wondering what a *web server* is anyway — and why do you need one? Surely you've dealt with a restaurant waiter/waitress-type server before, but what's the difference and all the fuss about? Well, the difference between a restaurant waiter/waitress and a web server is that one is a person and the other is a computer — unless, of course, you're here from the future, where robots run all the fast food joints.

A web server is a lot like a restaurant waiter: A restaurant waiter stands around until someone wants to order something; then he takes the order, runs to the kitchen to get it filled, and brings back the food to the customer. A web server does the same thing — except instead of taking and delivering orders for food, a web server takes and delivers orders for web pages and other web-related files.

If you've already heard of file servers, you may be wondering what's so special about a web server? A file server also takes and delivers orders for files . . . Well, a web server is *like* a file server, but it has some magical properties all its own! Remember how I said that your network needs to be running the TCP/IP protocol to support your intranet? (If you don't remember, go back and take a look at the section "What Do You Need?" earlier in this chapter.) Well, the web server is a big reason why you need the TCP/IP protocol — TCP/IP is the language that web servers use to communicate with the computers requesting files. Don't misunderstand — some file servers use TCP/IP, too, so this protocol's not the only thing that makes web servers magical. What makes them truly magical is that they know how to listen for orders from web browsers such as Internet Explorer and Netscape Navigator. If you spend time on the Internet, you're probably already familiar with a browser. Figure 1-7 illustrates how a Web server communicates with a web browser. I take a more in-depth look at web browsers in Chapter 3.

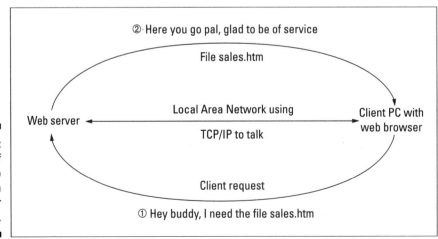

Figure 1-7:
The role of
the web
server in
your
intranet.

② Here you go pal, glad to be of service

File sales.htm

Local Area Network using

TCP/IP to talk

Web server ← → Client PC with web browser

Client request

① Hey buddy, I need the file sales.htm

Now that you have a better understanding of how a web server generally works, I review a few specific web server applications in the following sections. I hope to help you choose the web server with the right fit for your organization. If you've ever worn shoes that are too small, you know how painful walking can be with the wrong equipment. You need to choose shoes that fit right to be comfortable. Choosing the right web server is like choosing the right pair of shoes: Make the right choice and you're comfortable and happy; make the wrong choice and you get corns.

What's Microsoft Internet Information Server all about?

Microsoft Internet Information Server (IIS) is one of the big-boy web servers. IIS runs only under Windows NT. If you need to support a large organization on your intranet and you need hefty power and security, Windows NT and Internet Information Server are definitely the way to go. Internet Information Server comes at the right price — it's free with Windows NT. As with everything else these days, IIS has a Web site that enables you to download the latest version and find out the latest information. The IIS Web site is at the following address:

```
www.microsoft.com/iis
```

Just as with any choice you make in life, choosing a web server has both an upside and a downside. Sometimes, if you're lucky and you cross your fingers, the upside outweighs the downside. Table 1-2 lists the advantages and disadvantages of using Microsoft Internet Information Server as your intranet web server.

Table 1-2	The Pros and Cons of Using Internet Information Server as Your Intranet Web Server	
Advantage/Disadvantage	**Description**
Advantage	Internet Information Server provides very good security. Combined with Windows NT Security, it can act like a bulldog and keep employees from getting at files they shouldn't be accessing. If you have a small company or department, the level of security on your server may not matter much. Just remember: Putting a computer on a network can sometimes be like leaving the keys in the ignition of your new Jaguar — just too tempting for some people to resist.

(continued)

Table 1-2 *(continued)*

Advantage/Disadvantage	*Description*
Advantage	More power! Because Microsoft Internet Information Server works so closely with Windows NT, it can run very fast. If you have a big company or department, this feature can be a very important consideration. Everyone hates to wait on computers, and you can never have enough speed.
Advantage	Microsoft Internet Information Server can keep close track of every time someone accesses it. It can tell you who accessed it, when it was accessed, and what was accessed. The server does so by keeping a *log* (a record of user activity). This feature can be important if you're planning on putting sensitive information on your intranet. Use common sense in placing information on your intranet, however. A goofy employee (the same guy who wears lampshades on his head at the company parties) may be tempted to publish your boss's embarrassingly low IQ on your intranet, and that could be *sensitive information* that you don't want floating around.
Advantage	Microsoft Internet Information Server works closely with Windows NT. This close partnership can enable you to protect each file that you make available separately.
Disadvantage	Internet Information Server and Windows NT can be difficult to understand and manage. Unless you're up to a serious task or really need the power and security, Personal Web Server, which I review in the following section, may be a better choice for you.
Disadvantage	The cost of the hardware and software you need to run Microsoft Windows NT and Internet Information server can be high. If you're working on a tight budget because your boss thinks his new leather chair is more important, Internet Information Server may not be your best choice.

What's Microsoft Personal Web Server all about?

Microsoft Personal Web Server is the little guy's web server. It runs under the Windows 95 operating system. Personal Web Server is a great way to start building your intranet without spending a lot of cash — you most likely already have Windows 95 up and running, so you can mesh Personal Web Server right in. Sure, it's not as powerful as Internet Information Server, but it definitely stands up to the rigors of a small company or department. If you're just testing the intranet waters, Personal Web Server is a great option.

Personal Web Server has its own advantages and disadvantages, as I list in Table 1-3.

Table 1-3   The Pros and Cons of Using Personal Web Server as Your Intranet Web Server

Advantage/Disadvantage	Description
Advantage	Personal Web Server works with the hardware and software you probably already have. Personal Web Server may be the most cost-effective choice if you're working with a tight budget. If cost is a major factor in your web server decision, starting small and working your way up to Internet Information Server does make sense. You can easily move what you've created with a Personal Web Server setup over to an Internet Information Server setup if you outgrow your proverbial shoes.
Advantage	If you have a number of departments in your organization, you can easily give each department its own web server. Setting your network up this way gives each department more control and doesn't cost as much as a centralized Internet Information Server setup.
Disadvantage	Unlike Windows NT, which is designed from the ground up to share files with lots of users, Windows 95 is limited in how quickly it can process multiple requests. Because Personal Web Server runs with Windows 95, you don't get the same quick response to multiple user

(continued)

Table 1-3 (continued)

Advantage/Disadvantage	Description
	requests as you do with Internet Information Server and Windows NT. If you don't expect tons of people to use your intranet, however, the Windows NT/Windows 95 difference probably isn't a problem. But if you expect a lot of users (more than 20 or so), Personal Web Server running with Window 95 probably doesn't cut the mustard.
Disadvantage	Personal Web Server can't run in conjunction with some of the more advanced applications. Internet Information Server, for example, can work with another application — Index Server — to search all types of intranet files. Index Server doesn't work with Personal Web Server.

Other web servers

Like that of a fine wine, the choice of a good web server can be a matter of taste and price. Even though Internet Information Server and Personal Web Server are free, they're certainly not the Strawberry Ripple of the web server world. Other choices certainly do exist — just take a look at Table 1-1 at the beginning of this section. Each server offers its own unique set of advantages and disadvantages, but they all do the same basic thing: process requests for web files. Keep in mind that you're just getting started, and the choice you make isn't permanent. You can always move to something better down the line after your intranet takes off.

I can't possibly review every web server on the market. If you're still unsure which web server to use for your intranet, ask around. Find out what other people you know are using for their intranets. They may have some insights as to why their choice was good or bad. Table 1-4 lists some general advantages and disadvantages of using other web servers.

Table 1-4   The Pros and Cons of Using Another Web Server as Your Intranet Web Server

Advantage/Disadvantage	Description
Advantage	Another web server may fit in with what your company Information Systems department already has in place. IS departments like to protect their turf, so if you're setting your intranet up outside their control, you may need to clear things with them first.

Advantage/Disadvantage	Description
Advantage	Other web servers can offer better features in some areas, such as improved security or speedier performance. One can argue this point for a long time, but in the end, all web servers get the job done in pretty much the same way.
Disadvantage	Other web servers may not be free. You get what you pay for, right? Well, that's not always true — just because a web server is free doesn't mean that it's bad. And just because you must pay for a particular web server doesn't mean that you should overlook it.
Disadvantage	If you're looking to stay up with the latest and greatest improvements with Windows, some web servers may lag behind. Of course, being a bit behind is not always such a bad thing, because being on the so-called bleeding (buggy) edge can hurt a lot of the time.

In this chapter I show you how to install and configure Internet Information Server and Personal Web Server. I choose these Microsoft web server examples mostly because they are free and because they work well with the Microsoft Windows 95 and Windows NT platforms. These platforms are usually in use somewhere within most organizations. Using UNIX as the platform for your web server requires more technical expertise and is probably a task that's best left to the technical gurus of your company.

Walking through an Internet Information Server Installation

You can use Internet Information Server only with Windows NT. Usually, it's installed as part of your Windows NT Version 4.0 installation. If you're not sure whether Internet Information Server is installed on your computer, you can easily check. Just follow these steps:

1. **Click Start⇨Settings⇨Control Panel.**

   The Control Panel appears.

2. **Double-click the Network icon.**

   The Network dialog box appears.

3. **Click the Services tab to display the list of Network Services, as shown in Figure 1-8.**

A Network Service is just a way to communicate with other computers. If a service appears in this list box, your computer knows how to talk in that language. If the list contains Microsoft Internet Information Server 2.0, you're all set and you don't need to waste your time here — close the dialog box and head on over to the following section, "Taking It for a Test Drive." If you don't see the Internet Information Server item listed, you need to spend about 10 minutes going through the next set of steps in this chapter.

Internet information server is installed

Figure 1-8: The Network dialog box, showing the network services currently installed.

4. **Click on the OK button to close the Network dialog box.**

The latest version of the Internet Information Server is available at the Microsoft Web site at the following address:

```
www.microsoft.com/iis
```

Setting up Internet Information Server is painless — I promise. You can install it in just a few mouse clicks by following these steps:

1. **Double-click the IIS Setup application shortcut icon on your desktop.**

   A shortcut to the IIS Setup application should appear on your desktop if you didn't originally install Internet Information Server along with Windows NT. Go on to Step 2.

   If you can't find the IIS Setup application shortcut on your desktop, you can start the IIS Setup application from the Network Control Panel. Follow the preceding set of steps to access the Services tab of the Network dialog box (refer back to Figure 1-8). Then carry out the directions in the following substeps.

   a. **After you're at the Services tab of the Network dialog box, click the Add button to add a new Network Service.** The Select Network Service dialog box appears, as shown in Figure 1-9.

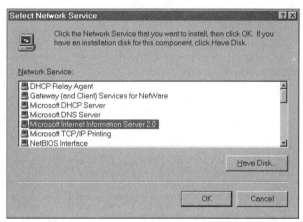

Figure 1-9:
The Select Network Service dialog box, which you use to add the Internet Information Server service to your system.

   b. **Next, click the Microsoft Internet Information Server 2.0 item in the Network Service list box.**

   c. **Click OK to continue with the installation.**

   The Internet Information Server Installation — Files Needed dialog box appears, as shown in Figure 1-10.

2. **Grab your original Windows NT Version 4.0 CD-ROM, pop it in your CD-ROM drive, and then specify the path to the I386 directory on the CD in the Installed from text box of the Internet Information Server Installation — Files Needed dialog box as shown in Figure 1-10.**

   If, for example, your CD drive is drive E, you need to enter **E:\I386** in this text box.

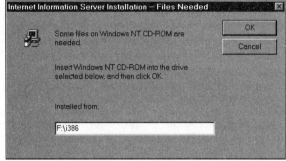

Figure 1-10:
The Internet
Information
Server
Installation–
Files
Needed
dialog box.

3. Click OK to continue with the installation.

The Microsoft Internet Information Server 2.0 Setup dialog appears. This dialog box is just a warning asking you to make sure that any other applications you're running are closed. So if you have something else running, go close it and then come back to this dialog box.

4. Click OK to continue with the installation.

The Microsoft Internet Information Server 2.0 Setup dialog box appears. You can select the parts of Internet Information Server you want to install here. The items already selected by default in this dialog box are what you need to run the server.

5. Select the optional components that you want to install from the Options list box in this dialog box by clicking the box next to the items in the list to put an X in those boxes.

Following are brief descriptions of some of the options in this dialog box:

- **The Internet Server Manager** options enable you to set up Internet Information Server after you're done (you need this one).

- **The World Wide Web (WWW)** options are what you need to run the web server (definitely select these options).

- **The FTP (File Transfer Protocol)** option enables you to create directories where you can share files (you need this one).

- **The ODBC (Open Database Connectivity)** option is a fancy way to keep information about who's using the Internet Information Server in a database.

- **The Gopher** option is an older way to provide information on the Internet. It was what people used before the web pages (HTML) became popular. You have no reason to install the Gopher option.

6. Click OK to continue with the installation.

The Publishing Directories dialog box appears, as shown in Figure 1-11. Any files placed in these directories can be used by the service listed. Files put in the World Wide Web Publishing service, for example, can be accessed by any web browsers. The default directories listed in this dialog box should be fine for your purposes.

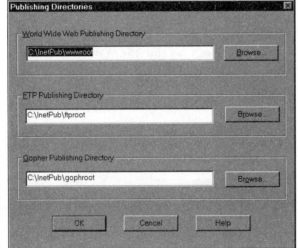

Figure 1-11:
The
Publishing
Directories
dialog box.

7. Click OK to continue.

The installation program copies the Internet Information Server files to your computer. After these files have been copied and the installation is complete, the Microsoft Internet Information Server 2.0 Setup dialog box appears, letting you know that the setup was completed successfully.

8. Click OK to end this boring process.

Excellent! You've just installed Internet Information Server. I don't know about you, but I'm going to Disney World!

Taking your new web server for a test drive

Installing the Internet Information Server creates a new program group that contains the Internet Information Server applications. The main controlling

Internet Information Server application is called the *Internet Service Manager*. To start the Internet Server Manager, follow these steps:

1. **Click Start⇨Programs⇨Microsoft Internet Server (Common)⇨ Internet Service Manager.**

   The Internet Server Manager application starts. The Internet Service Manager main screen displays the services that are currently running, as shown in Figure 1-12.

   The WWW service is the World Wide Web service — the service that's essential to enabling others to access your web files.

2. **If the State column doesn't say that the WWW service is running, highlight the name of the computer in the Computer column for the row that contains the WWW service.**

3. **Choose Properties⇨Start Service from the menu options to start the WWW service.**

   Great! Now you have a fully active web service.

Service column ———   ┌— State column

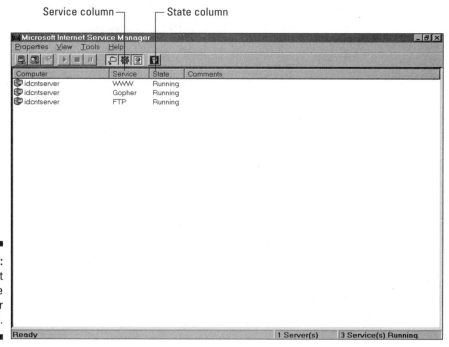

Figure 1-12:
The Internet
Service
Manager
application.

The WWW service offers a number of properties, which I review briefly in the next few paragraphs. I come back to the Internet Information Server administration features in Chapter 2.

To view the WWW service properties, follow these steps:

1. **In the Internet Service Manager, highlight the computer name in the Computer column for the row that contains the WWW service.**

   If the Internet Server Manager application is not running, click Start⇨Programs⇨Microsoft Internet Server (Common)⇨Internet Service Manager.

2. **Choose Properties⇨Service Properties from the menu bar to open the WWW Service Properties dialog box.**

   Now you're in control of your web server. From the Service tab, you can, among other things, control how Internet Information Server handles security.

3. **Click the Directories tab to display the version of this dialog box shown in Figure 1-13.**

   From this version of the dialog box, you can control the directories that the Internet Information Server uses to publish your intranet content.

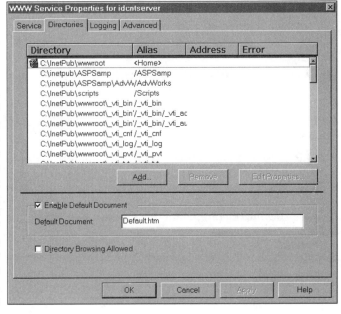

Figure 1-13:
The
Directories
tab of the
Internet
Information
Server's
WWW
Service
Directory
Properties
dialog box.

4. Click the Logging tab to display the version of this dialog box shown in Figure 1-14.

From this version of the dialog box, you can decide whether Internet Information Server tracks user activity — you can check up on who's accessing your intranet web server, when they're accessing it, and what files they're accessing. I discuss web server logging in more detail in Chapter 13.

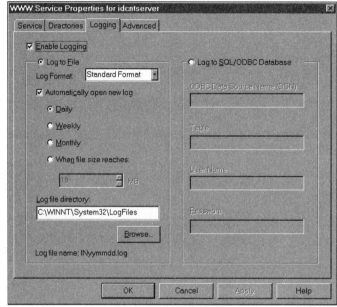

Figure 1-14:
The Logging tab of the Internet Information Server's WWW Service Properties dialog box.

5. Finally, click the Advanced tab to display the version of this dialog box shown in Figure 1-15.

From this version of the dialog box, you can limit the people who can access your web server. To limit someone's access, you need to know the *IP address* of the user you want to prevent from accessing your web server. An IP address is like a telephone number, so you can block users who have specific telephone numbers, area codes, or exchanges from accessing your web server.

6. Click the OK button to close the Service Properties dialog box.

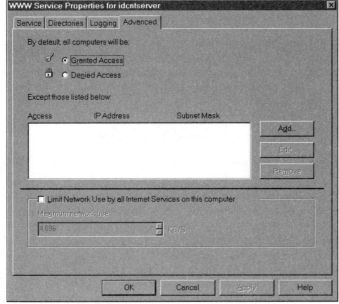

Figure 1-15:
The
Advanced
tab of the
Internet
Information
Server's
WWW
Service
Properties
dialog box.

Walking through a Personal Web Server Installation

You can use Personal Web Server only with Windows 95. Unlike Internet Information Server and Windows NT, however, this server doesn't come with Windows 95. You need to get Personal Web Server from the Microsoft Internet Explorer Web site at the following address:

```
www.microsoft.com/ie
```

Compared to installing Internet Information Server, Personal Web Server is a walk in the park. The current version of Personal Web Server is Version 1.0a. If you download Personal Web Server from the Microsoft Web Site, make sure that you put it in a directory that you can remember. I like to make a directory called \DOWNLOAD for all the files I download from the Internet; that way, I know where to find them later. You need to run only one file you download to install Personal Web Server To do so, follow these steps:

1. Click Start⇨Run.

The Run dialog box appears.

2. **Enter the path and name for the Personal Web Server setup application in the Run dialog box.**

   If you download the server from the Web, for example, you may enter **C:\DOWNLOAD\PWS10A.EXE** in the Run dialog box. You see the computer zip through, unpacking files and then installing them. After the installation is complete, you see the final dialog box asking you if you want to restart your computer so that your new settings will take effect.

3. **Click the Yes button to restart your computer.**

   Awesome! You've just installed Personal Web Server! Put your feet up, relish in your cool achievement, and wait a moment while your computer restarts.

Taking your web server for a test drive

Did you enjoy your break? The next step is to make sure that Personal Web Server installed itself and is running correctly. As shown in Figure 1-16, a Personal Web Server icon now appears on the far-right side of your task bar.

Figure 1-16:
You can access the Personal Web Server configuration dialog box from the Windows 95 taskbar.

You can double-click the Personal Web Server icon to open the Personal Web Server Properties dialog box, as shown in Figure 1-17. The Properties dialog box is where you can become the master of your web server domain, as explained in the following list:

   ✔ **The General tab** of the Properties dialog box enables you to view and modify where to put your intranet web files to make them available to your users; you can get access to more Help in this dialog box by clicking the More Details button.

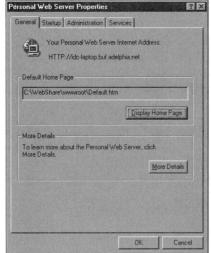

Figure 1-17:
The General
tab of the
Personal
Web Server
Properties
dialog box.

✔ **The Startup tab** is where you can start or stop the Personal Web Server, as shown in Figure 1-18. The Startup area should say that the Personal Web Server is now running. If your server is not yet running and the Start button is enabled, click it to fire up Personal Web Server. After your Personal Web Server is running, you're ready to enable users to start accessing your web files.

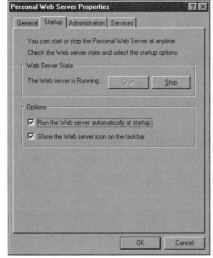

Figure 1-18:
The Startup
tab of the
Personal
Web Server
Properties
dialog box.

> ✔ **The Administration tab** of the dialog box is next, but I review web
> server administration in Chapter 2, so skip this tab for now.
>
> ✔ **The Services tab** of the dialog box is as shown in Figure 1-19. From here,
> you can control how the HTTP (Hyper Text Transfer Protocol — just a
> fancy way of saying web server) and FTP (File Transfer Protocol — the
> language your intranet uses to transfer files) start up: manually or
> automatically as your computer starts.

If you make any changes to any settings on these tabs of the Properties
dialog box that you'd like to save, click the OK button; otherwise click the
Cancel button to throw away your changes.

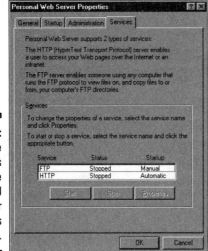

Figure 1-19:
The
Services
tab of the
Personal
Web Server
Properties
dialog box.

When Bad Things Happen

Luckily, web servers are pretty simple applications. If you walked through
the test drive for the web server you installed without problems, you should
be all set. In the end, however, Murphy's law always has a way of proving
itself. Table 1-5 tries to anticipate Murphy's law by listing some common
web server problems and solutions. If you can't find the answers to your
problems in Table 1-5, try the Microsoft Technical Support Web site at the
following address:

www.microsoft.com/support

In the following table, PWS means Personal Web Server, and IIS means
Internet Information Server.

Table 1-5	Common Personal Web Server and Internet Information Server Problems and Solutions
Problem	*Solution*
Why can't I access my web server?	**PWS/IIS answer:** You're just a little ahead of things here. Chapter 3 discusses web browsers and shows you how to test them out with your web server. The major cause for not being able to access your web server is usually network-related. Recall how you found out the name of your computer near the beginning of this chapter? Make sure that you're using the right computer name in trying to access your web server.
Where do I put web pages?	**PWS answer:** PWS sets up a directory for your web files; by default, this directory is C:\WEBSHARE\WWWROOT. Any files that you place in that directory can be accessed through your web server. I show you how to add more directories for your web files in Chapters 2 and 4.
	IIS answer: IIS sets up a directory for your web files; by default it's C:\INETPUB\WWWROOT. You can add new directories by using the WWW Server Properties dialog box that I review in the "Taking your web server for a test drive" section earlier in this chapter. I show you how to add more directories for your web files in Chapters 2 and 4.
How do I control my web server?	**PWS answer:** You can set up much of your Personal Web Server configuration through a web browser. I haven't discussed how to do so yet, but you can get to the PWS administration features from the Personal Web Server Properties dialog box, as I explain in Chapter 2.
	IIS answer: All Internet Information Server administration is done from the Microsoft Internet Service Manager, as I discuss in the "Taking your web server for a test drive" section earlier in this chapter. Click Start⇨Programs⇨Microsoft Internet Server (Common)⇨Internet Service Manager to start the Internet Service Manager application.

Where To Next?

Whew! You've covered a lot of ground in just this one chapter on getting started, but now that you have the core of your intranet established, you can start to have some fun. Now that you have your web server set up, the next step is to figure out what kind of information you want to make available on your intranet. You really need to think about this subject, so put on your thinking cap — your decisions involve many business and cultural considerations. Uh-oh, sounds as if the old corporate bureaucracy is rearing its ugly head. . . . Well, maybe just a little, but you're on a roll, and the opposition needs more than a little red tape to stop you now!

Chapter 2
Getting Ready for Battle

● ●

In This Chapter
▶ Developing a plan for your corporate intranet

▶ Identifying appropriate intranet content

▶ Wrestling your intranet web server into submission

▶ A review of intranet web content and how to stay organized

● ●

*A*fter the excitement of getting a hot new toy up and running — your *own* intranet web server! — you're probably starting to think about all the neat things you can start to make available. Although getting caught up in the moment and enjoying your accomplishment is great, you need to get back to reality for just a moment or two. Before you run off too far with your ideas, you need a plan. You know what a plan usually involves: the most dreaded corporate beast in existence — meetings. Before you run out of the room in sheer terror, don't worry. Everything's going to be all right. I show you how to develop a plan for your company intranet so that you can impress your boss, win the admiration of your coworkers, and land yourself a big fat raise!

Developing a Plan

Well, maybe I have a tendency to exaggerate a little. Nonetheless, to do things right, you need to know where you're going and have some sort of idea of how to get there. Your intranet can play an important role in getting your company to work together and distribute information, or it can become a disorganized mess that's hard to use and doesn't provide anything mean-ingful. In my experience, the difference between success and failure of a project usually comes down to good planning. Everyone wants to be a winner and create winning projects, right? You have a few key questions to consider, the answers to which can help lead you down the path to success when you develop your intranet plan:

✔ Who's going to use the intranet information?

✔ How is the information going to get on your intranet?

✔ Does each department have its own intranet server, or does your system have one centralized server?

✔ Who's responsible for your intranet?

✔ How is your company structured? Does this structure support the kind of team dynamics that an intranet can bring to a company?

Almost nothing is free these days, and that includes your intranet. Beyond the obvious hardware and software costs (which I show you how to keep down), you need to think about the cost of the people you need to develop intranet content and manage your intranet if things go wrong. You also need to remember how quickly technology changes these days. That hot new computer or software product you have today will look as old and antiquated as a horse-drawn buggy in as little as a few months. Make sure that you have a budget that accounts for these technology changes and people costs. Without the right funding, you may have a hard time getting your intranet off the ground, much less keep it going.

Ready, aim . . .

Fire! And that's not a word most employees like to hear. So how can you avoid it by creating a successful intranet that wows your boss and co-workers? Answer: by being prepared with a good plan. Every good plan begins with a goal. In this case, think about the goals of your intranet. Is your intranet in place to perform any of or all the following functions:

✔ Facilitate corporate communication?

✔ Provide a uniform and easy way to access corporate information?

✔ Empower your employees with corporate information that's always been too difficult to access quickly?

✔ Provide a way for people to meet easily without leaving their desks?

Your intranet may be designed to do some of or even all of these things, or maybe you have a few unique needs that I don't mention. Whatever the case, defining your intranet goals helps you to focus and make the right choices.

The next thing you need to do is to look at your organization. How does your organization accomplish your needs today — if, of course, they're accomplished at all? Make sure that what you're proposing fits into your organizational structure and goals. You need to make sure that your intranet design and goals remain consistent with your overall corporate goals. An intranet can empower employees, maybe even turn them into superheroes, but your organization needs to support this metamorphosis.

Intranets can enable employees to act on their own instead of waiting around for someone to tell them what to do. In many corporations, the Information Systems (IS) department still holds the information cookies and also has complete control of who gets what. An intranet thrives on *information democracy* — freely accessible information that resides within the workers' grasp.

Most of all, remember that the most successful intranets are those that work to solve specific organizational challenges — and also work within the current organizational maze. You may find that getting your organization to change for your intranet is difficult — at least initially. People are reluctant to change, no matter whether change is bad or good. If you're starting a corporate intranet and expecting to make sweeping changes in the way your company works, be aware that you're climbing a steep hill.

An intranet most likely brings about organizational *evolution* instead of a *revolution*. Your company is likely to change as it uses your intranet, and as a result, you're presented with more ideas. So remember that what you start out with today should be viewed as a work in progress that, with a little care and support, affects your company in ways you haven't thought of yet.

The keys to a successful intranet include:

- ✔ Making sure that the goals of your intranet fit within the corporate goals.
- ✔ Limiting initial changes, because the intranet has to be allowed to develop at a natural pace within the organization.
- ✔ Keeping the focus of your intranet specific and tight — working to solve specific challenges and goals.

Building a team

A good way to start planning your intranet is to put together an intranet design team with a representative from each part of your company. Make sure that you include someone from management, too — they're the ones who spend the money. Help everyone on your team become part of the solution you create with your intranet by including them in this early design process. Another important point is to include training in your planning process. What's the point of having the hottest and best new technology if no one knows how to use it? Keep this point in mind as you design your intranet as well — the easier your intranet is to use, the less training your employees need down the line. These early adopters and developers of the intranet plan are destined to become your greatest crusaders as your intranet grows in the future, helping to promote its use and helping to train other users.

Even though creating an intranet development team is a great way to get everyone involved in the process, you still need a leader — someone who's respected and can help bring everyone together and maintain focus if disagreements arise. (You *know* that's going to happen, too — getting 12 people in the same room to agree about very much of anything is not an easy task.) Make sure that your leader is someone who understands the technology — if not, buy the poor soul a copy of this book right now! Your intranet leader also needs to understand your company's goals and have enough responsibility and respect within the company to make decisions that stick.

Brainstorming

Now's the time to put on your thinking cap and let your thoughts run wild. Think about everything you'd like to do with your intranet. Looking for a few examples to get you started? Here are just a few things your intranet can provide:

- ✔ A structured way to make corporate information and documents easily available to everyone in the company.
- ✔ A backbone to improve corporate communication through e-mail and video conferencing.
- ✔ Ways to sift through large amounts of information and documents to easily find what you need.
- ✔ A mechanism for making the latest corporate news and information easily available — through television-like broadcasting (push technologies).
- ✔ A way to access all information in a similar manner. After a user knows how to use one area of your intranet web site, ideally the user should automatically understand how to use other areas.

Think of all the additional information and resources you'd like to make available. Now make a list of your best ideas. Focus in on two or three of your ideas that you think provide the best balance between benefit to the intranet's users and ease of implementation. Make these your initial goals. After you accomplish these goals, you can go back to your list with what you learned. Make changes to your goals — remember that this project is a work in progress. Pick a couple more and work toward those goals. Rome wasn't built in a day, and your intranet certainly isn't going to become everything you hope and dream for in a weekend.

The real power of your intranet is derived from keeping things simple. Let your intranet and your organization evolve together. Your intranet changes itself to meet the needs of your organization, and your organization changes itself, too, to adapt to the new, better, and quicker ways an intranet can help people get their jobs done. Don't be afraid to think *big*, but also don't be afraid to think *small*. What do I mean? Well, at this point, don't be afraid to throw out your big ideas for what you'd like to do with your intranet, but also don't overlook the smaller, simpler things that you can do with your intranet. Starting out small helps you iron out the technical details and provides something that people can use to start building their confidence.

What's the other guy doing?

Another great way to think about what you'd like to do and can accomplish with your intranet is to look at what the guy down the block is doing. Do you have friends in other companies that have corporate intranets set up? Ask them how they use their intranet and what they like and dislike about it. You can benefit from other people's experiences — this approach is the best way to avoid making the same mistakes others made and to capitalize on the same successes they enjoyed. You may also want to check out some of the following Web sites that can show you what a corporate intranet can accomplish:

- ✔ Microsoft Guide to Intranets Web site: `www.microsoft.com/intranet`
- ✔ Netscape Intranet Solutions: `home.netscape.com.comprod/at_work/index.html`
- ✔ Intranet Design Magazine: `www.innergy.com`
- ✔ Intranut: `www.intranut.com`
- ✔ The Complete Intranet Resource: `www.intrack.com`
- ✔ The Intranet Journal (SM): `www.intranetjournal.com`

Make sure that you check out Appendix B, "How Can I Find Out More? A Guide to Intranet Resources" for a list of Internet resources with more intranet information.

Getting ready

Getting your intranet web server up and running, the subject of Chapter 1, is just the first step. You also need to make sure that each employee's computer is up to the task of supporting your intranet. I discuss employee PCs (hardware and configuring) and the web browsers that need to run on those computers in Chapter 3.

After you have the foundation (web server) and plumbing (network wiring) in place for your intranet, your next step is to start identifying and gathering the information (intranet web content) you require. I find that a useful step at this point is to start by creating rough examples (such as lists, diagrams, and elementary web page examples) — you don't need anything fancy. You need to have an idea of the types of information you want to display and perhaps how you want to display it. This process starts you on the path to creating standards and identifying what information is to be available on your intranet.

Your next step is to develop a plan to tell employees that your intranet is available and show them how to use it. You may need to include scheduled training sessions. I think that the best way to train people is with a few shorter training sessions over a period of time rather than a weekend intranet intensive. Show employees how to perform basic tasks and send them off. Let them come back to you with questions and help them build on their knowledge. Growing employees into your intranet enables them to feel more comfortable and gives you time to build the more complex features they eventually want. As employees learn the intranet, they not only want more from it, but begin to add to it to satisfy their own intranet needs.

Another part of getting ready for your intranet includes thinking about ways to monitor how well your intranet works after it's up and running. Some suggestions include the following:

- ✔ Conduct short reviews with employees to get their feedback.

- ✔ Build places into your intranet where people can give feedback and suggestions.

- ✔ Quickly react to positive and thoughtful suggestions.

Supporting your intranet while you're creating it is important, but having a plan to support your intranet after it's up and running is even more important. I talk about how to take care of your intranet in Chapter 12.

Getting on your SOP box

Standard Operating Procedures (SOP) — sounds like a whole bunch of red tape, doesn't it? Well, your SOPs don't need to be. Although structure can often stifle creativity, creativity without a little structure can lead to thousands of finger painting artists run amok. You at least want some basic things in place to ensure that your intranet site runs smoothly. Some of these procedural items include the following:

- ✔ **Plan on things changing often.** Your business is dynamic and your intranet most likely needs to reflect that. The capability to deliver timely information is the key to your intranet. Stale information, like stale bread, just doesn't taste good. You need to appoint key people to keep the information in their areas up to date.

- ✔ **As much as possible, try to make things look and feel consistent.** Don't stifle the creative initiative of your fellow employees — their contribution is your best asset to developing your intranet. If everything on your intranet looks too different from page to page, however, people are likely to have a harder time finding what they want (and knowing what they're doing). A consistent interface can also help decrease your training effort and enable people to learn how to use things faster. Templates for the creation of web pages, as I discuss in Chapter 4, can often help ensure that your intranet web pages look the same.

✔ **Choose the right tools for the job.** In Chapter 4, I show you how to create intranet web pages by using Microsoft FrontPage, and in Chapter 6, I show you how to create intranet web pages by using Microsoft Word and Microsoft Excel.

✔ **Include intranet standards as part of intranet training.** Make sure that employees understand your intranet goals and what you expect. An intranet opens up a new freedom to express information — make sure that you set some limits on what is and isn't acceptable. For example, company handbooks and reports are acceptable — your family vacation pictures are probably not.

✔ **Standardize your web tools.** Unlike with the Internet, you have total control over the tools that your employees use to create stuff for your intranet and that they use to view your intranet content. Standardizing your Web browsers (as I discuss in more detail in Chapter 3) and web content creation tools (as I discuss in Chapters 4 and 6) and building your intranet around these tools helps to keep things consistent and simple.

Where do you want to go?

Where do you see your intranet going over the medium to long term? Predicting what the hot new technological trends may be is pretty difficult, but I think I can safely say that intranets are going to survive in one form or another well into the future. Obviously, your intranet isn't going to be everything you want it to be from day one. So set reasonable goals and expectations — not always an easy thing to do if management wants it all done yesterday. A key to making your intranet successful is to set goals that are realistic and achievable. If your company has a 1,000-page product catalog, hundreds of human resource documents, links to customer and product databases, and so on that all need to be available on your intranet, everyone needs to realize that this task can't be completed overnight. On the other hand, fulfilling your ultimate intranet goals may not be as difficult as you think. In Part II, I show you how to take a lot of the information your company's already created and quickly make it accessible on your intranet. Remember that the purpose of your intranet is to create magic with your corporate information — turning information into ideas and knowledge and, in turn, taking that information and knowledge and creating new products and opportunities.

Picking Your Content

After you identify the information you want to make available through your intranet, the next step is to determine what information you have and where you have it. I like to call this step taking an *information audit*. Your information audit doesn't need to be a detailed account of all your information — and no, you don't need to hire a CPA to perform an information audit.

How do you go about performing an information audit? Well, a good way is to think about the people who work in your company. How does the information currently flow? You may not be used to thinking about information in this way. A rough sketch of your organization and its departments may help you visualize information flow. How does the information generated by each department feed and combine with other departments? Figure 2-1 shows an example of such a diagram. Your diagram doesn't need to be anything fancy; you can even scratch it out on the back of your napkin during your lunch break at the local burger joint.

After you identify some of your information flow, you can also see who's responsible for what. As I discuss in the "Building a team" section earlier in this chapter, identifying a person from each area of your organization to be responsible for keeping their area's information up to date is very important. The intranet advantage comes from having the most current information available, and a part of your intranet's goals is to enable employees to make decisions on their own with the most current information available.

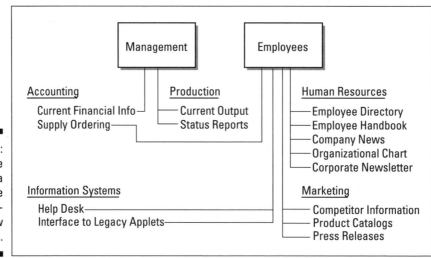

Figure 2-1:
An example
of a
corporate
information-
flow
diagram.

Your intranet can realize its full potential only if everyone is contributing on a consistent and timely basis — easy in the beginning, because everyone views the intranet as a new and interesting novelty. Your long term goal is to keep the "wow" factor going, and this goal comes to pass only if employees discover new and interesting ways to use the intranet on their own. During much of this time, you need to provide support to the people responsible for making the most current information available, helping them to focus more on the information and less on the technical details as they continue to learn the system. If you want to learn more about creating intranet content, *Intranet Publishing For Dummies* by Glenn Weadock (IDG Books Worldwide, Inc.) is a great place to get started.

So, where does your intranet information come from? Most of it probably comes from stuff that many departments already have available but that currently isn't easily accessible on demand by other departments. Things that you send memos for today can become e-mail messages and web pages tomorrow. Losing a piece of paper and then, in turn, losing all the information written on it is all too easy. With e-mail and intranet web pages, information lasts longer and can be easier to find later if an employee really needs it. Information on your intranet is always located in the same place, right where people can find it — not floating around from desk to desk or falling off bulletin boards because you're out of pushpins.

Make an assessment of the information you already have. Identify what you want available on your intranet and then use the right tools to get it there. This information may reside in existing Word or Excel documents, in a database, or on other computer systems. In Chapter 6, I show you how to use this existing information and quickly make it available on your intranet.

Taking Charge of Your Web Server

In Chapter 1, I show you how to install your web server and make sure that it's up and running. Then you quickly breeze through the administration facilities provided by Microsoft Personal Web Server and Microsoft Internet Information Server. In this section, I take a closer look at some of the more important features of each, as follows:

- How to control web server access.
- Where to store intranet information.
- How to make your intranet web site secure.
- How to keep track of who's accessing what on your intranet.

One of the nice features of both Personal Web Server and Internet Information Server, as I discuss in Chapter 1, is that they provide the capability to perform administrative tasks through a web browser. I discuss web browsers, which can be used to view Internet and intranet content, and the user side of things in more detail in Chapter 3, but what you need to know is that a web browser is a program that you use to look at web content. Using a browser to perform web site administration is really neat, because after your web server is up, running, and accessible, you can perform administrative tasks from any computer on your intranet that has a web browser installed.

To keep things simple, I just focus on the Personal Web Server and Internet Information Server administration features in this chapter that are likely to be important to you, and you shouldn't need to worry about any administrative features I don't discuss. If you want to dig deeper, however, try the online help of the particular software you're using. I know it's full of a lot of technical mumbo jumbo, but it's a place to start.

Personal Web Server power

You can configure many aspects of Personal Web Server including how it handles the following features:

- ✒ *Authentication* (just a fancy way of saying how the server makes sure users are who they say they are by asking for a user name and password).

- ✒ The directories you use to store your web files.

- ✒ How the server keeps track of who accesses what files.

Personal Web Server provides access to its administration features through a web browser. You need to have either Internet Explorer or Netscape Navigator installed before you can access Personal Web Server administration features. If you don't have a web browser installed, jump ahead to Chapter 3, and return here after you have your web browser installed. You can access the Personal Web Server from your task bar or from the Control Panel by following these steps:

1. **Click Start➪Settings➪Control Panel.**

   The Control Panel appears.

2. **Double-click the Personal Web Server icon to open the Personal Web Server properties dialog box.**

3. **Check to make sure that your web server is running and is configured to start up automatically by clicking the Services tab of the
Personal Web Server Properties dialog box (Figure 2-2).**

Check the HTTP (Hyper Text Transfer Protocol) service in the Service
list box. Its status should read Running.

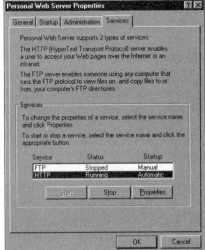

Figure 2-2:
The
Personal
Web Server
Properties
dialog box,
displaying
the
Services
tab options.

4. **If the status of the HTTP service reads** Stopped, **highlight the HTTP
item and then click the Start button.**

5. **Click the Properties button to display the HTTP Properties dialog
box, as shown in Figure 2-3.**

Make sure that the Automatic radio button is selected (that is, a dot
appears in the button) in the Startup Options area — this setting
ensures that the web server starts each time your system starts. If not,
click the button to select it.

6. **Click OK to save your changes, if any, and return to the Personal
Web Server Properties dialog box.**

To review the Personal Web Server administrative features, click the
Administration tab.

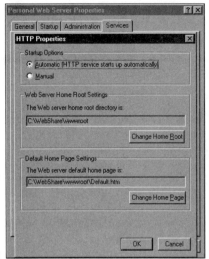

Figure 2-3:
The HTTP
Properties
dialog box.

7. **Click the Administration button to start your web browser and gain access to the Personal Web Server administrative features.**

   The main administrative web page appears, as shown in Figure 2-4. On this page, you find links to manage the Web service, the FTP (File Transfer Protocol) service, and Local Users. Other Personal Web Server-related links also are available on this page.

8. **Click the WWW Administration link to display the web page (this web page resides on the system where your Personal Web Server is installed) shown in Figure 2-5.**

   From the Personal Web Server WWW service administration web page, you can control how users access your web server. To start out, you're on the Services tab page, which has the following options:

   - **The Connection time out text box** determines the number of seconds a user waits for a request before it *times out* (which means that the web server gives up and returns an error). By default, the web server waits 600 seconds (10 minutes). You may find that this is too long for the web server wait — when this amount of time elapses the web server returns a time-out error. If you begin to experience these errors, you may need to consider upgrading your web server hardware with a particular focus on upgrading the speed of your process and amount of memory.

   - **The Maximum connections text box** enables you to specify the maximum number of requests that users can make of the web server at the same time. By default, the web server can handle 300 requests at the same time. If more requests are made, the web server returns an error message to the person making the request.

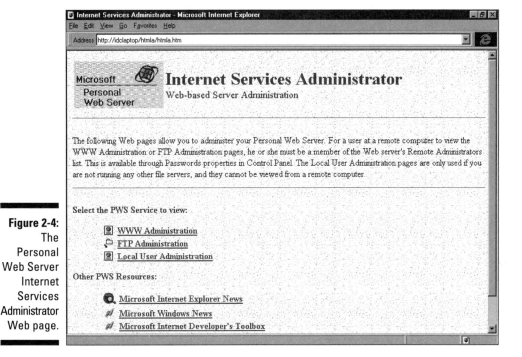

Figure 2-4:
The
Personal
Web Server
Internet
Services
Administrator
Web page.

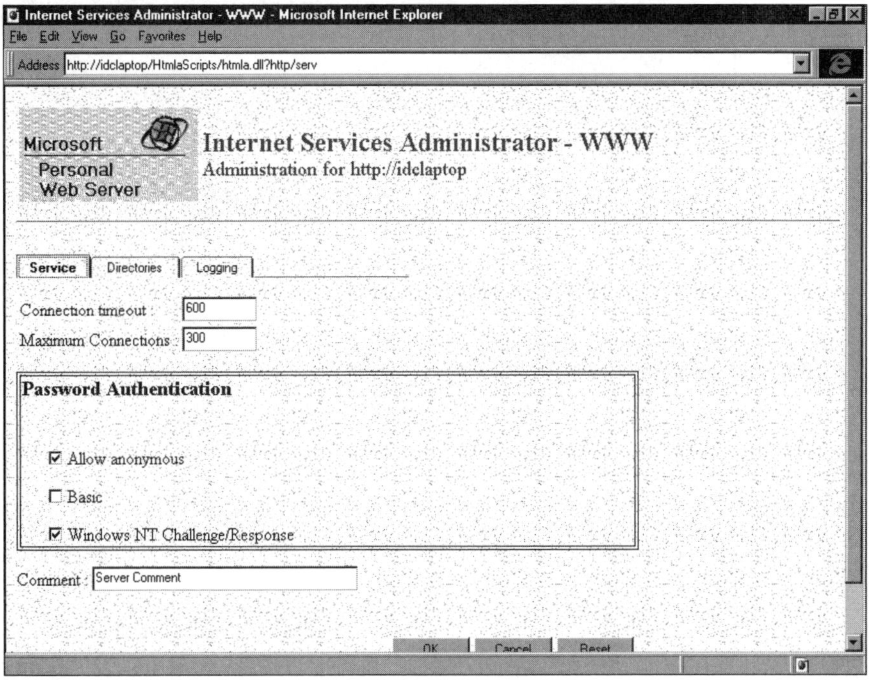

Figure 2-5:
The Internet
Services
Administrator -
WWW
web page.

- **The Password Authentication** area controls how the web server handles passwords. This feature comes into play when the server makes sure users are who they say they are.

  If the **Allow anonymous** check box is selected, anyone can access the web server without needing to supply a user name and password.

  If the **Basic** check box is selected and your web server requests a password to access a web page, the password isn't encrypted or scrambled, which means that you face a slim chance that a nerd genius could intercept user names and passwords supplied to Personal Web Server. In Chapter 11, I discuss how to secure your intranet web pages.

  If the **Windows NT Challenge/Response** check box is selected, the web server accepts encrypted passwords. Only users of the Internet Explorer web browser can send passwords this way.

- Anything you type in the **Comment text box** shows up on the logging reports (see Chapter 12 for more info).

9. **Click OK to save any changes.**

10. **Click the Directories tab to display the Directory Administration web page, as shown in Figure 2-6.**

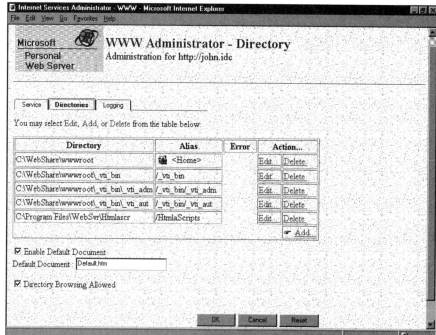

Figure 2-6:
The WWW Administrator - Directory web page.

From this web page, you can control the directories on the system on which you installed the Personal Web Server, provided those directories are accessible to the web server. The features you can change are described in the following list:

- **The Alias column** allows you to give the directory on the same row an alias. If the C:\Program Files\WebSvr\Docs directory, for example, is aliased as /Docs and the web server is accessed as `http://idclaptop`, you'd use the URL (Uniform Resource Locator) `http://idclaptop/Docs` to access that directory from your web browser.

- Click the **Add** link at the end of the table to add new directories.

- If the **Enable Default Document** check box is selected, then each time a web server directory is accessed without specifying a specific filename, the file named in the Default Document text box automatically appears. If, for example, the DEFAULT.HTM file is in the C:\Program Files\WebSvr\Docs directory, that file automatically appears if a browser accesses `http://idclaptop/Docs`.

- If the **Directory Browsing** check box is selected and a default web page file, such as DEFAULT.HTM, isn't in the directory, the user can then view all the files contained in the directory. This level of access may not be a good idea if you're trying to provide access only to specific web files. In Chapter 11, I discuss how to secure your intranet web pages.

11. **Click OK to save any changes.**

12. **Click the Logging tab to display the Logging Administration web page, as shown in Figure 2-7.**

The features you need to know on this page are as described in the following list:

- If the **Enable Logging** check box is selected, web server log files are created. To log or not to log: Take a look at the note at the end of this set of numbered steps for some things to consider regarding the logging feature.

- If the **Automatically open new log** check box is selected, a new file is created every day, week, month, or whenever the log file reaches a certain size, as you specify by selecting the appropriate radio button.

- The **Log file directory** text box is where you enter the directory in which you want the log files created. Logging files track web server usage — keeping account of who accessed a web page, which web page they accessed, and when they accessed it. I discuss web server logging in more detail in Chapter 12.

13. **Click OK to save your changes.**

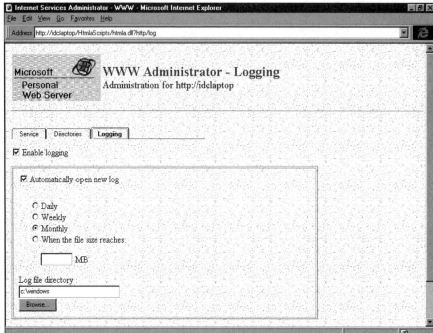

Figure 2-7:
The WWW
Administrator -
Logging
web page.

Depending on how often users access your web server, these log files can become quite big — a line of text is added to the log *each time* someone accesses your web server. You need to remember to periodically delete these files — or you may choose not to create them at all if you're not planning on ever looking at them.

Supervising Internet Information Server

I cover a bunch of the Microsoft Internet Information Server administration information in Chapter 1. Interestingly enough, many of the web server administration dialog boxes available to you in Internet Information Server are very similar to the web pages provided by Personal Web Server. You can access the Internet Information Server Manager by following these steps:

1. Click Start➪Microsoft Internet Server (Common)➪Internet Server Manager.

The Internet Server Manager appears. The main Internet Server Manager window displays a table that contains a row for each service currently running on the system.

2. **Click the Computer Name for the row that contains the WWW service to view the WWW Service properties.**

3. **Choose Properties⇨Service Properties from the Service Manage menu bar to open the WWW Service Properties dialog box, as shown in Figure 2-8.**

   The Service tab is selected by default. On the Service tab of this dialog box, you can change the following features:

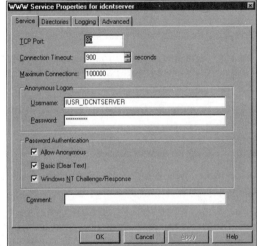

Figure 2-8:
The Service
tab of the
WWW
Service
Properties
dialog box.

- **The Connection time out** text box determines the number of seconds a user must wait for a request before it *times out,* (which means that the web server gives up and returns an error). By default, the web server waits 900 seconds (15 minutes). You may find that this is too long for the web server wait — when this amount of time elapses the web server returns a timeout error. If you begin to experience these errors, you may need to consider upgrading your web server hardware with a particular focus on upgrading the speed of your process and amount of memory.

- **The Maximum connections** text box enables you to specify the maximum number of user requests that can be made of the web server at the same time. By default, the web server can handle 100,000 requests at the same time (many more than Personal Web Server). If more than 100,000 requests are made at one time, the web server returns an error message to the person making the request. The actual number of requests your web server can handle effectively at one time is also limited by the hardware on which your web server runs.

- **The Password Authentication** area controls how the web server handles passwords. This feature comes into play whenever the server makes sure that users are who they say they are.

  If the **A̲llow Anonymous** check box is selected, anyone can access the web server without needing to supply a user name and password.

  If the **B̲asic (Clear Text)** check box is selected and your web server requests a password to access a web page, the password isn't encrypted or scrambled, which means that you face a slim chance that a nerd genius could intercept user names and passwords supplied to Personal Web Server. In Chapter 11, I discuss how to secure your intranet web pages.

  If the **Windows N̲T Challenge/Response** check box is selected, the web server accepts encrypted passwords. Remember that only Internet Explorer clients can send passwords this way.

- Anything that you type in the **Comment** text box shows up on the logging reports.

4. **Click the A̲pply button to save any changes.**

5. **Click the Directories tab to display the version of the WWW Service Properties dialog box shown in Figure 2-9.**

   From this dialog box, you can control which directories on the system on which the Internet Information Server is installed are accessible to the web server. An alias just assigns an alternate (usually shorter) name to a directory.

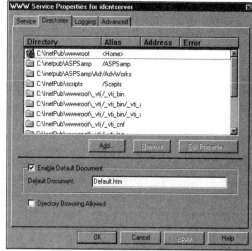

Figure 2-9:
The Directories tab of the WWW Service Properties dialog box.

6. **Click the Add button to make a new directory available.**

   In Chapter 4, I show you how you can use Microsoft FrontPage to manage your web directories.

7. **Click the Logging tab to display the Logging tab of the WWW Services Properties dialog box, as shown in Figure 2-10.**

   The features you can change are on this tab are described in the following list:

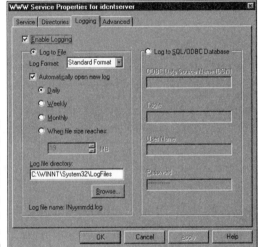

Figure 2-10:
The Logging
tab of the
WWW
Service
Properties
dialog box.

- If the Enable Logging check box is selected, web server log files are created every time someone accesses your server.

- If the Automatically open new log check box is selected, a new file is created every day, week, month, or whenever the log file reaches a certain size, as you specify by selecting the appropriate radio button.

- The Log file directory text box is where you enter the directory in which the log files are created.

8. **Click the Apply button to save your changes.**

Once again, depending on how often your web server is accessed, these log files can become quite big — a line of text is added to the log *each time* a user accesses your web server. You need to remember to periodically delete these files — or you may choose not to create them at all if you're not planning on ever looking at them. In Chapter 12, I discuss web server log files in more detail.

Web File Directories

As you create your intranet site, you need to create all sorts of files, including web pages, graphics, Word or Excel files, and maybe even programs written in Java or VBScript. I show you how to create various intranet files in Part II. You may find that keeping all these files organized is quite a challenge. Having a messy web server is usually not a good idea, unless you're partial to messes (and so is everyone else who must use it). Sorting through all the various files can become difficult if they're all thrown in one location. By using the Directory Administration features of your web server, however, you can create separate directories for each of these file types.

If many departments are accessing the same web server, you may also decide to create directories for each department. To create a new directory that a particular department can access from your web server, you need to access the Directory administration feature of the web server you're using. To do so, follow these steps:

1. **Access the web page or dialog box in your server that enables you to add a new directory.**

   If you're using Personal Web Server, you need to access the administrative web pages, as described in the steps in the section "Personal Web Server Power," earlier in this chapter, and then click the Directories tab to display the WWW Administrator – Directory web page (refer to Figure 2-8). Then you need to click the Add link button on this web page to display the WWW Administrator – Directory Add web page, as shown in Figure 2-11.

   If you're using Internet Information Server, you need to access the Directories tab in the WWW Service Properties dialog box, as I describe in the steps in the section "Supervising Internet Information Server," earlier in this chapter (refer to Figure 2-9). Then click the Add button to open the Directory Properties dialog box, as shown in Figure 2-12.

2. **Enter the name of the new directory to which you want to allow access — for example,** C:\WebShare\wwwroot\Accounting **(you can use the Windows Explorer to create a new directory).**

   In Personal Web Server, enter this new directory name in the Directory text box near the top of the page. In Internet Information Server, enter this new directory name in the Directory text box at the top of the dialog box. Other options function as described in the following list:

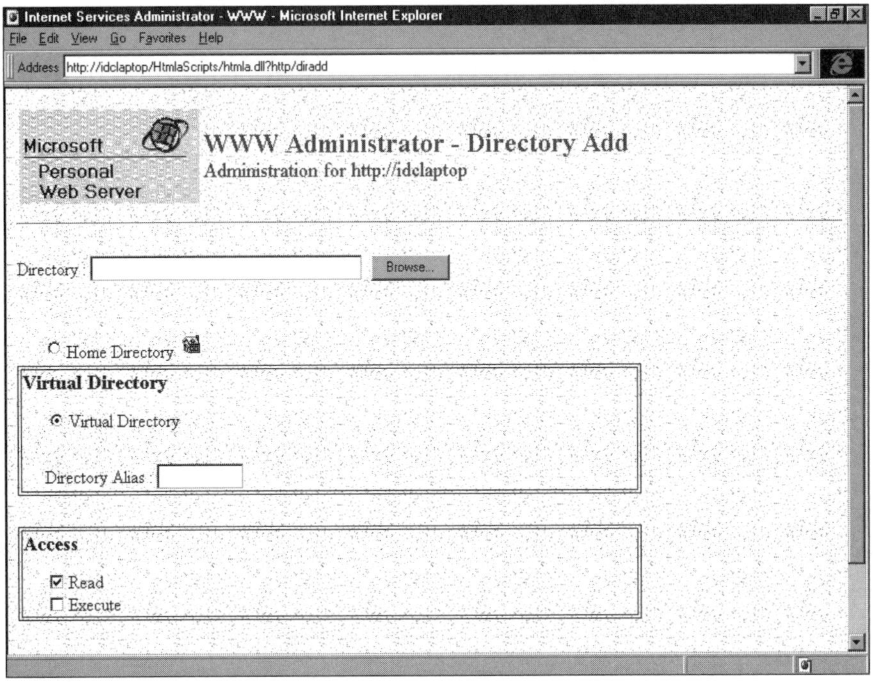

Figure 2-11:
The WWW
Administrator -
Add
Directories
web page
for Personal
Web Server.

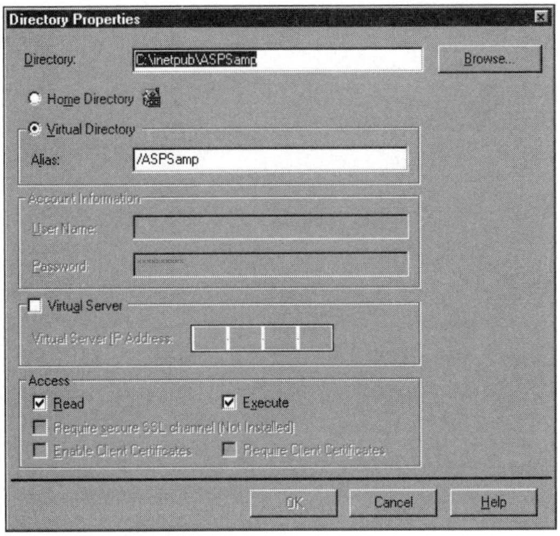

Figure 2-12:
The
Directory
Properties
dialog box
for Internet
Information
Server.

- If the **Virtual Directory** check box or radio button is selected, you can display a web server alias. An alias is just another name (usually shorter) that is used to refer to the directory.

- If the **Read** check box is selected, users can read files in the directory.

- If the **Execute** check box is selected, users can run programs in this directory.

3. Click OK to save your new Web Server directory.

If you're using Personal Web Server, the OK button appears at the bottom of the web page — click it and you're done.

Chapter 3

What about Your Users?

*W*hat *about* your users? Well, they're the ones for whom you're building your intranet, so you need to make sure that they have access to your intranet, right? A big factor in the success of your intranet is how fast users think it's working. People hate to wait — and hate to wait even more when using computers. Although a part of the speed equation is how much information your users need, another big part involves the computers that everyone's using. If your company has a bunch of computers more than two or three years old, those machines may not be up to the intranet task. If you haven't figured it out already, creating an intranet is going to keep you close to the cutting edge of hardware and software.

Minimum Requirements

Getting your intranet up and working for your users takes a mixture of hardware and software. Most companies made the move to give their employees personal computers long ago — if your company is in the minority, what are you waiting for? For your intranet to become all that it can be, each employee must have a computer to participate. Each computer needs the right combination of hardware and software, as I describe in the following sections.

Hardware

I really hate making specific hardware recommendations, because hardware changes so fast. I can give you some minimum requirements, but again, I'd like to talk about selecting computers for your users based mainly on price. Today, a typical PC that's powerful enough for your intranet costs between $1,500 and $2,500. Unless you're buying computers from Fast Eddie's Computer Emporium and getting taken for a fast ride, you can expect any name-brand computer priced in this range to get you what you need. Okay, I promised to give you some general types of requirements you need in your users' computers; here they are:

- ✔ **A CD-ROM** is useful for installing applications. In the "How to be a Network Dictator" section later in this chapter, I talk about how to install and update your users' computers without visiting each and every computer.

- ✔ **A mouse** (not a little squeaky thing — a pointing device!).

- ✔ **At least a 15-inch monitor with a Super VGA graphics card.**

- ✔ **Last, but not least, a network card.**

Software

Luckily, much of the software your users need comes at the right price — free. Many readers, plug-ins, and other intranet programs continue to be free, except for the time you spend waiting for the file to make it through your network. You may need to consider a few things with user software, however, starting with the operating system — the heart of the computer. Although you can still use older versions of Windows (3.x) on your intranet, many intranet programs don't run under the older version. Basing your intranet on Windows 3.x-based machines can be temperamental at best. Consider upgrading to Windows 95 if you're not there already — doing so enables you to run the latest and coolest intranet programs and offers much better networking support.

The other key piece of intranet software every user needs is a web browser. I show you how to select and install a web browser in the "The Basics" section a little later in this chapter.

Going beyond the minimum equipment

I'm referring to some of the extras you can add to the computers on your system to make your and your users' intranet experience even more thrilling. I show you how to use all these cool things in Part II, but I'm giving you a head start on getting this stuff together. Although the following extras definitely increase your costs, they can make a big difference in the things you can do with your intranet:

- ✔ **A faster processor.** Your computer can never go fast enough, so push this device as close to the edge as you can reasonably afford. Although a processor running at 200 MHz seems fast today, it's going to be only average a year from now.

- ✔ **Additional RAM.** Computers love to gobble up memory. Adding extra memory can often have a bigger positive effect on a computer than adding a faster processor. Try to move up to 32MB of RAM — or more, if possible.

- ✔ **A larger monitor.** Staring at a small screen all day can make anyone turn cross-eyed. A larger monitor, 17-inch or better, can make almost anything look better.

- ✔ **A sound card with speakers, a microphone, and a camera.** These are really the bells and whistles of your intranet — they can be used for some of the cooler applications you can deploy, but they aren't really required for most of your day-to-day office tasks. A sound card, microphone, and camera are primarily used to conduct virtual meetings over your intranet.

Are All Your Users Hooked Up to a Network?

Before you can begin, you need to answer one very important question: Are all your users' computers hooked up to the network? I know that I asked this very same question as you installed your web server in Chapter 1, but it's very important to check each user's computer for this same connection. Your intranet is dead in the water if nobody's computer is connected to it.

Yep — they're hooked up!

Great! You're all set. You just need to make sure that your users' computers are using the right language (TCP/IP) to talk on the network. If your users' computers are running Windows 95 — you can check whether your users' computers are running the TCP/IP protocol by following these steps:

1. **On the user's computer — Click Start⇨Settings⇨Control Panel.**

   The Windows 95 Control Panel appears.

2. In the Control Panel window, double-click the Network icon.

The Network dialog box appears with the Configuration tab open, as shown in Figure 3-1.

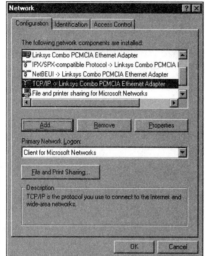

Figure 3-1:
The
Windows 95
Network
dialog box.

3. Check the list box at the top of the dialog box that lists which network components are installed.

If the words TCP/IP appear on the same line as Ethernet Adapter, as shown in Figure 3-1, you're all set! The computer shouldn't have any problems talking to your web server and other computers on your network. If you can't find the TCP/IP option or are unsure whether the TCP/IP protocol is installed, you may want to find out from your resident computer guru. You need to have the TCP/IP protocol up and running on your users' computers before you can continue.

Nope — they're not hooked up!

Bummer. You need to get the computer hooked up to the network before you can proceed. In Chapter 1, I briefly review how to set up your network. Remember: You need a network card for *each* user's computer that you want to connect to your intranet. Again, if you're still unsure how to get your company's computers networked together, consult one of your company's computer experts. Undoubtedly, you need to work with them to get things off the ground. If you're the one who must get things done and you don't know where to start, *Networking For Dummies,* 2nd Edition, by Doug Lowe (IDG Books Worldwide, Inc.) offers a good beginning.

The Basics

Although your web server may be the core of your intranet, a web browser offers the way in to your intranet. A web browser is the application your users run to view the information you publish on your intranet. You need to consider a number of things in choosing the web browser that's right for you and your company. In the following sections, I review your web browser choices and show you how to get each of your options up and running.

Picking a browser

Choosing a web browser can become as big a crusade as choosing your web server. Basically, you have only two real options for a web browser for your intranet: Netscape Navigator or Microsoft Internet Explorer. For many, the choice becomes a matter of personal taste, but you need to be aware of a few key differences between the two. Table 3-1 lists the pros and cons of using Internet Explorer, and Table 3-2 lists the pros and cons of using Netscape Navigator.

Table 3-1 The Advantages and Disadvantages of Internet Explorer

Advantage/Disadvantage	Description
Advantage	Microsoft Internet Explorer supports ActiveX controls, which are small programs that can run inside your web browser. The important thing to realize about ActiveX controls is that they're specifically designed to run under Windows 95 and NT. ActiveX controls can make your intranet web pages look cool and offer increased functionality — such as access to databases and displaying non-HTML files.
Disadvantage	Internet Explorer supports ActiveX controls. Although this feature can be great and nifty, it's also a big disadvantage because ActiveX controls can be a security risk. For example, ActiveX programs can write to users' hard drives. I've heard a few reports of ActiveX controls that do nasty things to your system — such as examine the contents of your hard drive and delete files. Although on a self-contained intranet that you control you don't need to live in fear, you still need to be aware of the security risks.

(continued)

Table 3-1 *(continued)*

Advantage/Disadvantage	Description
Advantage	Internet Explorer completely supports VBScript and JavaScript scripting languages. VBScript and JavaScript can enable your users to interact with your intranet web pages. VBScript is a lot like the Visual Basic programming language. If the programmers at your company are already familiar with Visual Basic, they can apply much of what they already know in using VBScript.
Disadvantage	Internet Explorer runs only under Windows (including 95, 3.*x*, and NT) and Macintosh operating systems.

Table 3-2   **The Advantages and Disadvantages of Netscape Navigator**

Advantage/Disadvantage	Description
Advantage	Netscape Navigator runs on a number of platforms, including Windows (all versions), UNIX, Macintosh, and OS/2. This feature can be very important if your company has a number of different types of computers that all require intranet access.
Disadvantage	Netscape Navigator doesn't provide built-in support for ActiveX controls. Netscape Navigator does, however, support plug-ins that enable you to run ActiveX controls from within Netscape Navigator. Try NCompass labs at www.ncompasslabs.com for more information about their ActiveX-enabling plug-in. Supporting ActiveX controls adds an extra step in your Web browser setup, but may be worth the effort, depending on what you want to do.
Advantage	Netscape Navigator is smaller, because it doesn't include built-in ActiveX support, and is slightly faster than Internet Explorer.
Disadvantage	Netscape doesn't support the advanced password-scrambling mechanisms provided by Microsoft Personal Web Server and Internet Information Server.
Advantage	The Gold edition of Netscape Navigator includes a built-in web page editor. By using this feature, your users can use a single program to view your intranet as well as create new content.

Ideally, you design your intranet to support both web browsers. However, if you're looking to take advantage of some of the latest features or are interested in providing the best possible look and feel to your intranet, you're better off picking one and sticking with it. Unlike the Internet, you have complete control over your intranet, how people access it, and the browser they use to access it. Picking one web browser can help keep your support and development costs down.

Internet Explorer

The latest release version of Internet Explorer is Version 3.02, which includes fixes for recently discovered security problems in Version 3.0. As browsers improve and new features are added, you want to make sure that you keep up to date with the latest releases. A good Internet information resource to help you keep up with the latest stuff is at www.browsers.com.

Internet Explorer is available on the CD-ROM included at the back of this book and also available as a free download from the Microsoft Internet Explorer Web site at www.microsoft.com/ie. You can run Internet Explorer on computers less powerful than what I describe earlier in this chapter, but that doesn't mean that doing so is a good idea for your intranet. In any case, Internet Explorer's minimum system requirements include the following:

- ✔ At least an 80386 processor.
- ✔ At least 8MB system memory.
- ✔ A minimum of 5MB free disk space and up to 10MB, depending on the features you want to install. I recommend allocating the full 10MB when installing Internet Explorer.

After you connect to the Internet Explorer Web site, you see a button or some text that you can click to get to the download page. The Microsoft Web site download process is pretty painless. Just make sure, however, that you note the name of the file you're downloading and pay close attention, because you can choose from several different versions of Internet Explorer for Windows 95 and Windows 3.1. I usually download new files to a special directory I call DOWNLOAD.

If you need help downloading applications from the Internet, go to Appendix B, "A Guide to Intranet Resources," where I show you how to get the latest Internet downloads. If you need help accessing the applications on the included CD-ROM, go to Appendix C, "What's on the CD," where I show you how to get to and install the stuff included on the CD.

Internet Explorer Version 4.0

Microsoft has recently released the beta of Internet Explorer Version 4.0. Microsoft calls it a "developers release," and as of the time I write this chapter, the program's certainly not ready to install for everyday use on your intranet. I suggest that you make a computer available for testing the latest browsers and other software that you're thinking about using on your intranet. That way, you can evaluate new products before you have every single user on your intranet wondering why they're constantly installing new software that doesn't even work. Most often, you want to stick with the final, tested, and true software releases for your intranet to avoid potential software bugs. Because the window to your intranet is through the web browser, bad software locks everyone out and can undermine your entire intranet project. In other words, be patient for the latest version of Internet Explorer!

The new version of Internet Explorer is expected to provide a number of new and exciting features, including the following:

✔ **Integrating the web browser into your desktop through Active Desktop.** You can have a number of web pages open and displayed as part of your desktop.

✔ **Built-in support for push technologies**, which automatically send the most current information to your web browser, without you needing to explicitly ask for it. I discuss Push technologies and your intranet in Chapter 9.

✔ **Built-in web page editing capabilities**, which enable your users to publish their own web pages on your intranet more easily.

✔ **Works seamlessly with e-mail and conferencing applications.**

✔ **Closer integration with Windows 95 and NT**, with the integration of Windows Explorer and Internet Explorer, enabling you to view your intranet and local hard drive as a combined resource.

Clearly, the latest version of Internet Explorer is going to blur the line between your intranet and the files stored on users' PCs. Your intranet will begin to appear more and more like something that's built into your users computers and less like some distant place where information is stored. Hold on just a little, however, until Microsoft releases the final version and then wait just a bit longer until a few of the bugs are worked out before making Version 4.0 the browser on your intranet. After a little time to get the bugs worked out, this latest version of Internet Explorer should make your intranet easier to use and an even more valuable resource. Visit the Microsoft Internet Explorer Web site at www.microsoft.com/ie for the latest Internet Explorer version information.

Installing Internet Explorer

Ready to install and fire up Internet Explorer? Follow these steps:

1. **Go to the directory where the Internet Explorer installation file is located, either in the directory where you saved it when you downloaded it from the Internet, or on the CD-ROM included with this book.**

To get to Windows Explorer, click Start➪Programs➪Windows Explorer.

2. Double-click the installation file in the Windows Explorer.

The License Agreement dialog box appears, giving you the standard legal mumbo jumbo.

3. Click the Yes button to continue with the installation.

Don't worry — you haven't agreed to a life of Microsoft servitude by agreeing to the licensing agreement. At least, I don't think so. The Internet Explorer installation wizard unpacks the program files. A dialog box appears asking you to select which optional components to install.

4. Click the Yes button to open the Optional Components dialog box.

5. Select the components that you want to install by clicking the check box next to each one.

If you're trying to save some extra disk space, you can choose not to install some of these components. The full version of Internet Explorer includes:

- **Internet Mail** for e-mail through the browser (see Chapter 6)

- **Internet News** for reading Internet news groups, which are bulletin-board type discussions

- **NetMeeting** for video conferencing over an intranet

- **ActiveMovie** for viewing video clips through the browser

- **HTML Layout control** for adding ActiveX controls to web pages

I recommend installing all of these if you have the space on the user's computer. Otherwise, none of them are absolutely necessary for the browser to work.

6. Click OK to continue with the installation process.

The features you select are added to your installation, and the Installation Status dialog box appears. You can monitor the process of the Internet Explorer installation as the files fly into your hard drive.

During the installation process, a Version Conflict dialog box may appear, telling you that a more current version of a file used by Internet Explorer is already installed. In most cases, you need to choose Yes and keep the more current version of the file. In all likelihood, other applications on your system rely on the most current version of the file, and replacing it with an older version may cause problems.

After the installation process is complete, a final dialog box appears asking you if you want to restart your computer.

7. Click the Yes button to finish the installation process and restart your computer.

8. **Kick your feet up, sit back, and relax while your computer restarts.**

   Congratulations, you've just installed Internet Explorer! In the following section, I show you how to make sure that everything is working correctly.

Getting Internet Explorer going

Now that you have Internet Explorer installed, you need to take a little time to make sure that everything is working correctly. Internet Explorer adds a shortcut to your desktop and also appears in your Start menu. So fire up those engines! Just follow these steps:

1. **Double-click the shortcut on your desktop or click Start⇨Program Files⇨Internet Explorer.**

   By default, Internet Explorer tries to connect to the Microsoft Web site. If you're not connected to the Internet, an error message box appears, but don't worry.

2. **Click the OK button to continue.**

   The default blank web page loads. In the "Do you have a server?" section of Chapter 1, I talk about finding out the name of your Web server. Now is the time that you need to use that name.

3. **In the Address text box, at the top of the Internet Explorer window, type the following text:**

   http://*yourservername*

   You need to enter the text that appears only in bold here just as it appears. The ***yourservername*** part(shown here in bold italics) is the name of your particular web server. I have Personal Web Server based web server running on a computer called IDCLAPTOP, for example, so I'd type **http://idclaptop** in the Address text box. If you're running Personal Web Server, the default web page appears, as shown in Figure 3-2. If you have any problems accessing your web server, jump ahead to the "When Bad Things Happen" section later in this chapter, where I discuss possible problems and solutions. In Chapter 4, I show you how to use FrontPage to create your own intranet web pages.

To have your intranet web server home page open by default each time you start Internet Explorer, load Internet Explorer on the user's computer and follow these steps:

1. **Go to View⇨Options to open the Options dialog box.**

2. **Click the Navigation tab to display the Navigation options, as shown in Figure 3-3.**

3. **Click the Use Current button to make your Personal Web Server default page your Start Page.**

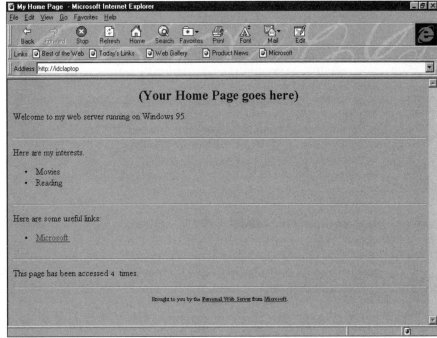

Figure 3-2:
Internet
Explorer
displaying
the default
Personal
Web Server
home page.

4. Click OK to save your changes.

Now, each time you start Internet Explorer, your intranet web server home page opens automatically.

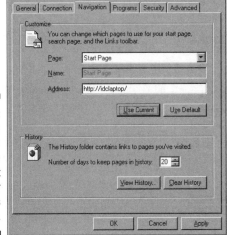

Figure 3-3:
The
Navigation
tab of the
Internet
Explorer
Options
dialog box.

Netscape Navigator

Your other Web browser choice is Netscape Navigator. The Gold version of Netscape Navigator includes a built-in web page editor — a big advantage if you plan to rule your intranet as a pure democracy and enable users to publish as well as access documents. The current Gold release is Version 3.01, and you need to purchase it from a store or from the Netscape Web site at www.netscape.com. The beta version of Netscape Navigator is available as a free download from the same site, but you need to remember that betas are only good to give the software a test drive — don't expect your users to rely on beta versions. Netscape Navigator's minimum system requirements include the following:

✔ At least an 80386 processor.

✔ At least 6MB of RAM.

✔ A minimum of 10MB free disk space, depending on the features you select to install.

Netscape Communicator Version 4.0

Like Internet Explorer, Netscape also has a new web browser version waiting in the sidelines — Netscape Communicator Version 4.0. At the time I write this chapter, this latest version of Netscape is available only as a preview release, and the cautions I outline in the Internet Explorer sidebar, earlier in this chapter, apply here as well. You need to be wary of the latest, newest versions of products that have been available for only a few weeks. Often, the bugs in these programs can make them extremely frustrating to use. You're best off just being patient and waiting for the dust of the newest software to settle a bit — talk to other people who run intranets and see what their experience has been. After the coast seems clear, go ahead and upgrade!

Netscape Communicator is a suite of components that work closely together and includes the following features:

✔ **The Netscape Navigator Web browser,** which includes support for the latest HTML features (*HTML* being the HyperText Markup Language — the code and "tags" you use to create Web pages) and improved security.

✔ **An e-mail client,** Netscape Messenger, which includes an integrated spell checker and support for encryption. Encryption allows you to send messages which can only be read by the intended reader.

✔ **Netscape Collabra and Conference,** which you can use to hold virtual meetings over your intranet.

✔ **Netscape Calendar,** which is a group scheduling tool which allows a group of users to schedule meetings and appointments.

✔ **Netscape Composer,** a Web page editing tool which gives users an easy way to create their own web pages.

Visit the Netscape Web site at www.netscape.com for the latest Netscape Communicator information.

After you connect to the Netscape Web site, you see a button or some text that you can click to get to the download page. The Netscape Web site download process, similar to the one for Internet Explorer, is fairly painless. Just make sure that you note the name of the file you download, and that you download it into a directory that you can remember (I usually create a special directory named DOWNLOAD). (The download file for the latest complete version of Netscape Navigator Gold Version 3.01 for Windows 95 or NT is called G32E301P.EXE.)

Installing Navigator

Ready to install and fire up Netscape Navigator? Follow these steps:

1. **Go to the directory where the Netscape Navigator installation file is located.**

   You can use Windows Explorer to locate and access the directory. (Aren't you glad you created that DOWNLOAD directory now?) To get to Windows Explorer, click Start⇨Programs⇨Windows Explorer.

2. **Run the installation application: Double-click on the installation file in the Windows Explorer.**

   The Netscape Navigator Installation dialog box appears on screen.

3. **Click Yes to continue with the installation.**

   The Welcome dialog box appears, warning you to close any programs you currently have open, so snap to it — close any other programs that are currently running.

4. **Click the Next button to continue.**

   The Choose Destination Location dialog box appears. You can choose to install Navigator in a directory other than the default, C:\PROGRAM FILES\NETSCAPE\NAVIGATOR, but I don't recommend doing so.

5. **Make life easy on yourself and keep the default directory by clicking the Next button to continue.**

   If you're installing the complete Gold version, your next visual treat is the Question dialog box. This dialog box asks you whether you'd like to install CoolTalk. CoolTalk is an Internet/intranet phone application that you can use to talk with people over your intranet in real time, kind of like a phone system over your computer network.

6. **To install CoolTalk, click Yes; otherwise click No to continue.**

   The Netscape Navigator installation process continues regardless of your choice.

   If you choose to install CoolTalk, a Question dialog box appears, asking whether you'd like to install the CoolTalk Watchdog. If, in addition to your fledgling intranet, your users' computers (or the network at large) are also hooked into the Internet, I suggest you click the Yes button. If your intranet is *not* connected to the Internet, I suggest you click the No button to continue. Simply explained, the Watchdog application isn't some junkyard dog — it simply enables other intranet/Internet users to call you whenever your computer's on.

7. **Click <u>Y</u>es to install the CoolTalk Watchdog; otherwise, click <u>N</u>o.**

The Question dialog box shown in Figure 3-4 appears next. This dialog box asks you whether you'd like to connect to the Navigator Web site to complete your installation process. Connecting to this site really isn't required to complete your installation — it just sends you some registration information. Remember, you're only be able to connect to this site if you are connected to the Internet.

8. **Click <u>N</u>o for now.**

After you start up Navigator later, you can connect to the Netscape Web site and get the spiel.

Another dialog box appears asking whether you'd like to view the README release notes file now. If you're interested in reading the release notes, go ahead and click the Yes button. The sky doesn't fall, however, if you click the No button to skip the notes for now.

Figure 3-4:
The
Netscape
Navigator
Question
dialog
box.

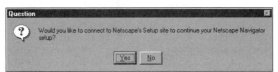

9. **Click <u>Y</u>es to read the release notes; click <u>N</u>o to skip the notes and continue.**

The Information dialog box shown in Figure 3-5 graces your screen next. Congratulations! The Netscape Navigator installation process is complete!

10. **Click OK to complete the installation process.**

Figure 3-5:
The
Netscape
Navigator
Information
dialog box.

In the following section, I show you how to make sure that everything is working correctly.

Getting Netscape Navigator going

Now that you have Netscape Navigator installed, you need to make sure that everything is working. The time is here for you to take Navigator for a test drive:

1. **Click Start⇨Programs⇨Netscape Navigator Gold 3.01⇨Netscape Navigator Gold.**

   The Netscape License Agreement dialog box appears.

2. **Click the Accept button.**

   Don't worry. Netscape has shorter terms of servitude than Microsoft Internet Explorer. Netscape Navigator tries to connect to the Netscape Web site by default. If you're not connected to the Internet, an error message box appears — but don't worry; just click the OK button to continue. You need to dig up the name of your web server — check in the "Do you have a server?" section of Chapter 1, where I talk about finding the name of your web server, if you don't know the name or don't have it written down.

3. **In the Location text box, at the top of the Netscape Navigator window, type the following:**

   http://*yourservername*

   You need to enter the text that appears only in bold just as it is here. The ***yourservername*** part (in bold italics here) is the name of your particular web server. For example, my web server is Internet Information Server which runs on a computer called IDCNTSERVER, so I type **http:// idcntserver** in the Location text box. If you're running Internet Information Server, the default web page appears, as shown in Figure 3-6. If you have any problems accessing your web server, go to the following section "When Bad Things Happen," where I discuss possible problems and solutions. In Chapter 4, I show you how to use FrontPage to create your own intranet web pages — so you don't have to look at the boring default home page provided by your web server.

To have your intranet web server page open by default each time you start Netscape Navigator, follow these steps:

1. **Choose Options⇨General Preferences to open the Preferences dialog box, as shown in Figure 3-7.**

2. **Enter the address of your intranet server in the Browser Starts With text box.**

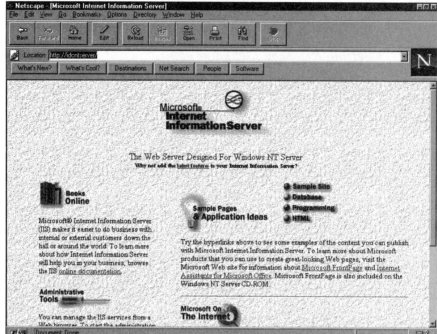

Figure 3-6:
Netscape
Navigator,
displaying
the default
Internet
Information
Server
home page.

Figure 3-7:
The
Netscape
Navigator
Preferences
dialog box.

3. Click OK to save your changes.

Now, each time you start Netscape Navigator, your intranet web server home page opens automatically.

When Bad Things Happen

Your web browsers are unlikely to be the direct cause of any problems. But you're here at this section anyway, aren't you? Well, don't despair — everything's under control. If you're having problems accessing your web server from your Web browser, Table 3-3 lists the answers to some common problems you may encounter.

Table 3-3	Common Web Browser and Web Server Problems and Solutions
Problem	*Solutions*
Can't find your web server?	If you're getting an error on your user's computer stating that your web server can't be found, you need to check your network. Make sure that all your network cables are secure. If you're using coaxial networking cables, make sure that a terminator (a little metal cap) is connected to both ends of the cable. Try another user's computer — if it's also having a problem finding your web server, you may have a bigger network problem and you probably need some help from your local network guru.
HTTP/1.0 500 Server Error	You get this error if your web server isn't allowing people to log on. Make sure that your web server is configured for anonymous logon and that the Windows NT Challenge/Response option check box is *not* checked. I review web server administration and how to configure the Challenge/Response option in the "Personal Web Server power" and "Supervising Internet Information Server" sections in Chapter 2.

How to Be a Network Dictator

If your company has a lot of computers that need to access your intranet, you may want to consider tools that help automate the process of configuring a large number of computers and installing software. Microsoft provides software called Systems Management Server, which runs on a Windows NT server. Systems Management Server can help manage your organization's PCs from one centralized location and includes such features as the following:

✔ The capability to configure and install software from a central location.

✔ The capability to troubleshoot problems with network computers from a central location.

✔ The capability to schedule software installations and upgrades when everyone is out of the office.

✔ The capability to create an inventory of the hardware and software installed on your intranet.

The Microsoft Systems Management Server Web site, at www.microsoft.com/smsmgmt, provides additional information. I recommend checking out this site if you think that the features I described may be useful to your company. If you're not a systems administrator, however, you may want to leave these tasks to them.

Where to Next?

Now that you have your web browser installed on one computer, you know how to install it on every computer that you want to be able to access your intranet. You also got a chance to see your default web server home page, and it was ugly and useless, wasn't it? Well, the focus of Part II of this book is to show you how to start designing your own web pages by using Microsoft FrontPage and to continue reviewing other cool applications that you can run on your intranet.

Part II
Using Your Intranet to Achieve World Domination

The 5th Wave   By Rich Tennant

BOB'S DECISION NOT TO BE CONNECTED TO THE CORPORATE INTRANET CAUSED SOME SUSPICION ON THE PART OF THOSE WHO WERE.

In this part . . .

This part is the heart of *Building an Intranet For Dummies* — I mean, isn't everyone's goal to rule the world? If you get your corporate intranet up and running quickly, you may just have some extra time to work toward world domination, not to mention the advantage you need to keep it.

This part takes on the key hot intranet technologies and tackles them one at a time. I cover each technology independently so that you can select the one that's right for you when you need it, and jump right in. To begin the discussion of each key technology, I review what the technology is all about, who would use it, why you want it, where to find it, what you're going to need (on both the client and server side), and what the nerds say about the technology in order to give you the essential background you need before you begin.

Chapter 4

Web-Ward Ho!

. . . .

. . . .

*A*fter you have your web server set up and your users can access it with their web browsers, you're ready to hit the fun stuff. The easiest way to get information out on your intranet is by using web pages. You create web pages by using *HTML* (HyperText Markup Language). If you've ever used an older version of WordPerfect, you may remember the Reveal Codes option, which enables you to see your word-processing file with all the formatting commands. HTML is very much like those WordPerfect formatting commands — the commands, or *tags* as they're called, tell your web browser how to display the web page.

Luckily, you don't need to become an HTML wizard to start creating useful, cool intranet web pages. You can use any of a bunch of different *web page editors*. A web page editor lets you create web pages just as easily as you create a document with a word processor or a spreadsheet program.

Making Sure that You Have the Right Stuff

You and anyone else on your intranet can create intranet web pages from any connected computer by using a web page editor and a web browser. As long as your computer is powerful enough to run a web browser, it should be powerful enough to run a web page editor.

Some of the currently available web page editors (and their associated Web sites) include the following:

- ✔ Microsoft FrontPage 97: `www.microsoft.com/frontpage`
- ✔ HoTMetaL Pro: `www.softquad.com`
- ✔ Netscape Navigator Gold: `www.netscape.com`
- ✔ HotDog Pro: `www.sausage.com`

As is true of a lot of things involving computers, picking an HTML editor is a matter of personal preference. I focus on Microsoft FrontPage 97 in this chapter because it provides tools that help you manage your intranet web site, wizards that automate the process of creating web pages, and tools to visually design your web pages. If you decide to check out some of the other web page editors, I have some suggestions for choosing a web page editor that will work for you:

- ✔ **Easy to use.** Choose a web page editor that's easy to use and doesn't require you to have an in-depth knowledge of HTML (unless you're into that kind of stuff).

- ✔ **Intranet web site management.** Managing the links and all of the web pages contained in your web site can be a tedious process — look for a web page editor that provides the ability to manage your web site.

- ✔ **Syntax checker.** Make sure your web page editor only allows you to create web pages that use correct and complete HTML code.

- ✔ **Spell checker.** An integrated spell checker is a great addition.

- ✔ **Provides templates.** Templates provide a skeleton for the design of your web page and can help you get started quickly.

Cutting through the Technobabble

Web page technical terms mostly involve convoluted tongue-twisters that sound pretty cool if you say them at some programmer's cocktail party but never seem to make any sense in real conversation. Table 4-1 is your guide to decoding the technical mumbo-jumbo of web page design.

Table 4-1	**Web Page Design Terms and Standards Decoded**
What the HTML Guru Says	**What the HTML Guru Really Means**
CGI	*Common Gateway Interface (CGI)* is a way to process form information, perform searches of your web site, and other neat things. CGI scripts are mostly written by serious programmers.
Forms	A *form* is just a page with a way for a user to enter information. You can create web page forms by using text boxes, list boxes, check boxes, and radio buttons. If you combine forms with a little scripting, you have a way of collecting information from your web site viewers and picking it up back on the web server.
Frames	*Frames* are separate little windows that you can create on your web pages. You can use frames to divide your web pages into logical sections. For example, you can divide a page into two frames, one for links to major pages within your intranet and the other to display those pages. That way, the links to the major areas of your intranet are always visible and available in the browser.
HTML	*HyperText Markup Language* is the language you use to create web pages. Many web page editors enable you to visually create web pages and then generate the HTML code for you behind the scenes. HTML tells the web browser how every piece of text and image needs to appear.
Image maps	An *image map* lets you to create an image with different regions that users can click to link to other web pages.
Links	*Links* are the key element of web pages — they are what you use to navigate through a web site. Text links usually appear in a different color and are underlined when you see them in your web browser. Image links often have a border around them. If you click a link, you're sent to the web page specified by that link.
Scripting	*Scripts* are little programs that you can put inside your web pages to enable your users to interact with the page. VBScript and JavaScript are common examples of scripting languages. CGI scripts run on your web server, while VBScript and JavaScript scripts typically run on the user's web browser.

(continued)

Table 4-1 *(continued)*

What the HTML Guru Says	What the HTML Guru Really Means
Tables	HTML *tables* are gridlike tables that you can use to display information in an organized manner. Think of the thing that you're reading right now. . .
Tags	In discussions of HTML, the term *tag* may come up. No, people aren't talking about price tags; they're talking about *HTML tags*. HTML tags control how each element on your web page appears. Many times, HTML tags appear in pairs. If the tags <B> and </B> are used, for example, any text that appears between them appears in bold as you view the web page in your browser.
WebBots	*WebBots* are a feature of Microsoft FrontPage that allow you to automate certain tasks. For example, you can use WebBots to time- and date-stamp your web pages, automatically update your web pages at specified times, generate a table of contents for your web site, or a number of other little tasks.

Designing Your Intranet Site — What to Include

So you're ready to start thinking about your intranet web site. What kind of information do you want to make available? Here are a few ideas to help get you started:

✔ **Information from your human resources department.** You know those big bulky employee manuals and benefits information packets that no one ever has a chance to read until they have a problem? Your intranet is perfect for human resources issues — the information is in one place and easily updatable as it changes.

✔ **The latest accounting and financial information.** Everyone needs to keep an eye on the bottom line.

✔ **Answers to the most common company-wide computer questions.** Sometimes intranet web pages with reference information are called *FAQs,* for *Frequently Asked Questions.* In fact, some companies not only answer computer questions, but also conduct the majority of their computer training right through their intranet! This type of training is known as Intranet-Based Training, or IBT for short. *Intranet Publishing For Dummies,* by Glenn Weadock (IDG Books Worldwide, Inc.), is a great resource for more information IBT.

✔ **Organizational charts.** You can post these so that you can see how far from the top you really are or, more likely, how close to the bottom.

✔ **Employee directory information.** You can even include employee pictures so that you know which one of those guys down the hall is really Joe Blow.

✔ **The latest company news, press releases, and upcoming events.** Instead of wasting the time and paper to distribute memos and other paper based information, you can simply put this information on your intranet web site for immediate access.

Designing and Managing a Web Site with Microsoft FrontPage 97

Microsoft FrontPage 97 provides a visual tool that helps you design intranet web pages and manage your web site. FrontPage 97 provides a number of wizards that you can use to automatically create anything from a single web page all the way up to an entire web site with just a few clicks of your mouse. Although I can't show you all the subtleties of creating web pages with FrontPage, I do show you how to use the wizards and other whiz-bang tools that FrontPage provides to help you quickly get your intranet site off the ground. If you get turned on by this chapter and you want a more in-depth look at FrontPage, check out Asha Dornfest's *FrontPage Web Publishing & Design For Dummies* (IDG Books Worldwide, Inc.).

Getting up and running with FrontPage 97

Installing Microsoft FrontPage is a fairly painless process. Follow these steps to install the commercial version of FrontPage:

1. **Place your FrontPage 97 CD-ROM in your CD-ROM drive.**

   The installation process should start as soon as you put the CD-ROM into your drive. If the installation starts automatically, the FrontPage

Installation dialog box appears as shown in Figure 4-1. If it doesn't start automatically, run the Setup application on the CD-ROM driver from Windows Explorer or the good old DOS prompt, as follows:

a. Click Start⇨Programs⇨Windows Explorer.

The Windows Explorer appears.

b. Double-click the CD-ROM drive icon.

c. Double-click the SETUP.EXE file in the right-hand area of Windows Explorer.

The FrontPage Installation dialog box appears, as shown in Figure 4-1.

Figure 4-1:
The
FrontPage
97 Setup
dialog box.

2. Click the FrontPage 97 Installation button to get started.

The Welcome dialog box appears on-screen.

3. Click the Next button to continue.

The FrontPage registration dialog box appears and you're asked to enter your name and company name.

4. 'Fess up and tell who you are and where you're from by entering that information in the Name and Company Name text boxes and clicking the Next button to continue.

The Confirm FrontPage Registration dialog box is displayed showing the name and company name you entered. FrontPage now asks you whether you're lying or made a mistake.

5. If you're absolutely sure that you know your name and where you work, click the Yes button.

Software doesn't assume anything (except that you know how to use it . . .). The Microsoft FrontPage CD Key dialog box is displayed asking you for your CD key.

6. **Enter your CD key in the CD Key edit box.**

   The *CD key* is the code on the back of your CD-ROM case.

7. **Click OK.**

   The Destination Path dialog box is displayed and you're asked where you want to install the FrontPage files.

8. **To accept the default directory, C:\PROGRAM FILES\MICROSOFT FRONTPAGE, click the Next button to continue.**

   You should accept the default directory. The Setup Type dialog box appears.

9. **Select the Typical installation option and click the Next button.**

   FrontPage begins its long and arduous journey to find a web server. In Chapter 1, I give you the lowdown on web servers — if you don't have a server installed, you may want to read that chapter. If FrontPage finds a server, it's listed in the next dialog box that appears. FrontPage then installs the FrontPage Server Extensions.

9. **Click the Next button to continue in the Installed Servers Detected dialog box.**

10. **The Start Copying Files dialog box is displayed, make sure that what you tell FrontPage to install is correct and then click the Next button to get on with the show.**

    If you're installing the FrontPage Server Extensions, you're asked to stop your web server for just a second while the extensions are installed.

12. **Go ahead and stop your web server — it restarts after the extensions are installed.**

    After the FrontPage files are installed, you're asked to restart your computer.

13. **The Setup Complete dialog box is displayed. Click the Finish button to complete the installation process.**

    If you installed the FrontPage Server Extensions a dialog box appears asking you to restart your system

14. **Click on the Restart button and relish in your victory for just a few minutes, because the fun is just beginning!**

FrontPage server extensions

If you installed FrontPage *before* you installed your web server, you need to re-install FrontPage and choose to install the Server Page extensions. The FrontPage server extensions provide a way for FrontPage to talk directly to your web server, and help you manage your web site. FrontPage server extensions are available for Personal Web Server, Internet Information Server, and other web servers. FrontPage server extensions for Personal Web Server and Internet Information Server are included with the FrontPage CD-ROM and are also available on the Microsoft FrontPage Web site at the following address:

```
www.microsoft.com/frontpage
```

Guide to creating your intranet web pages

Microsoft has made an Intranet Starter wizard available for a free download on the Microsoft FrontPage Web site at `www.microsoft.com/frontpage/wpp.htm`.

If you need help downloading applications from the Internet, see Appendix A. If you need help accessing the applications on the book's CD-ROM, see Appendix C.

The Intranet Starter wizard file that you download is called FPINTWIZ.EXE. After you have it on your hard drive, you can run the file from the Windows Explorer (or your DOS prompt); just follow these steps:

1. **Click Start➪Programs➪Windows Explorer.**

   The Windows Explorer appears.

2. **Go to your C:\DOWNLOAD folder and double-click the FPINTWIZ.EXE file.**

   The installation process begins! The installation process displays a dialog box asking you whether you'd like to continue.

3. **Click the Yes button.**

   The legal agreement for the software burns its way onto your screen.

4. **Click the Yes button to commit yourself to the wonderful world of FrontPage intranet design.**

   After the wizard files are installed, you're ready to rock 'n' roll. Another dialog appears letting you know that Intranet Starter wizard is installed.

5. **Click OK to complete the installation process.**

Guess what? You're done!

Intranet Starter wizard, step by step

The Intranet Starter wizard can help you create an intranet starter site in just a few minutes. If you're having trouble figuring out how to start designing your web site, the wizard can provide you with a quick start that you can customize for your own company or organization. Even if you end up creating your intranet site from scratch, the Intranet Starter wizard can give you an idea of what you can do on your intranet web site.

If you're back to this step-by-step process because you want to start over, that's okay — experimentation is the key to success! You can delete a previous web site if it's already open by choosing File⇨Delete FrontPage Web. A dialog box appears that asks whether you're sure that you want to delete your web site. If you're really, really sure, click the Yes button, and you're ready to start over fresh — without your older experiments laying around.

Although the following steps aren't themselves all that exciting, they get your intranet site up and running quickly, and *that* is exciting:

1. **Click Start⇨Programs⇨Microsoft FrontPage.**

   The Getting Started with Microsoft FrontPage dialog box appears, as shown in Figure 4-2.

2. **Click the From a Wizard or Template radio button and then click OK to get started.**

   The New FrontPage Web dialog box appears, as shown in Figure 4-3.

3. **Select Intranet Starter wizard from the Template or Wizard list box and then click OK to continue.**

   The Intranet Starter wizard starts, and you need to create a new directory for your intranet web pages. The dialog box shown in Figure 4-4 appears and asks you to enter the name of the new web server directory you want to create.

4. **Enter the directory name in the Web Server or File Location text box, and a name in the Name of New FrontPage Web text box and click OK to continue.**

   Now, isn't this a lot easier than using your web server administration tools to create a new directory? You can't continue the process until you provide a directory name, so make sure that you do. And your computer may churn away for a minute or so after you click the OK button, so be patient.

   Finally, the Intranet Starter wizard dialog box appears. This dialog box is just informational and clues you in on what to expect along the way.

Figure 4-2:
The Getting
Started with
Microsoft
FrontPage
dialog box.

Figure 4-3:
The New
FrontPage
Web dialog
box.

5. Click the Next button to continue.

A dialog box appears containing various options for the types of web pages that you can design, as shown in Figure 4-5.

6. Select the types of web pages that you want FrontPage to automatically generate by placing a check in the check box in front of each page type.

You can include information related to Human Resources, Information Technology, Accounting/Financial, Personal Online Information Center, Company News, Additional Departments, Table of Contents, and a Search page. If the check box next to an item is checked, FrontPage includes that page as part of your design process.

7. After selecting a page option in the list box, click the Page Settings button to open the Page Settings dialog box for the particular page you selected, as shown in Figure 4-6.

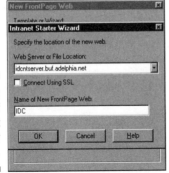

Figure 4-4:
Step 1 of
the Intranet
Starter
wizard.

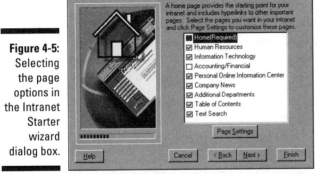

Figure 4-5:
Selecting
the page
options in
the Intranet
Starter
wizard
dialog box.

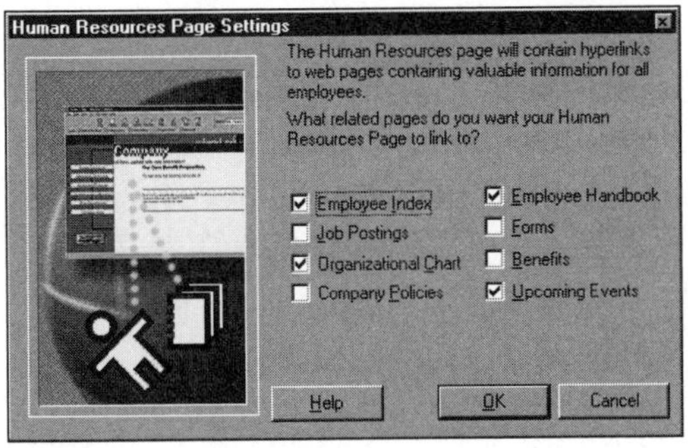

Figure 4-6:
The Page
Settings
dialog box.

In this dialog box, you can decide what information you want to include in that area of your intranet. Figure 4-6, for example, shows the Page Settings dialog box for the Human Resources option, in which I've selected four related pages of information I want my Human Resources page to link to.

8. **Click OK button to save your Page Settings options or click Cancel to discard them.**

   You return to the Intranet Starter wizard dialog box that you just left. You can select more page types and determine what to include on them by using the Page Settings dialog box or you can continue to the next step.

9. **After you make all your page type selections and you're happy with them, click Next to continue.**

   The dialog box shown in Figure 4-7 appears.

10. **In this dialog box, choose the information that you want to appear at the bottom (footer) of your web page by selecting the appropriate check boxes.**

    Each item you select (click to place a check in the box) is included in the footer.

11. **Click Next to continue.**

    Next, you're asked to provide the name of your company and your mail address, as shown in Figure 4-8.

12. **Enter your company name and mailing address information into the respective dialog boxes and click OK to continue.**

    The dialog box shown in Figure 4-9 appears.

    FrontPage can keep a To Do list of things that you need to complete for your intranet web site.

13. **Check the Display To Do List check box to have this handy list appear automatically when the Intranet Starter wizard is finished.**

    Guess what? You're almost done!

14. **Click the Finish button to create your intranet web site.**

After the Intranet Starter wizard has a chance to churn out your web site to your specifications, you're sent to the FrontPage Explorer, as shown in Figure 4-10. Here you can view your web site graphically. Each icon represents a web page or other document, such as a Word, PowerPoint, or Excel document. Clicking the +(plus) in the upper left-hand corner of any icon expands the graphical view of your web site, showing you how all your intranet web pages link together. Double-clicking any web page icon starts the FrontPage Editor.

Figure 4-7:
Choosing
what
type of
information
you want to
include in
your web
page
footers.

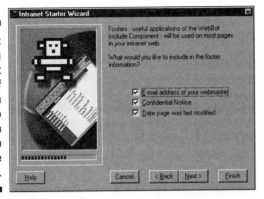

Figure 4-8:
Filling
in your
company
and web-
master
address
info.

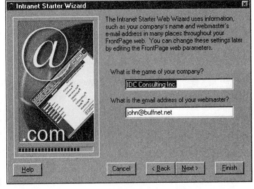

Figure 4-9:
Choosing
whether
you want
FrontPage
to display a
To Do List
of items
that you still
need to
finish.

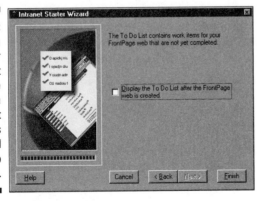

Editing your intranet web pages

FrontPage Explorer offers a nice way to see how each document on your site links together and helps you keep your site organized. Figure 4-10 highlights the different types of icons in the graphical view of your web site. At the core of the intranet site that you create by using the Intranet Starter wizard is your intranet home page. Begin by double-clicking the Home Page icon to open the FrontPage Editor, as shown in Figure 4-11. The FrontPage Editor works a lot like Word or WordPerfect in that it enables you to edit the text and images that appear on the web page in a straightforward manner.

The home page that you can automatically create by using the Intranet Starter wizard has a little taste of all the things you can do by using the FrontPage Editor. On your intranet home page, you can see links to other pages, images, static text, and WebBots. You need to fill in your own information, as indicated on the template home page. If you need to make any changes, just click the item that you want to change and then type or draw your changes. The big thing to remember is that you can always change things, and starting over is really easy, too.

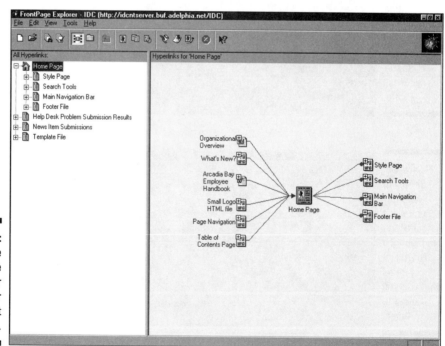

Figure 4-10:
The
FrontPage
Explorer
view of your
intranet
web site.

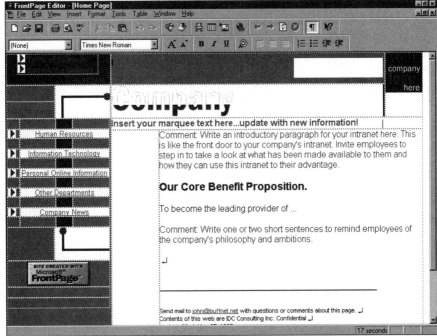

Figure 4-11:
Using the
FrontPage
Editor to
edit the
Intranet
Starter
home page.

The text that starts with the word Comment, is just that — it doesn't appear to visitors of your actual web page. If you move your mouse over that area of text, your mouse pointer turns into a little robot — that's because the comment is a FrontPage WebBot. Comments are only visible when you're designing your web page — they're useful for adding reminders and descriptions that you as the page designer may find useful. When you save your web page in FrontPage, the Comment WebBot saves your web page comments using the appropriate HTML comment tags, and visitors to your web page never know the difference.

All web page text, on the other hand, does appear on your finished page. If, for example, you highlight web page text with your mouse, such as the text that reads Our Core Benefit Proposition, and then start to type, you can enter a paragraph that describes what your intranet offers. You don't need to hit the Enter key after you reach the end of the line — FrontPage automatically wraps the line for you. Highlight the text that reads To become the leading provider of . . . to replace this text and enter your company's mission statement or goals.

Toward the top of your home page you find text that reads `Insert your marquee text here . . . update with new information!` This text area is a *marquee* component — any text that you put here scrolls sideways across your screen. Marquees scroll only as someone views your web page in Internet Explorer — if you view a marquee area in Netscape Navigator, it just appears as static text. Double-click the marquee text to display the Marquee Properties dialog box, as shown in Figure 4-12.

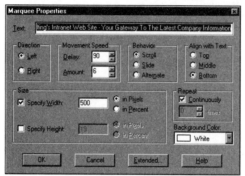

Figure 4-12:
The
Marquee
Properties
dialog box.

If you click your right mouse button anywhere on your home page, a pop-up menu appears. Choose the Page Properties menu option from this pop-up menu to display the Page Properties dialog box, as shown in Figure 4-13. In this dialog box, you can give your web page a title, specify an image to display as a background, and set margins for your web page.

In the Page Properties dialog box, click the General tab. You can enter a title for your web page in the Title text box. The title appears on the title bar of the viewer's web browser.

At the top right-hand side of your intranet home page, you can put your company logo. If you already have a company logo and you have the file for it, you can add the logo to your web page right now.

Selecting the right type of image file format for your web page is important:

✔ To display an image on a web page, it needs to be in one of two file formats. These formats are *GIF* (Graphics Image File) and *JPEG* (Joint Photographic Expert Group). Both of these file formats store your images in a special way that makes the files small and, therefore, quick for your users to download. If your logo isn't in one of these two formats, you need to go into your graphics program (most of them can make this conversion) and save your image as one of these file types or ask your art department (if you have one) to give you a file containing your logo in a GIF or JPEG format.

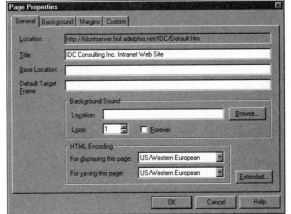

Figure 4-13:
The Page
Properties
dialog box.

✔ The best way to go is to use JPEG files to store full-color photographic
images and GIF files to store computer-drawn graphics or icons. Storing
full-color photolike images by using JPEG creates files that are smaller
than if you store them as GIF files. JPEG files make a mess of icons and
computer graphics — these images end up looking very spotty because
of how the files are compressed. JPEG works great with photos, however, because of the way the human eye works — the spottiness
doesn't affect photos the same way because you don't detect it with
your eyes. (It's actually a kind of optical illusion.)

Click the `Your Company Logo Here` image at the upper right of your page
with your right mouse button. A pop-up menu appears. Choose the Image
Properties menu item to open the Image Properties dialog box, as shown in
Figure 4-14. In the Image Properties dialog box, you can specify the image
file to use for your logo, the type of file used (GIF or JPEG), and the align-
ment of the image.

Click the Browse button next to the Image Source text box. The Image dialog
box appears. Click the Other Location tab to view the version of the dialog
box shown in Figure 4-15.

Click the Browse button next to the From File text box to find your image or
just enter the name of the image, including the directory path, in the From
File text box. Click OK to close the Image dialog box and click OK again to
close the Image Properties dialog box. If your logo looks too big or small,
you may need to resize it a bit. If you click the image, you see four little
black squares appear at each corner of the image. Click a corner and, while
holding the mouse button down, drag your mouse to make the image
smaller or bigger until it's the size you want.

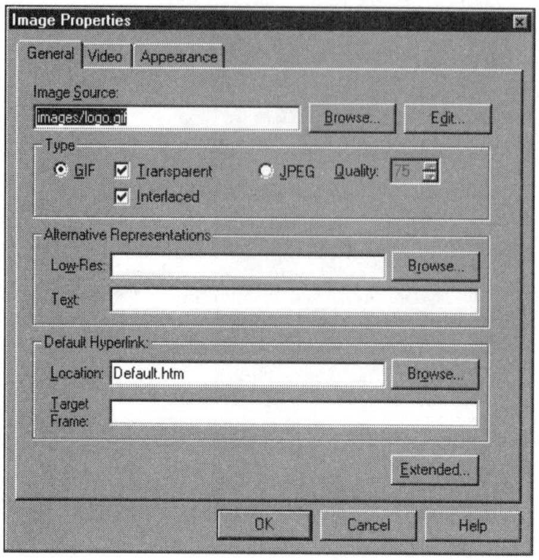

Figure 4-14:
The Image
Properties
dialog box.

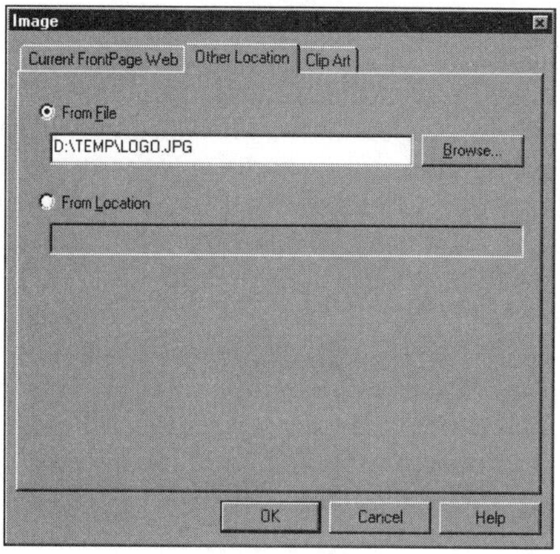

Figure 4-15:
The Image
dialog box.

FrontPage stores all web page images as part of your intranet web site in the same directory that you created on your web server for storing your intranet web using the Intranet Starter wizard. FrontPage automatically moves any file image you add to your web pages into your intranet web after you save your changes. Choose File⇨Save, and the Save Image To FrontPage Web dialog box appears, as shown in Figure 4-16. Click the Yes to All button to move all images you've added into the web server directory. This feature really simplifies a task that would be incredibly tedious otherwise — without FrontPage, you'd need to manually copy each of these files into the web server directory one at a time and fiddle around with a bunch of HTML stuff to make sure that you used the right filename and path. Whew! Good thing you don't need to worry about all that junk.

Figure 4-16:
The Import
Image to
FrontPage
Web dialog
box.

The last thing I review on the intranet home page are the links that appear at the left-hand side of the page. The Table of Contents and Search links appear at the top of this column, and the other department links appear below them. The links that appear here may be different for you, depending on the departments and other special features you chose to include as you ran the Intranet Starter wizard. If you move your mouse over these areas, you see your pointer turn into a friendly little robot — that's because these areas are actually WebBots. They aren't really on the home page but are stored as separate files. You can find these files in the FrontPage Explorer window: Choose File⇨Exit to return to FrontPage Explorer. Make sure that you save any changes you made if you're asked to.

The FrontPage Explorer window appears, as shown in Figure 4-17. The icons on the right-hand side of the window represent links to web pages that your intranet home page can call up directly. The links on the left-hand side represent web pages that are part of your intranet home page. The Search Tools icon represents the web links at the top left-hand side of your intranet home page, and the Main Navigation Bar icon represents the links below the search tools. If you double-click any of these icons, you can edit the link areas of your web pages.

Viewing your intranet creation

Now that you have the basic idea of how to customize the web pages you create by using the Intranet Starter wizard, you're probably eager to see what your home page actually looks like in your web browser. So go ahead and fire up your web browser.

Remember when you had to enter a directory name for the Intranet Starter wizard? You need to use that name now and enter it in the Address text box of your browser — something similar to the following name: `http://webserver/directory`, where `webserver` is the name of your web server and `directory` is the name of the directory you specified in the Intranet Starter wizard. In my case, my web server is called `IDCNTSERVER` and the directory I used was `IDC`, so I would use the address `http://idcntserver/idc`. (Notice that whether you use upper- or lowercase letters doesn't matter.) Figure 4-18 illustrates how my intranet home page looks in Internet

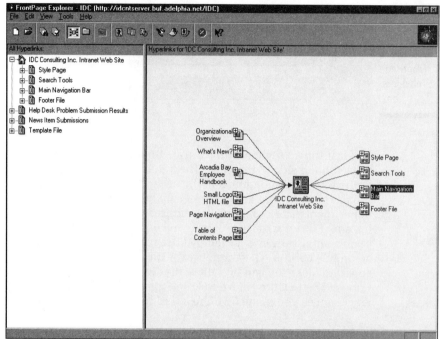

Figure 4-17:
The
FrontPage
Explorer
window.

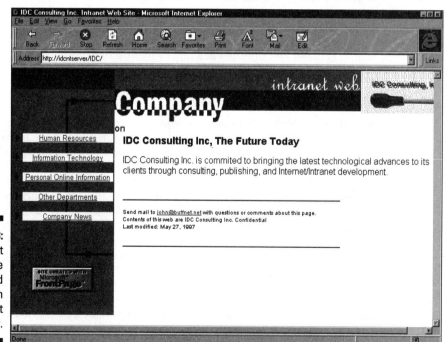

Figure 4-18:
My intranet
home page
as viewed
from
Internet
Explorer.

Explorer. If you're using Netscape Navigator, it looks very similar. Click all the links to explore the web pages you generated in Intranet Starter wizard. Play with the FrontPage Editor and Explorer to customize your web site. Don't be afraid to experiment and make mistakes — that's the best way to figure all this stuff out.

Creating forms fast

If you explore the web site you created by using the Intranet Starter wizard, you may run across a few web pages that contain text boxes, combo boxes, list boxes, radio buttons, and check boxes and wonder how to do use them. Pages with input areas for your users (such as these buttons and text boxes) are called *forms*. Here's the 30-second manager's guide to using FrontPage to creating a web page that contains a form — just follow these steps:

1. **From the FrontPage Explorer, choose Tools⇨Show FrontPage Editor.**

2. **After the FrontPage Editor is running, choose File⇨New to open the New Page dialog box, as shown in Figure 4-19.**

3. **Select the Form Page Wizard from the Template or Wizard list box and then click OK.**

   The Form Page Wizard starts.

4. **Click the Next button to continue.**

   The Form Page Wizard dialog box shown in Figure 4-20 appears.

5. **Give a name to the form page file (in the Page URL text box) and a title (in the Page Title text box) and then click Next to continue.**

6. **Click the Add button to open the dialog box containing a list of questions, as shown in Figure 4-21.**

   A dialog box appears containing a list box from which you can select from predefined questions and types of input information.

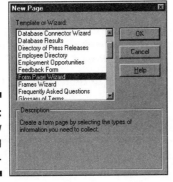

Figure 4-19:
The New Page dialog box.

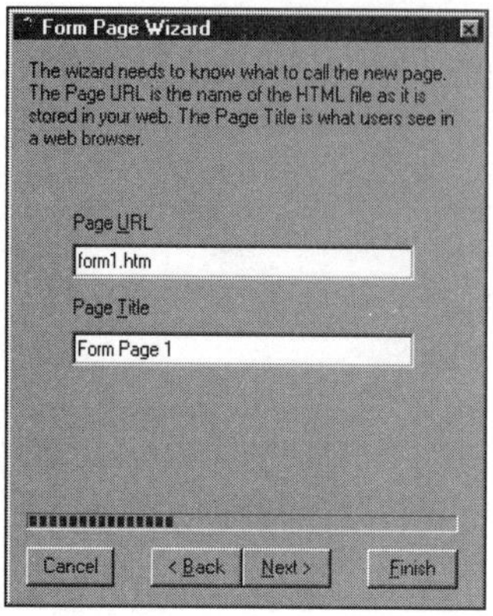

Figure 4-20:
Enter the name and title of the web page form you're creating.

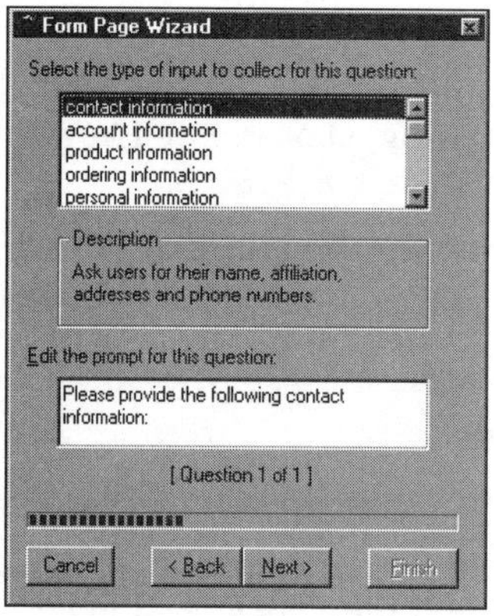

Figure 4-21:
The Form Page Wizard's list o' questions dialog box.

7. **Select a single question from the list at the top of the dialog box or select a group of questions and then click Next to continue.**

   Select the Contact Information collection of questions, for example, and click the Next button to continue to another dialog box. The Input Type dialog box appears, as shown in Figure 4-22. You can select the items you want to collect from the user for the question group you selected.

8. **In the Input Type dialog box add or remove any fields for your form by selecting or deselecting the appropriate check boxes, click Next to continue after you have made your selections.**

9. **Click the Add button to add additional form fields or click the Finish button to generate your form questions.**

   The form you create appears in the FrontPage Editor, as shown in Figure 4-23. Whew! That was fast — but I did promise the thirty-second version. Creating forms is pretty easy — you just did it in nine short steps!

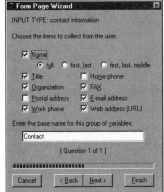

A quick guide to Bots

If you've worked through any of the other sections in this chapter, you've already come across a few FrontPage WebBots. WebBots are little helpers, like robots, that automate some of the tedious processes you encounter as you create web pages. You can add a WebBot to your web page by choosing Insert⇨WebBot Component from the menu bar. Table 4-2 describes the WebBots you have available in FrontPage.

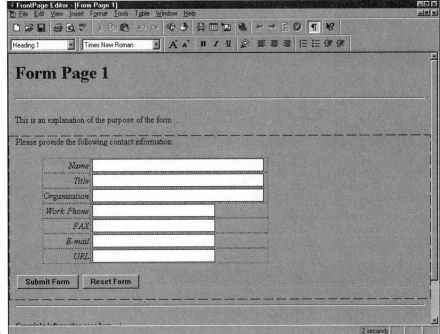

Table 4-2	The WebBot Components Available in FrontPage 97
WebBot	**Description**
Confirmation Field	Displays the contents of a form field as the user submits it.
Include	Includes the contents of another web page in the current web page.
Scheduled Image	Includes an image that appears only for an amount of time you specify. This feature is useful if you have an image that you only want to show for a couple of days, a week, or until some date after which the image is no longer needed or current.
Scheduled Include	Includes the contents of another web page and displays them only for an amount of time. This feature is useful if you have a web page that you only want to show for a couple of days, a week, or until some later date after which it will no longer be useful.
Search	Includes a form on your web page that enables your users to perform text searches.
Substitution	Displays the value of a web page or web page *property*, such as the Author or Description of the web page.
Table of Contents	Automatically displays a current table of contents for your web site. The contents are updated automatically each time you change your web site.
Timestamp	Automatically shows the time and date of the last change to a web page.

When Bad Things Happen

Bad things can happen in life, and bad things can happen if you use FrontPage to create web pages. Table 4-3 lists the answers to some common problems you may encounter as you use Microsoft FrontPage. For even more help with FrontPage, try the Microsoft FrontPage support Web site at

www.microsoft.com/frontpagesupport

Table 4-3 Common Microsoft FrontPage Problems and Solutions

Problem	*Solutions*
Can I use FrontPage without accessing a web server?	You can't access the full functionality of FrontPage without access to a web server, but you can still use the program. I recommend that you still install at least Personal Web Server even for just the machine you're working on so that you can at least get to use all the cool FrontPage features.
I can't access my web server from FrontPage.	If you're not using Microsoft Personal Web Server or Internet Information Server as your web server, you may not have the appropriate FrontPage Server Extensions installed for your web server. Visit the Microsoft FrontPage web site (`www.microsoft.com/frontpage`) to download the appropriate extensions for the web server you're using.
I'm not using Internet Server or Personal Web Server — are the FrontPage Server Extensions available for my web server?	Probably — the Microsoft FrontPage Web site Information lists the web servers that support Front Page Extensions. Point your browser to `www.microsoft.com/KB/ARTICLES/Q161/1/58.htm`.

Chapter 5

We're Not in HTML Anymore, Toto!

• •

In This Chapter

▶ Getting your stuff to look good without any fancy-schmancy HTML

▶ Zapping your Word, Excel, and PowerPoint documents into HTML fast

▶ Taking your documents for a tumble with Adobe Acrobat

▶ Curing the document-conversion blues

• •

You know all those employee manuals, financial spreadsheets, product catalogs, and company newsletters you have lying around? Wouldn't you like to be able to wave a magic wand over all that stuff and instantly turn it into something that you can view with your intranet browser? Well, you're in luck — the magician is in today.

Do You Have the Right Stuff?

In this chapter, I show you two ways to pump out documents that are ready for your intranet use:

✔ By using tools provided in Microsoft Office 97.

✔ By using Adobe Acrobat for documents that you don't have in an Office 97 application.

You may already use Office 97 in your company for all the day-to-day document chores. You probably don't have the Adobe Acrobat publisher, but by the time you're done with this chapter, you may want to get your hands on a copy. Using Office 97, you can easily convert your existing files into HTML (*HyperText Markup Language* — the language that web browsers understand) and even create new HTML web pages with it. Sounds neat, doesn't it? Well, as is true of everything else, you always have those tradeoffs.

A really quick HTML history lesson

Way back in time, when Ronald Reagan was still president and you had spiked hair and a nose ring (what — you mean you *still* have those?), a group of really smart dudes who knew a lot about computers created a standard called *SGML*, which stands for *Standard Generalized Markup Language*. SGML was the prototype for *HTML* (*HyperText Markup Language*), which is what makes today's web pages work. A few years later, a bunch of people working at CERN — the European Laboratory for Particle Physics — got their hands on SGML and thought, hey, we can make SGML smaller and use it to publish our latest research papers on the Internet. Thus HTML was born.

A couple of years after that, a guy named Marc Andreesen started to work at the NCSA (National Center for Supercomputing Applications) on a little project called *Mosaic*. Mosaic turned out to be the first graphical web browser, meaning that it could show pictures. Soon after, Marc split from NCSA and started this little company that you may have heard of called Netscape. Mosaic and Netscape both used HTML to display documents with pictures.

With the advent of these graphical web browsers and the desire to make the documents that they can display even cooler, HTML has slowly grown to encompass tables, different font sizes, and even the addition of programming code (by way of Java, JavaScript, and VBScript).

To keep everyone from running off and creating a bizillion different versions of HTML, however, the W3 Consortium was formed to set and maintain the standards for HTML. Every web browser works with the W3 standards, and you can pretty much view any HTML document in any web browser. Microsoft and Netscape still have some of their own special features that work only in their own browsers, but these features are slowly getting incorporated into HTML. HTML still doesn't enable you to exercise fine control over the look and layout of your documents, but I expect that future enhancements to HTML are going to offer you finer control, and that the difference between what people think of today as word-processing documents and web pages may someday be a pointless distinction.

HTML was never designed to display all the fancy fonts and formatting stuff that you can create with your trusty word processor. The idea behind HTML was to create simple pages that look pretty much the same on any web browser. Office 97 can do a pretty good job of moving your documents into HTML, but you can expect to lose a few things along the way. Most of the time, what you lose is no big deal — some fonts and certain other text and formatting elements are what you can expect to fall by the wayside.

Sometimes you absolutely need your documents to look *exactly* as they do whenever you view or print them from your word processor or some other application. This situation is where *Adobe Acrobat* helps you walk the tightrope. Adobe Acrobat lets you "print" your document from whatever application you used to create it into a special file that you can view by using the Adobe Acrobat Reader, a program that works with your web browser. Acrobat Reader reads these special files and recreates your documents exactly the same way they'd have looked if you'd printed them — kind of like an electronic copy machine. Later in this chapter, I show you how to use the Adobe Acrobat Publisher and get the Acrobat Reader to work with your web browser.

Where Can I Get It?

Both Office 97 and Adobe Acrobat are commercial applications, which means that you can't get your hands on them without plunking down some cash. The good news is that you probably already have and are familiar with Office 97. If you need the latest Office 97 information, you can get it at the Microsoft Office 97 Web site at the following address:

```
www.microsoft.com/office97
```

Adobe Acrobat is really made up of two parts, the Acrobat Publisher and the Adobe Acrobat Reader. The Acrobat Publisher is the stuff that you need to pay for — it's what converts your documents into viewable files. The Acrobat Reader, which is free (and included on the CD at the back of this book), takes the files that you create with the publishing tools and lets you view them. The Acrobat Reader can even run right inside your web browser. You can pick up and read more about Adobe Acrobat at the following URL:

```
www.adobe.com/acrobat
```

Cutting through the Technobabble

If the only wizard you know is named Merlin and a plug-in sounds like an air freshener, this section is for you. Table 5-1 takes you on a techno trip through the language of web document publishing.

Table 5-1   Web Page Design Jargon Decoded for Regular Folks

Technobabble	*In Plain Language*
Hyperlink	Hyperlinks, or more simply (and slangly) *links*, define the address to another web page. They usually appear as underlined, different-colored text in a web page that, after a user clicks it, sends the user to another web page. Good web-page designers make sure that the text of the link describes the page where the user is sent.
PDF	*PDF* stands for *Portable Document Format* — the format that Adobe Acrobat Publisher uses to save your documents for the Acrobat Reader.
Plug-Ins	A *plug-in* is an application — for example Adobe Acrobat Reader, which I discuss in detail in this chapter — that works with your browser to provide some extra functionality to your web browser. Plug-ins are available to enable you to listen to radio-like broadcasts in real time over your intranet or the Internet, view three dimensional worlds, or even view richly formatted documents, to name a few possibilities.
PostScript	*PostScript* is a language invented by Adobe that applications use to talk to printers. Adobe Acrobat makes use of PostScript in converting your documents so that Adobe Acrobat Reader can use them.
URL	A *URL* is a *Uniform Resource Locator*, the techie name for the address of a Web page. The most typical URLs you see look something like `http://website`. The `http://` part just means that you're looking for a document that's written using the HTML standards, and the `website` part is the actual address of where you can find that document.
Viewers	Sometimes you hear specific plug-in applications called *viewers*, because these programs enable you to look at specific types of files. The Adobe Acrobat Reader, for example, is a viewer that enables you to look at the contents of PDF files.
Wizards	*Wizards* are magical in that they save you a whole bunch of time. Microsoft Office provides a number of wizards that break down what would ordinarily be really complex and tedious tasks into simple step-by-step, point-and-click processes.

Getting the Word Out with Office 97

Ready to start pounding out intranet documents in Word 97? Cool — in the next few sections, I show you how to use the new Office 97 features to create intranet web documents in a jiffy by using Word, Excel, and FrontPage. Although you don't need to be an expert with Office 97 to do all this stuff, you're best off if you have at least some familiarity with one of the following applications: Microsoft Word, Excel, or PowerPoint. In Chapter 7, I review how to use Microsoft Access and other databases with your intranet.

Office 97 web page authoring tools

Before you can start using Office 97 to whip your intranet into shape, you need to make sure that you have the Web Page Authoring (HTML) tools installed.

To check whether the Web Page Authoring (HTML) tools are installed along with your copy of Office 97, follow these steps:

1. **Pop your Office 97 CD in your CD-ROM drive and run the SETUP application by clicking Start⇨Run and then typing** d:\setup **in the Open text box of the Run dialog box.**

   If your CD-ROM drive has a letter other than D, use that letter in place of D.

   The Microsoft Office 97 Setup dialog box appears, as shown in Figure 5-1.

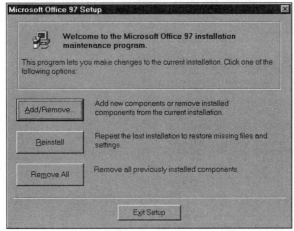

Figure 5-1:
The
Microsoft
Office 97
Setup
dialog box.

2. **Click the Add/Remove button to check whether the Web Page Authoring (HTML) tools are installed.**

   The Microsoft Office 97 - Maintenance dialog box appears, as shown in Figure 5-2.

3. **Make sure that the Web Page Authoring (HTML) option is selected (checked); if so, you're good to go — click the Cancel button to quit the installation process and then read the following paragraph; if not, continue on to Step 4.**

   You return to the Microsoft Office 97 dialog box, where you can click the Exit Setup button to quit the installation process.

4. **If the Web Page Authoring (HTML) option is not selected (checked), click the check box to select the option.**

5. **Click the Continue button to install the Web Page Authoring tools.**

6. **Click the Continue button to install the missing components.**

   A dialog box appears telling you that you're done.

7. **Click OK and you're ready for action.**

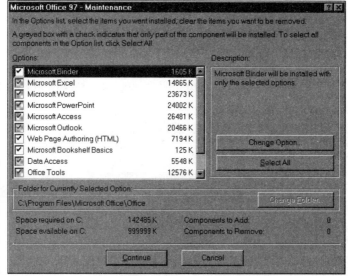

Figure 5-2:
The
Microsoft
Office 97 -
Maintenance
dialog box.

Publishing Word 97 documents

Of all the Office 97 applications, Microsoft Word 97 provides the most intranet publishing features, including the following:

- ✔ **Easy export to HTML.** You can save your Word documents as HTML files — as easily as that.

- ✔ **Web Page Wizards.** These devices enable you to create cool-looking web pages by wielding your fearsome mouse.

- ✔ **Formatting doo-dads.** Word 97 includes a gallery of neat-looking horizontal lines and bullets that you can use in your web pages.

- ✔ **Quick forms.** Word 97 offers the Form wizard to help you quickly create data entry forms and collection mechanisms for your web pages.

- ✔ **Easy hyperlinks.** You can easily create links to other documents, marquee-style scrolling text, and other advanced styles.

- ✔ **Easy tables.** Create tables faster than you can set the dinner table.

- ✔ **Easy browsing.** Word 97 enables you to do your intranet web browsing without ever leaving Microsoft Word.

Easy as Save As . . .

To save a document as a web page (HTML) from Word 97, you simply follow these steps:

1. **Choose File⇨Save as HTML.**

   The Save as HTML dialog box appears.

2. **Enter in the text box the name that you want to give your file.**

3. **Click OK to save your file.**

   Shazam — your document converts into 100 percent certifiable HTML.

You may notice that your converted document doesn't look quite the same as when you created it. The trick here is that HTML doesn't directly support the wide selection of fonts and formatting that's possible in Word 97. A lot of the basic things such as bold, italics, and tables stay the same. Certain other tricks like paragraph styles can get lost. While your converted document may not look exactly perfect, it's a good start and it takes almost no time to do it.

If you really need your document to look the same way it does when you have it on screen, you can use Adobe Acrobat as I discuss later in this chapter.

Word web wizardry

Word 97 provides the Web Page Wizard to help you quickly create a number of different web page styles. To start the Word 97 Web Page Wizard, follow these steps:

1. **Choose File⇨New from Word 97.**

   The New dialog box appears, as shown in Figure 5-3.

2. **Click the Web Pages tab.**

3. **Double-click the Web Page Wizard icon to open the Web Page Wizard - Type dialog box, as shown in Figure 5-4.**

   You can run through the various types of possible web pages and see an example displayed in the background. You can quickly create two and three column layouts, calendars, and personal home pages.

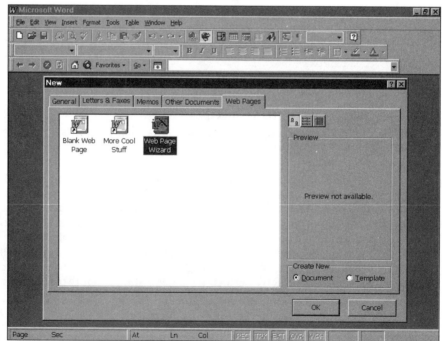

Figure 5-3:
The New dialog box where you select the Web Page Wizard.

Figure 5-4:
Selecting
the type of
web page
with the
Web Page
Wizard.

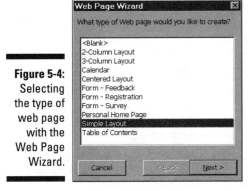

4. **Select the Personal Home Page Wizard and click the Next button.**

   The Web Page Wizard - Style dialog box appears, as shown in Figure 5-5.

Figure 5-5:
Choosing a
visual style
for your
web page
with the
Web Page
Wizard.

5. **You can choose from a list of a number of different visual styles for your web pages — select the style that tickles your fancy and then click the Finish button.**

   Now you can edit your web page just as you can any other Word 97 document.

Tool up from the toolbar

The Word 97 toolbar, as shown in Figure 5-6, offers a few tools to help you edit your new web page. Table 5-2 lists and describes the important Word 97 web page design toolbar items.

Table 5-2	The Word 97 Toolbar Items
Toolbar Item	*Description*
Address (URL)	The Address (URL) text box lets you specify a filename or URL of a web page you want to access.
Font	The Font combo box lets you pick the font for your web page text. Remember, however, that your font may get replaced by a different font as someone views your web page, depending on the web browser.
Font Size	Clicking the big A makes the font size of the currently selected text bigger, and clicking the little A makes the font size smaller.
Form design mode	Form design mode lets you interactively design forms, adding check boxes, radio buttons, list boxes, buttons, and text boxes, as well as other features.
Insert hyperlink	The Insert hyperlink button lets you create a link to another web page or area in your current document. A link to another area in the current document is sometimes called a *book-mark*, not to be confused with *Bookmarks* in Netscape Navigator, which are the same as Favorites (saved web page links) in Internet Explorer.
Recently visited web pages	This area automatically saves a list of the past ten or so web pages you've visited.
Saved web page links	The Favorites drop-down list box lets you save some of your favorite web pages so that you can return to them quickly.
Style	The Style combo box lets you specify the way text on your web page looks.
Web navigation	These buttons let you move through the web pages you've recently visited, stop the current web page from loading, and reload the current web page.
Web page preview	This button lets you preview your web page in your default web browser (Internet Explorer, Netscape Navigator, or Word 97).
Web toolbar	If you click the Web toolbar button, you access the third row of the toolbar, which contains the Web navigation buttons, Saved web page links, Recently visited web pages, and Address items.

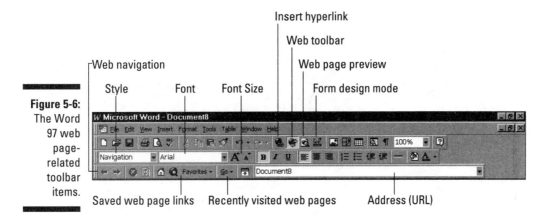

Figure 5-6:
The Word
97 web
page-
related
toolbar
items.

Wacky styles

Editing your web pages with Word 97 is really easy — you just do the same things you'd do if editing any other Word document. The only additional things you need to know are how to change the font/style of text and how to create hyperlinks, as I explain in the following section, "Word links."

If you created your personal home web page by using the Personal Home Page Wizard, as I describe in the numbered steps in the "Word web wizardry" section a little earlier in this chapter, you see some text at the top of your document that reads Insert Heading Here. Follow these steps:

1. **Highlight the text by using your mouse or the keyboard.**

   The Style combo box in the toolbar displays the style of the selected text — in this case, it reads Heading 1. HTML provides six different heading styles, Heading 1 (large) through Heading 6 (small).

2. **While the text is still highlighted, click the Style combo box to display the list of styles, as shown in Figure 5-7.**

3. **In place of the** Insert Heading Here **text, enter your name and change the text style to a size that you like — anything from Heading 1 to Heading 6 — by selecting that style from the Style list.**

4. **In place of the text that reads** Subheading **enter your position — again, you can change the font size to your liking as described in Step 3.**

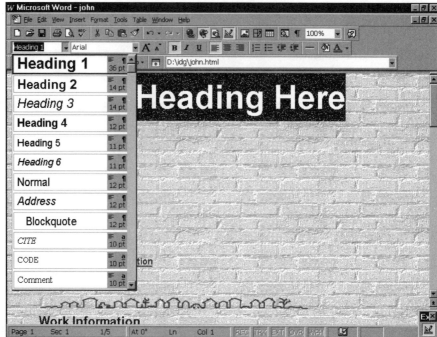

Figure 5-7:
The Word
97 web
page text
styles.

Word links

In the Contents area of the web page, you find some headings that are blue and underlined — these are *links*. If you view this web page and then click these links, you automatically jump to the associated area later in the web page. You can also create links that jump to other, completely new web pages. The Work Information link (underlined in blue at the top of the page), for example, links to the Work Information title that appears later in the web page. To check the link, highlight the Work Information link at the top of the web page and click the Insert HyperLink button in the toolbar to display the Edit HyperLink dialog box, as shown in Figure 5-8.

You can create or edit HyperLinks for any text selection the same way. In the Link to File or URL text box, you can enter the URL of another web page or simply specify another filename. In the Named Location in File text box, you can enter the name of a bookmark that appears on your web page. In the case of the Work Experience link, it connects to a bookmark called A. Not really an exciting name, but it works. Click the OK button to save any link changes.

Move your way down in the web page until you get to the Work Information area that appears in black. Highlight the Work Information text and select View➪Bookmark from the menu bar. The Bookmark dialog box appears, as shown in Figure 5-9.

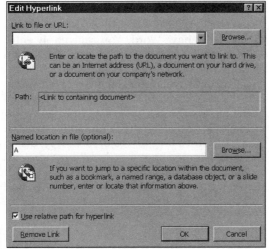

Figure 5-8:
The Edit
HyperLink
dialog box.

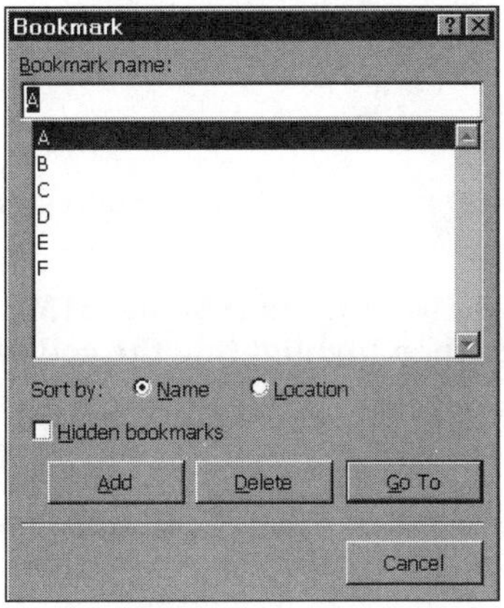

Figure 5-9:
The
Bookmark
dialog box.

The bookmark name, A, appears in the Bookmark Name text box. You can create a new bookmark for the selected text by entering a new name in the Bookmark Name text box and clicking the Add button.

You can continue to edit your web page by using these simple commands to add your own information. Don't forget to save your creation by using the File⊏>Save menu items and remember to experiment and have fun — you can't break anything and you can always start over.

The last word on web browsing

The last word about Word 97 is about the web browsing features it provides. Who needs a web browser if you have Word? You can simply enter the name of your intranet web server site or any other URL in the Address text box to view the web page. I wouldn't rush to throw out Internet Explorer or Netscape Navigator, however. The web browsing features in Word aren't currently up to par with the major web browsers (Word couldn't, for example, even display the intranet web site I create in Chapter 4 by using FrontPage 97), and unless you have a fast machine (a Pentium 166 or better) with a lot of memory (more than 16 Megabytes of memory), using Word this way can be really slow. I don't know about you, but I'd rather read the phone book than wait forever for a web page to load. If you view a web page by using Word as your browser, the web page opens in read-only mode, which just means that you can't make any changes.

Publishing Excel spreadsheets

To make an Excel spreadsheet available on your intranet, just use the Save as HTML command:

1. **Choose File⇨Save as HTML.**

   The Internet Assistant Wizard - Step 1 of 4 dialog box appears, as shown in Figure 5-10.

2. **Select the range of cells that you want to send to the HTML web page by clicking the Add button and then highlighting the cell range.**

3. **After you select the cells to send to the web page, click the Next button to continue.**

   The Internet Assistant Wizard - Step 2 of 4 dialog box appears, as shown in Figure 5-11.

4. **Click on the top radio button (Create an independent . . .) to create a complete web page, or if you want to add your Excel table to another web page, click the bottom radio button (Insert the converted . . .).**

   You can create the table in Excel, and then use FrontPage 97 to add the table to an existing web page. To make things simple for now, I suggest that you select the top radio button to create a complete web page.

5. **Click the Next button to continue.**

   The Internet Assistant Wizard - Step 3 of 4 dialog box appears, as shown in Figure 5-12. You can provide a title for the web page in the Title edit box, text to display at the top of the web page in the Header edit box, and text to appear below the header in the Description below header box. You can add horizontal lines before and after the data, and you can

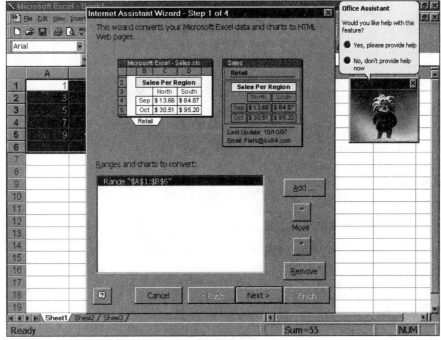

Figure 5-10:
The
Internet
Assistant
Wizard
Step - 1 of 4
dialog box.

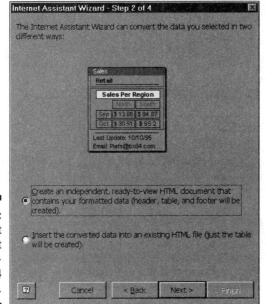

Figure 5-11:
The Internet
Assistant
Wizard -
Step 2 of 4
dialog box.

add the date of last update, the name of the person who created the web page, and that person's e-mail address in the respective edit boxes at the bottom of the dialog box.

6. Click the Next button to continue.

The Internet Assistant Wizard - Step 4 of 4 dialog box pops up, as shown in Figure 5-13. If you're saving the web page to a file, enter the filename in the File path edit box.

7. Click the Finish button to save your Excel information into a web page.

You can also use Excel to create web page forms (using the Tools⇨Wizard⇨Web Form menu items) and insert hyperlinks into cells (using the Insert⇨HyperLink menu options).

Publishing PowerPoint presentations

You can create web pages with Microsoft PowerPoint:

1. Choose File⇨Save as HTML. (See a pattern here?)

The PowerPoint Save as HTML wizard appears, as shown in Figure 5-14.

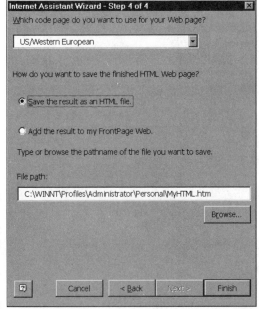

Figure 5-13:
The Internet
Assistant
Wizard -
Step 4 of 4
dialog box.

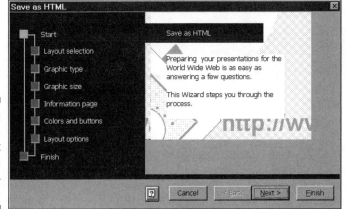

Figure 5-14:
The
PowerPoint
Save as
HTML
wizard.

2. Click the Next button to continue.

A dialog box appears in which you can select a layout for your web
page, as shown in Figure 5-15.

3. Select the New Layout option and click the Next button to continue.

A dialog box appears in which you can choose a style for your page, as
shown in Figure 5-16. You can create a web page that uses *frames*
(subwindows within your main browser window) or web pages that
don't use frames at all.

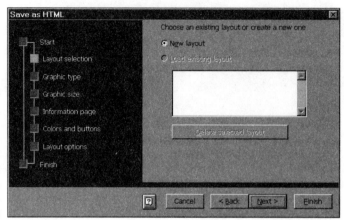

Figure 5-15:
Selecting a
layout in the
PowerPoint
Save as
HTML
wizard.

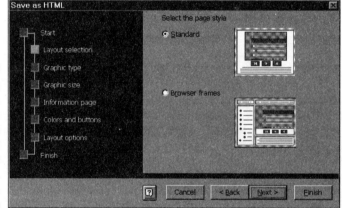

Figure 5-16:
Selecting a
page style
in the
PowerPoint
Save as
HTML
wizard.

4. Pick a style and then click the Next button to continue.

A dialog box that lets you choose graphic types for your web page
graces your screen, as shown in Figure 5-17. You can choose the type of
image for displaying each PowerPoint slide — either GIF or JPEG. For a
variety of reasons, GIF is best for small computer-generated images,
and JPEG is best for images that come from scanned photographs. (See
the sidebar "GIF and JPEG — What gives?" in this section for more
information). You can also choose to use the PowerPoint viewer. The
easiest option is to choose either the GIF or JPEG image formats.

5. Click the Next button to continue.

Another dialog box appears, letting you choose the resolution of the
graphics you want to create, as shown in Figure 5-18. Unless you
know the resolution of everyone's monitor in your company, you are

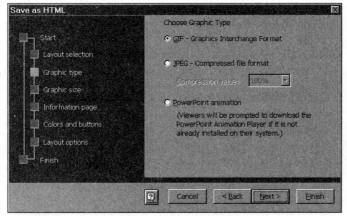

Figure 5-17:
Choosing a
graphic
type in the
PowerPoint
Save as
HTML
wizard.

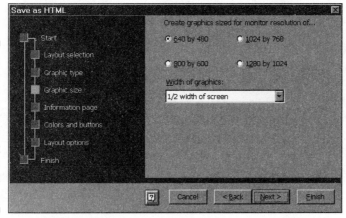

Figure 5-18:
Choosing a
resolution
for you
graphics
in the
PowerPoint
Save as
HTML
wizard.

best off picking the lowest value. In this case, 640 by 480. The width
of graphics combo box enables you to control how much of the
screen your graphics will take up.

6. Click the Next button to continue.

Surprise! Another dialog box is displayed, as shown in Figure 5-19. You
can enter your e-mail address and other information in the appropriate
edit boxes. If the Download original presentation check box is checked,
a button appears on the web page that allows the person viewing the
presentation to download the original PowerPoint presentation file.

7. Click the Next button to continue.

A dialog box appears allowing you to choose the colors for the pages
and buttons of your web site, as shown in Figure 5-20. If you like being

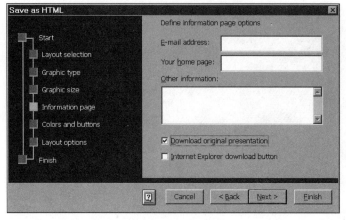

Figure 5-19:
Defining
your
information
page
options in
the
PowerPoint
Save as
HTML
wizard.

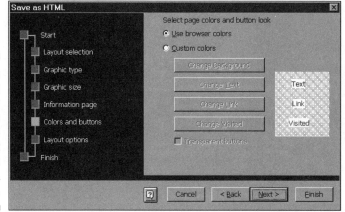

Figure 5-20:
Choosing
colors for
your web
site in the
PowerPoint
Save as
HTML
wizard.

artistic, you can select your own custom colors for the background, text, and links by selecting the Custom colors radio button, or you can use the default browser colors by selecting the Use browser colors radio button.

8. Click the Next button to continue.

Now you get to choose the button style for your web page in the next dialog box that appears, as shown in Figure 5-21. The buttons you choose help visitors to your web site navigate through its pages.

9. Select the radio button next to the button style you like and click the Next button to continue.

In the next dialog box that appears, you need to choose a standard layout for the buttons you chose, as shown in Figure 5-22.

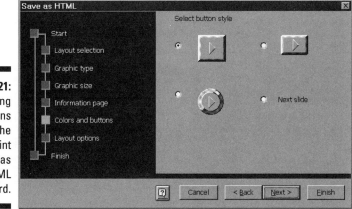

Figure 5-21:
Choosing
buttons
in the
PowerPoint
Save as
HTML
wizard.

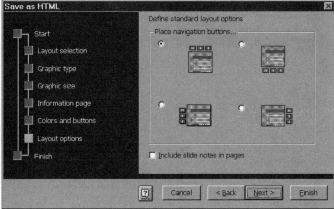

Figure 5-22:
Deciding
how to lay
out your
buttons
in the
PowerPoint
Save as
HTML
wizard.

10. **Click the radio button next to the style you like. If your presentation includes notes, you can include them on your web page by selecting the Include slide notes in pages option.**

11. **Click the Next button to continue.**

    Finally, in this last dialog box, you choose where to save your HTML folder, as shown in Figure 5-23.

12. **In the Folder edit box, specify the name of the folder where you want to save your presentation; click the Next button to continue.**

13. **Finally, the Finished! dialog box appears — click the Finish button to save your PowerPoint presentation as an HTML document. Whew! — those were a lot of steps — but your presentation is now ready for your intranet web site.**

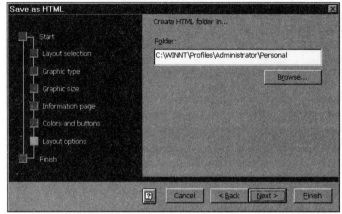

Figure 5-23:
Selecting a directory in which to save your completed HTML folder.

GIF and JPEG — What gives?

GIF (pronounced "jiff") stands for *Graphic Interchange Format.* Storing your images as GIF files makes them smaller, and therefore quicker for your web page users to download. The computer brainiacs call this process *compressing* a file. When you view a GIF image, you *uncompress* the file, and you get the whole image back out.

One neat thing about GIF files is that you can make their backgrounds transparent. You can place transparent background GIF images on a fancy background without leaving any annoying blank spots around the edge. Think of an image of a donut — with a standard image, the donut hole shows white (or some other color). With a transparent background GIF image, the donut hole can show through to whatever background you place your donut image on.

JPEG stands for *Joint Photographic Experts Group.* JPEG is another way to store images in a compressed file. So what's the difference between a JPEG and a GIF? Well for one, no

transparent background. The big difference, however, is *how* JPEG and GIF files are compressed.

When an image is saved in a GIF file and then displayed, all the pixels (the little dots) you had when you created your picture are still there when you uncompress and display the image. However, when you save an image as a JPEG file and then later display it, not all the pixels you had when you created your picture are displayed — some of the pixels are lost. However, because you only lose a few pixels, your brain doesn't notice the difference when you see the picture again. Losing a little bit of the image helps to make the files smaller. This type of compression, where you actually lose some of the original image, is called *lossy compression.*

Generally speaking, GIF images are great for computer-generated graphics and logos, or simple images. JPEG is good for scanned photographs.

What about My Other Stuff?

If you have documents in applications other than Office 97, or if you absolutely, positively, without a doubt need a document to always look like it does when it's printed out, then you want to use Adobe Acrobat. Adobe Acrobat works by intercepting the printing output of your application and converting that stuff into the Portable Document Format (PDF). The Adobe Acrobat Reader works with your web browser or as an application by itself to display these PDF files.

Adobe Acrobat

To get started with Adobe Acrobat 3.0, put your Adobe Acrobat CD-ROM in your CD drive and run the INSTALL program.

1. **The Welcome dialog box appears. Make sure that you close any other programs that are running; then click the Next button to continue.**

2. **The Licensing Agreement dialog box appears. Click the Yes button to get on with the process.**

   The Select Adobe Acrobat and Related Products dialog box appears.

3. **To create documents, you need to install the products selected by default — Acrobat Exchange, Acrobat Capture and Scan Plug-Ins, Acrobat Distiller, Acrobat PDFWriter, and Acrobat Catalog. Click the Next button to continue.**

   You see the Select Components dialog box.

4. **Install all the components selected by default. Click the Next button to continue.**

   (You need roughly 50MB of free disk space to install all the components.)

   The Choose Scanner Drivers dialog box appears. Adobe Acrobat can take documents that you scan and convert them into PDF files.

5. **If you have a scanner, select the scanner type from this dialog box. If you don't have a scanner, don't worry; you don't need to make a selection. Click the Next button to continue.**

6. **You're asked for the usual background information — name, company name, and serial number. Enter the information and click the Next button to continue. Confirm your information by clicking on the Yes button.**

   The Start Copying Files dialog box appears.

7. **Make any necessary changes to the Start Copying Files dialog box or bail out. Click the** <u>**N**</u>**ext button to install Acrobat.**

8. **After the files are installed, click the** <u>**F**</u>**inish button to complete the installation process.**

Using Adobe Acrobat Publisher

When you install Adobe Acrobat Publisher, the Acrobat PDFWriter is added to your system as a *printer* (even though it isn't physically a printer at all). If you want to convert your document to a PDF file, all you need to do is "print" your document to the PDFWriter printer by following these steps.

1. **Choose** <u>**F**</u>**ile**⇨<u>**P**</u>**rint.**

   The Print dialog box appears.

2. **Select the PDFWriter printer as your printer and click OK.**

   When you start the printing process this way, the Save PDF File As dialog box appears, as shown in Figure 5-24.

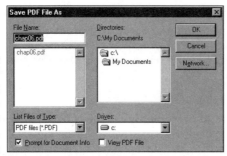

Figure 5-24:
The Save
PDF File As
dialog box.

3. **Type a name for the PDF file you want to create and then click the OK button.**

   The Acrobat PDFWriter Document Information dialog box appears, as shown in Figure 5-25. You can enter the title, subject, author, and document keywords in the appropriate edit box.

4. **Click the OK button.**

   You just created a PDF file — easy as pie!

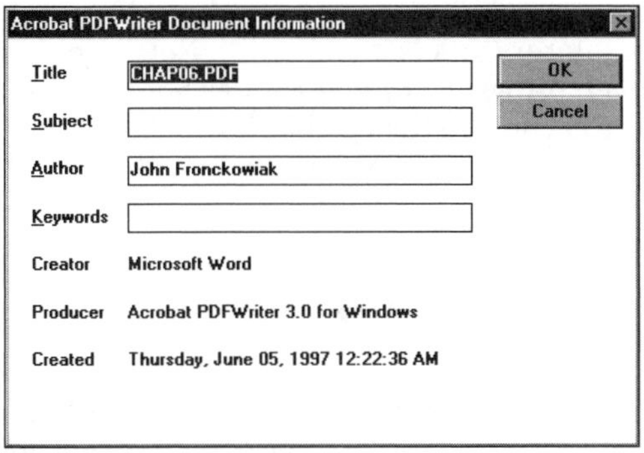

Figure 5-25:
The
Acrobat
PDFWriter
Document
Information
dialog box.

Using Adobe Acrobat Reader

You can easily add links to PDF files on the web pages that you create —
simply specify the PDF filename as the URL to link to. However, to view the
PDF link, Adobe Acrobat Reader needs to be installed on the client computer. You can get Adobe Acrobat Reader on a separate CD-ROM if you
bought the Adobe Acrobat Publisher software, on the CD-ROM included with
this book, and at the Adobe Web site:

`www.adobe.com/prodindex/readstep.html`

You can install Adobe Acrobat Reader in no time. If you download the Adobe
Acrobat Reader from the Adobe Web site, you can simply run the file
`ar32e30.exe`, and it takes you through the setup routine.

1. **When the Welcome dialog box appears, close any other programs
   that you have running and then click the ₦ext button to continue.**

   The licensing information appears.

2. **Click the Yes button to accept the license and continue.**

   A dialog box appears asking you to provide a directory in which to
   install the Adobe Acrobat Reader.

3. **Why mess with success? Keep the default and click the ₦ext button to
   continue.**

4. **After the files have been installed, the Setup Complete dialog box
   appears, and you can click the ₣inish button to complete the
   installation.**

   If the Display the ReadMe file check box is selected, the Acrobat Reader
   ReadMe file appears; otherwise you're done!

Adobe Acrobat Reader is registered as a *plug-in* for both Netscape Navigator and Microsoft Internet Explorer (this is good news). Now, each time you open a PDF file in your web browser Acrobat Reader automatically launches, as shown in Figure 5-26. You can use the toolbar buttons just below the Address edit box to navigate, zoom in and out, search, and print the PDF file.

When Bad Things Happen

Things always mess up, especially when you're on a deadline. Table 5-3 lists the answers to some common problems you may encounter when using Office 97 and Adobe Acrobat to publish documents on your intranet. For even more help with Office 97, try the Microsoft Office 97 support Web site at

```
www.microsoft.com/MSOfficeSupport
```

and for further help with Adobe Acrobat try the Adobe support Web site at

```
www.adobe.com/supportservice/custsupport/main.html
```

Table 5-3	Common Publishing Problems and Solutions
Problem	**Solutions**
My Word document doesn't look quite the same since I saved it as HTML.	Remember that HTML doesn't have quite the same formatting capabilities as a Word document. Some of your special formatting may be lost on complex documents. If you absolutely need your document to look the same, Adobe Acrobat is the way to go.
Loading PDF files in my browser takes a long time.	Adobe Acrobat tends to be a big application, especially when used with your web browser. PDF files are usually much bigger than HTML web pages, so they can take longer to download from your web server.

In this chapter, I just scratch the surface of intranet web publishing. If you really want to learn how to become an intranet web publishing guru, *Intranet Publishing For Dummies* by Glenn Weadock (IDG Books Worldwide, Inc.) is a great place to dig in deeper.

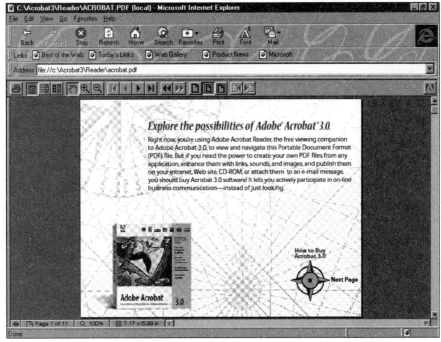

Figure 5-26:
Acrobat
Reader
opened as
an Internet
Explorer
plug-in.

Chapter 6

Getting the Word Out

• •

In This Chapter

▶ Serving up your corporate e-mail with the right mail server

▶ Running your e-mail life with Microsoft Exchange and Eudora

▶ Managing more than just your e-mail with integrated personal information managers

▶ Mediating postal strikes (what to do if your mail system goes down)

• •

*E*lectronic mail (generally referred to as *e-mail*) — love it or hate it, most people can't imagine life without it these days. How else can you send an important memo to everyone in your company in seconds? Lately, people even seem to exchange their e-mail addresses sooner than their phone numbers.

Setting up a corporate e-mail system takes more than giving each user a mail address and program that lets you read and send mail. Think about *snail mail.* (You get to coolly call the U.S. Postal Service "snail mail" after you start using e-mail.) The heart of the postal system is the post office — a place where all the letters come in and are then distributed to all the right homes. Well, the heart of a corporate e-mail system is called a *mail server,* and it performs the same function that a post office performs: The mail server holds new messages as they come in and routes them to the right people. The only differences are that your mail server doesn't ask for a postage hike every couple of years and you don't need to lick any stamps.

In this chapter, I show you how to get a corporate mail server up and running and how to get Microsoft Exchange and Eudora (two popular e-mail clients) working with your server. I also show you how you can use *personal information manager* software to keep track of that dentist appointment you have next week, that never ending list of things you need to do, and those important notes you took the last time you were on the phone doing business with Mr. Big.

Who Uses E-Mail and Why Do I Want It?

Electronic mail lets you communicate messages to other people through your computer. Big deal. You're probably thinking that you can do the same thing with a telephone or a fax machine. Well, e-mail can be better than both a phone call and a fax. If you make a phone call, the person you want to talk to must be there (unless that person has an answering machine — but who likes talking to a tape?). And both faxing and phone calls require the receiving phone line to be free.

And think about your end: Incoming phone calls require your immediate attention. You must talk to the person right as the call comes in or suffer the incessant ringing. This situation can be a real pain, especially if you're trying to get your work done.

In addition, e-mail is much better than phoning or faxing for the following reasons:

- E-mail is written down, making your message clear and explicit.
- You don't need to read your e-mail right away; you can wait for a time that's convenient for you.
- E-mail can include a *subject* line. You can use the subject line to inform recipients of the urgency or subject matter of your messages.
- You can send other information — called *attachments* — with your e-mail messages. These attachments can be other files, like word processing documents or spreadsheets.
- Reaching someone directly by e-mail is usually easier than by phone. In a large company, you can easily send an e-mail message to a manager who may normally be impossible to reach by phone.
- You can easily send a message to many people at once.
- When employees take the time to write out the messages they need to send, they are usually more clear than in verbal communications.

A typical mail message is made up of three basic parts: the address of the person who sent the message, the *subject* of the message (what the message is about), and the message text. A typical e-mail message looks like this:

```
Date: Fri, 11 Jul 1997, 19:26:26 +0100
To: john@buffnet.net
From: Bill Clinton <president@whitehouse.gov>
Subject: Congratulations on Building Intranets for Dummies

Dear John,
I would like to personally congratulate you on the comple-
tion of Building an Intranet for Dummies.
Your friend,
Bill
```

Do You Have the Right Stuff?

E-mail systems are made of two basic pieces: a *mail server* and a *mail client*. The *server* is the computer that actually receives the e-mail and redistributes it to the addressees — just as the post office does with snail mail. A mail *client* is a program that enables you to send and receive mail messages through the mail server — it's really that simple. A mail client can also help you organize all the mail messages you receive and send. Each user in your company needs a mail client to send and receive mail.

A mail server stores all the messages that you're supposed to receive until you pick them up. Your mail client program usually checks with the sever every once in a while to see whether any new mail is sitting on the server for your e-mail address.

If someone uses a mail client, he logs on to the mail server, which then identifies the person by user name and password. In some cases, logging on to the corporate network gives access to e-mail as well; in other cases, logging on to the e-mail server is a separate process. The mail server then knows to give the user the mail that's addressed to him — just as the post office delivers the mail sent to you to your home (most of the time).

To run a corporate e-mail system, you need a mail server in addition to a mail client program on each user's computer. Usually, you want to run your mail server on a system that's solely dedicated to the task. You generally want the same type of fast computer for your e-mail server as you use for your intranet web server. In smaller companies, you can have both running on the same computer, but remember that the more work your server must do, the slower things run — and nothing is more frustrating to your users than a slow network. Most mail servers require you to run an operating system with built-in networking support — for example, Windows NT or UNIX.

In this chapter I show you how to get your corporate e-mail system off the ground using the Microsoft Exchange Server, and Microsoft Exchange and Eudora e-mail clients. While Microsoft Exchange server is a very good choice if you're developing your e-mail system from scratch around a Windows NT server, you probably want to consult with your corporate IS department to determine if you already have an e-mail system in place, or if they prefer another system. Some of the various e-mail systems that are commercially available are:

- ✔ **cc:Mail from Lotus Development Corporation:** www.lotus.com
- ✔ **Microsoft Exchange Server:** backoffice.microsoft.com
- ✔ **Netscape Suitespot:** www.netscape.com
- ✔ **Novell Groupwise:** www.novell.com
- ✔ **UNIX Mail Services:** Already bundled with your UNIX operating system.

I have a few suggestions for choosing the e-mail system that's right for you:

✔ **Under what type of operating system will your corporate e-mail system run?** Each mail system has it's own operating system and hardware restrictions.

✔ **How many users do you need to support?** Some mail systems can scale up to many more users — UNIX mail systems have been supporting large numbers of users for years. You may have additional hardware considerations, such as memory and disk space, as your mail system scales up to handle more users.

✔ **Do you need the ability to send and receive e-mail from people outside of your company?** If the answer is yes, you need to make sure that your mail system supports Internet connectivity. Be sure to read about extranets in Chapter 13, and security issues in Chapter 16 if you plan to go this route.

Where Can I Get E-Mail?

A number of mail servers and mail clients are available for your intranet. In this chapter, I show you how to get up and running by using Microsoft Exchange Server, Exchange Client, and Eudora. Eudora also provides a mail server called WorldMail Server. Microsoft provides an evaluation version of Microsoft Exchange Server and Client at the Microsoft Exchange Web site at www.exchangeserver.com/trial.

The Exchange Server application is provided as a self extracting program (which just means that when you run it, all the files necessary to install the program are created) called ntexch.exe. The Exchange Client application is provided as a self-extracting program called outlook.exe.

Eudora provides an evaluation version of WorldMail Server and Eudora client at the Eudora Web site www.eudora.com.

And another great e-mail program may be sitting right under your nose — if you use Netscape Navigator as your web browser, you already have a terrific e-mail client included! You can read more about the current version of Netscape Navigator in Chapter 3, and the follow-up program, Netscape Communicator in Appendix A.

I can't possibly review every e-mail program that's available today. If you're interested in checking out all the latest e-mail programs out there, try the Electronic Mail category on the Yahoo! Web site at www.yahoo.com/Computers_and_Internet/Software/Internet/Electronic_Mail.

Cutting through the Technobabble

To help you keep your electronic mail POPping, your gateways humming, and your inbox full, take a look at Table 6-1, which helps decode the jargon-orama that surrounds electronic mail systems.

Table 6-1	Electronic Mail Elaboration, Education, and Enlightenment
Technobabble	***Decoded***
Attachment	An e-mail *attachment* is a file that you tag onto your e-mail message. The attachment can be a picture or another file, such as a spreadsheet or word processing document.
Connector	*Connectors* are used by Microsoft Exchange Server to connect to mail clients other than Microsoft Exchange. Microsoft Exchange Server provides a POP connector for Eudora, for example, and for Netscape-mail clients as well.
Filtering	Some mail clients provide *filtering* options to help you automatically sort mail messages — you can put all the messages from Aunt Edna and your boss in separate places.
Gateway	A *gateway* is a computer that connects two networks together. If your internal mail system is hooked up to the Internet, the connection between the Internet and your internal mail system is generally accomplished using a gateway.
Inbox	Just like the inbox on your desk, your e-mail *inbox* is where the incoming mail you pick up from the server sits until you choose to read it.
MIME	I'm not talking about Marcel Marceaux here — *MIME* stands for *Multimedia Internet Mail Extensions.* MIME is a way to encode normal text mail messages so that you can include attachments such as pictures, formatted text, and sound files.
MTA	An *MTA* is a *Message Transfer Agent,* used by Microsoft Exchange to send messages from one mail server to another.
Outbox	Again, like the outbox on your desk, your e-mail *outbox* where the mail is stored that you're still waiting to send.
PIM	Great — another pesky TLA (Three Letter Acronym). A *Personal Information Manager (PIM)* is an application that you can use to manage mail, to-do lists, contact information, and lots of other information you use on a day-to-day basis. Microsoft Outlook is an example of a PIM.

(continued)

Table 6-1 *(continued)*

Technobabble	Decoded
POP	*POP* is the *Post Office Protocol.* POP is a way for e-mail clients such as Eudora and Netscape mail to read mail from a mail server.
SMTP	*SMTP* means *Simple Mail Transfer Protocol,* which is a way for a mail client to send mail to a mail server.
X.400	*X.400* is another protocol, like SMTP, that networks use to send mail between a client and mail server. Because X.400 isn't as simple to use as SMTP, it's not used very often.
X.500	*X.500* is a protocol used by some mail servers. It has the advantage of letting you look up user information — kind of like calling directory assistance for your mail server.

Serving Up E-Mail

The heart of your corporate e-mail system begins with your mail server, as Figure 6-1 shows.

Each user in your company uses an e-mail client to access the e-mail server in order to send and receive mail. The most common way for e-mail clients and servers to communicate is as described in the following list:

✔ **Checking for mail:** The e-mail client connects to the e-mail server to see whether any new mail is there. The e-mail server first asks the user for some ID to make sure that the user is allowed on the system. The most common ID system asks for a user name and a password — often, you hear this process referred to as *authentication*. After the user's identity is confirmed, the e-mail server sends back any waiting messages. The POP protocol is one of the most common ways that mail clients check for mail on the mail server.

✔ **Sending mail:** The e-mail client has a message to send to another user. The e-mail client takes the text and any extra attachments that go along with the text and packages them up as the e-mail message. The most common way to package up a mail message is by using MIME. The packaged message is then sent to the e-mail server, usually by using the SMTP protocol. One interesting thing to notice here is that, after *sending* mail, the e-mail server doesn't ask users to identify themselves. This little quirk has been exploited at times by hackers and other users with less-than-honorable intentions.

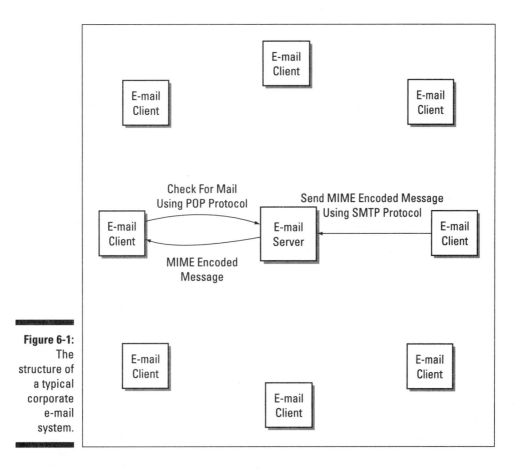

Figure 6-1:
The
structure of
a typical
corporate
e-mail
system.

What the heck is a protocol?

A *protocol* is a way of bringing some order to communications. Suppose, for example, that you hear your phone ringing; you rush to pick the phone, and the first thing you do after that is to say, "Hello," or something similar. After you exchange information with the person on the other end, you usually say, "Good-bye." The "Hello" and "Good-bye" can loosely be thought of as a protocol — all your communications begin with a *Hello*, you send your message, and then you indicate that the message is complete with a *Good-bye*. If you answer a phone call with "Blueberry" and end with "Desk," you're not using the correct protocol for a phone conversation. E-mail protocols work the same way, bringing structure and order to electronic mail messages and enabling two computers to exchange messages.

Pick your e-mail poison — Microsoft Exchange Server and others

Building a corporate e-mail system starts with an e-mail server. As with web servers, web page editors, and graphics software, your choice is based on personal preference and the features you need. Key e-mail server features to look for include the following:

- *Scalability,* which just is a fancy way of saying the server can grow with your company

- Support for standard e-mail protocols such as SMTP and POP

- The capability to work within your current networking environment

- Manageability and easy administration

- Built-in security

- Possible additional features such as:

  - News server capabilities (the capability to read and send bulletin board-like messages)

  - User information directory services (like a phone book for looking up users)

Besides the obvious capability to read and send messages, some key e-mail client features you may want to look for include the following:

- **The capability to manage the messages you receive and send by sorting them into folders.** Some e-mail clients support automatic filtering of mail messages, meaning that the messages are automatically sorted into folders based on a number of different factors, such as who sent the message, a word that appears in a message, or the message subject line.

- **Compatibility** — the e-mail client needs to work with your e-mail server.

Installing Microsoft Exchange Server

Before you can begin setting up Microsoft Exchange Server Version 5.0, you need to make sure that your system is up to the task. The requirements for running Microsoft Exchange Server include the following:

- **Windows NT Server and a fast computer.** At least a 133 MHz Pentium system, with at least 32MB of RAM for Windows 95 and 16MB of RAM for Windows NT. If you're using Windows NT Version 3.51, you also need Service Pack 5 installed. With Windows NT Version 4.0, you need Service Pack 2 installed. (Service Packs are updates to the Windows NT operating system.)

✔ **A lot of disk space!** At *minimum* you need 150MB of free disk space, but 300MB or more is *highly* recommended. The disk space is where all the incoming messages are stored — I recommend at least 10MB of free disk space on the server per user who needs to access it.

✔ **A CD-ROM drive to install Exchange Server.**

Ready to begin installing Microsoft Exchange Server Version 5.0? Roll up your sleeves and dig in:

1. **Pop your Microsoft Exchange Server 5.0 CD in the CD-ROM drive and run the Setup application, or run the file you downloaded.**

   If you're running Windows NT on a Pentium based system, run the Setup application in the \SERVER\SETUP\I386 directory. If you're running Windows NT on a Digital Equipment Corporation Alpha-based system, run the Setup application in the \SERVER\SETUP\ALPHA directory. If you downloaded the Microsoft Exchange Server demo from the Microsoft Exchange Server Web site then you should simply run the ntexch.exe application.

   You must be logged in using the Administrator account before you start the installation process.

   The Microsoft Exchange Server Setup dialog box appears. You're reminded to close any other applications you currently have running.

2. **Click OK to continue with the installation.**

   The Microsoft Exchange Server Setup installation-type dialog box appears. You're best off selecting the dialog box's Complete/Custom option to install all the Exchange Serve components. The Typical option installs the basics needed to run your mail system, but the Custom/Complete option allows you to provide access to your mail system over your intranet (TCP/IP-based) network. Finally the Minimum option is just the bare bones minimum you need to run the Exchange Server.

3. **Click the Complete/Custom button to continue with the installation.**

   The Microsoft Exchange Server Setup - Complete/Custom dialog box appears, as shown in Figure 6-2. All of the Exchange Server options are installed if you continue with the Complete/Custom option.

4. **Click the Continue button to continue with the installation.**

   If you're running Internet Information Server as your intranet web server on the same machine that you're installing Exchange Server on, a dialog appears telling you that Internet Information Server services

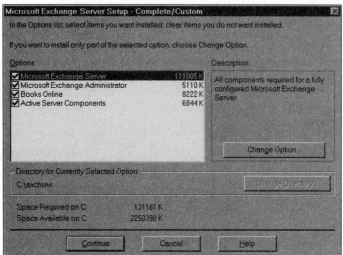

Figure 6-2:
The
Microsoft
Exchange
Server
Setup -
Complete/
Custom
dialog box.

will be stopped temporarily. Internet Information Server stops while Exchange Server is installed, meaning that no one can access your intranet web server until the installation is complete. Try to install Exchange Server during off hours, when people aren't using your web server.

5. Click the OK button to continue.

You're next asked to provide your CD-Key. The CD-Key is usually on a sticker on the back of the case that contains your CD.

6. Enter the 10 digit number from the little orange sticker and click OK to continue.

The Microsoft Exchange Server Product ID dialog box is displayed next.

7. Click OK to continue with the installation.

The Choose Licensing Mode dialog box appears, as shown in Figure 6-3. Just as you need a license for your dog, you need to purchase a license for each user who's going to use the Exchange Server. Exchange Server offers two types of licensing modes: *Per Server* and *Per Seat*. With Per Server licensing, you buy a license for each user who needs to connect to the Exchange Server at the same time. With Per Seat licensing, you buy a license for each computer that can access the Exchange Server. Purchasing Per Server licenses is generally cheaper, because not everyone in your company is always connected and reading mail.

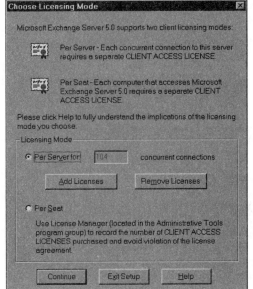

Figure 6-3:
The Choose
Licensing
Mode
dialog box.

8. **Select the appropriate licensing mode radio button — Per Server or Per Seat.**

   If you select the Per Server mode, you also need to click the Add Licenses button to access the New Client Access License dialog box. Enter the number of licenses you bought in the Quantity text box, and click the OK button to continue. You're asked to confirm your license purchase in the Confirm License dialog box. Click the I agree check box and then click the OK button to continue.

9. **Click the Continue button in the Choose Licensing Mode dialog box to continue with the installation.**

   The Organization and Site dialog box appears, as shown in Figure 6-4. The Create a New Site radio button is selected by default. You're creating a new mail site for your company, so the default option is fine.

10. **Make any necessary changes to your Organization Name and Site Name (to name your e-mail server) as they appear in the text boxes and then click OK to continue with the installation.**

    You're now asked to confirm that you want to create the new Exchange Server site for the organization and site you just specified.

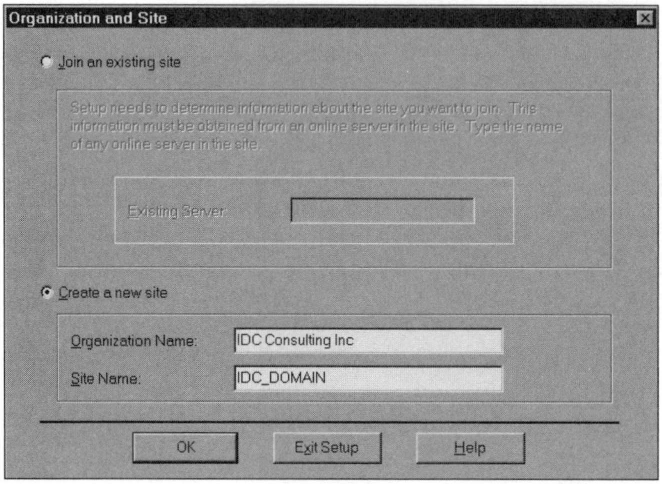

Figure 6-4:
The
Organization
and Site
dialog box.

11. Click the Yes button to continue with the installation.

The Site Services Account dialog box appears, as shown in Figure 6-5. You need to provide a Windows NT account name and password that's to be used to manage the Exchange Server. By default, the Windows NT Administrator account is used for this purpose.

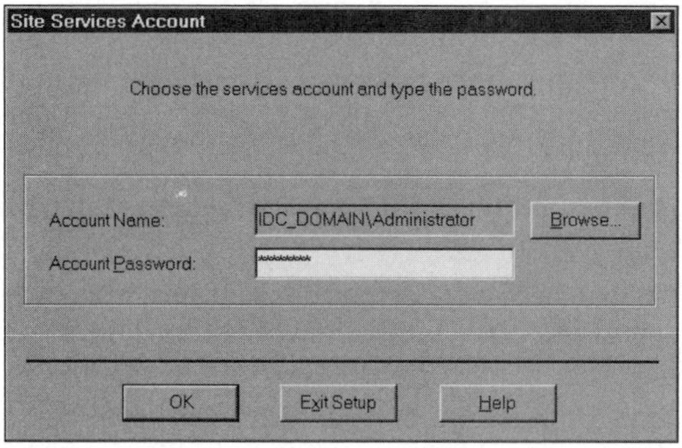

Figure 6-5:
The Site
Services
Account
dialog box.

12. Enter the Administrator Password in the Account Password text box and then click OK to continue.

Make sure that you don't forget the Administrator password for your Windows NT Server system. You have no way of getting the password back if you forget it; your only safe recourse is to re-install Windows NT.

The Exchange Server files copy onto your system. This process takes a while (remember — you're installing more than 100MB of files!), so go get a cup of coffee or a soda. By the time you come back, the files should be copied. The Microsoft Exchange Server Setup complete dialog box appears, as shown in Figure 6-6.

Figure 6-6:
Installation
is complete.

13. **Click the Exit Setup button.**

If you press the Run Optimizer button, Microsoft Exchange cleans up the area it uses to store messages — making sure that any messages which are no longer needed are deleted.

Congratulations! You now have a mail server up and running!

Installing a mailbox

Start by digging a hole about 2 to 3 feet deep; then fill it with concrete and set a post in the concrete. Oh, you want to know how to install a *Microsoft Exchange e-mail* mailbox? To do so, you need to perform the following steps for each user who needs a mailbox:

1. **Run the Microsoft Exchange Administrator Application: Click the Start button and choose Program Files⇨Microsoft Exchange⇨ Microsoft Exchange Administrator.**

The Connect to Server dialog box appears, as shown in Figure 6-7, asking you for the name of the mail server you want to connect to. Click the Browse button if you can't remember the name you gave to your system. Select the server name from the Servers list box in the dialog box that appears and then click OK to continue.

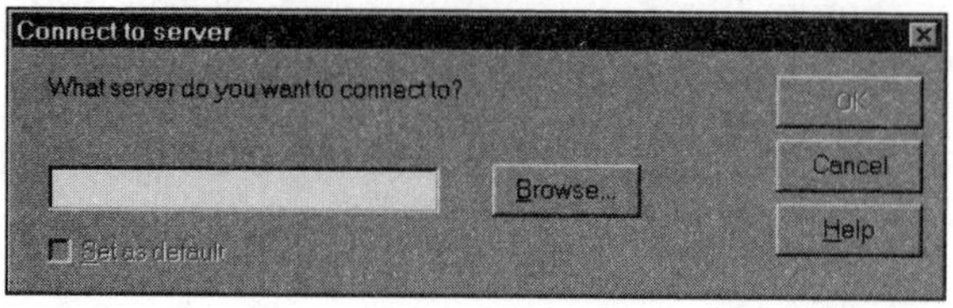

Figure 6-7:
The
Connect to
Server
dialog box.

2. **Click OK in the Connect to Server dialog box to start the Exchange Administrator.**

   The Exchange Administrator starts.

3. **To begin creating a new mail box, choose File⇨New Mailbox from the menu bar.**

   If a dialog box appears asking you to switch to the recipients container, just click OK to continue. The Properties dialog box appears, as shown in Figure 6-8. The General tab is selected by default.

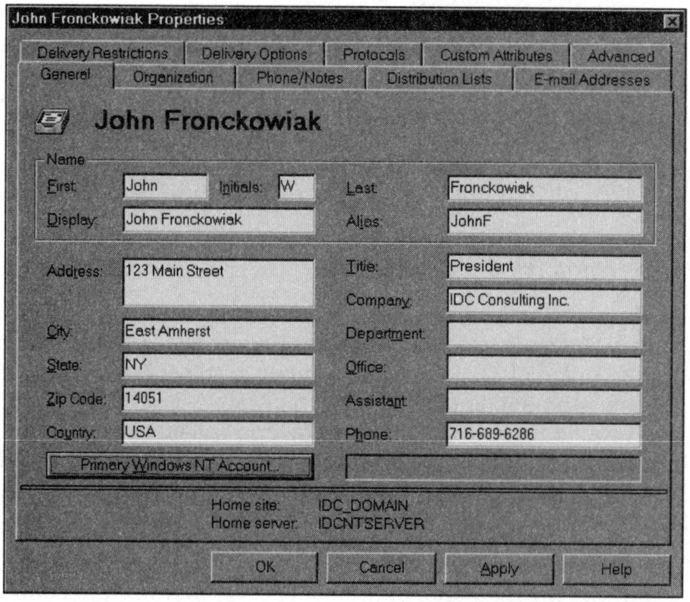

Figure 6-8:
The General
tab of the
Properties
dialog box.

4. Fill in the name and address information in the appropriate text boxes.

The user's alias is automatically created by using the First Name and the first initial of the Last Name. An alias is just another name people can use for you when they send you mail. You can change the user's alias, but make a note of it, because you need to remember it to set up Eudora Light (or any other POP mail client).

Each user who has a mailbox needs a Windows NT account setup.

5. Click the Primary Windows NT Account button.

The Primary Windows NT Account dialog box appears, as shown in Figure 6-9. If this user doesn't have an account set up already, select the Create a New Windows NT Account radio button and click OK to continue. If the user has an account already set up, click the Select an existing Windows NT account radio button and click OK — and jump to the end of these steps, because you're done!

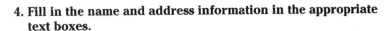

Figure 6-9:
The Primary
Windows
NT Account
dialog box.

The Create Windows NT Account dialog box appears, as shown in Figure 6-10.

Figure 6-10:
The Create
Windows
NT Account
dialog box.

6. Make any changes necessary to the account name and click OK to continue.

A dialog box appears stating that the user was assigned a blank password that the user needs to change after logging on for the first time.

7. Click OK to close this dialog box and then click OK in the Properties dialog box to finish creating the mailbox.

Congratulations — you just created your first e-mail mailbox. You need to repeat this process for each user who needs a mailbox, which may take some time — but at least you need to do it only once for each user!

If you need more help with setting up and maintaining user accounts in Windows NT Version 4.0, *Windows NT 4.0 For Dummies,* by Andy Rathbone and Sharon Crawford (IDG Books Worldwide, Inc.), is a great place to find out more!

Ordering Up E-Mail

Now that you have your e-mail server up and running smoothly, you need to get your e-mail clients ready to do your users' evil bidding. You can use Microsoft Exchange Server right out of the box with a number of different e-mail clients because the program supports the popular POP mail protocol — you don't need to do any special fiddling to support Eudora, Netscape, or a variety of other programs.

Although both Microsoft Exchange and Eudora let you read and send e-mail using the Exchange Mail Server, Eudora and many other e-mail clients access the Exchange Mail Server a little differently than the Microsoft Exchange client does. If you use the Exchange client with the Exchange Mail Server, your users need to log on to the Windows NT Server where the Exchange Server is running. The Exchange Server understands who you are based on the fact that you've logged on using the Windows NT security mechanisms. Eudora, on the other hand, uses the POP protocol to connect to the Exchange Server. If you're using Eudora, the mail server directly asks for a user name and a password each time a user reads mail.

Guide to setting up an Exchange client

Microsoft Exchange Server includes the Microsoft Exchange e-mail client. Follow these steps to set up Microsoft Exchange:

1. **Close any applications currently running (except Windows).**

2. **Put your Microsoft Exchange Server 5.0 CD in the CD-ROM drive and the run the** Setup **application in the \CLIENT\Win95 directory for Windows 95, or the \CLIENT\WinNT\I386 directory for Windows NT with a Pentium Processor, or simply run the** outlook.exe **application if you downloaded the Microsoft Exchange Client demo from the Microsoft Exchange Web site.**

   The Microsoft Exchange Setup dialog box appears.

3. **Click the Continue button to continue with the installation.**

   The Name and Organization Information dialog box appears.

4. **Enter your name and company name and click OK to continue.**

   A dialog box appears asking you to confirm your name and company name.

5. **Click OK button to continue with the installation (if you think you know how to spell your own name and you are reasonably sure that you know what company you work for).**

   The Microsoft Exchange Setup select installation directory dialog box appears.

6. **You shouldn't need to change the default directory, so just click OK to continue with the installation.**

   The Microsoft Exchange Setup installation type dialog box graces your screen.

7. **Click the Complete button to install the Exchange Client with typical installation options.**

   After the Exchange files are installed, a dialog box pops up to tell you that the setup is complete.

8. **Click OK and you're done.**

Congratulations — you just installed the Microsoft Exchange client!

Taking Exchange Client for a test drive

The next step is to test out your Microsoft Exchange e-mail client and make sure that you can send and receive e-mail — that's the point of this whole exercise after all. You need to be at the computer of a user who already has a mailbox set up on the Exchange server. Make sure that the user whose computer you're using is already logged on to the Windows NT server where Exchange Server is installed. Then follow these simple steps:

1. **Start up the Exchange e-mail client by clicking Start⇨Programs⇨ Microsoft Exchange⇨Microsoft Exchange.**

2. **To make sure that you're connecting to the Exchange Server to access your e-mail, choose Tools⇨Services.**

   The Services dialog box appears, as shown in Figure 6-11.

3. **If Microsoft Exchange Server appears in the list in the Services dialog box, click OK.**

   Microsoft Exchange client appears, as shown in Figure 6-12. Your mail folders appear on the left side of the window, including your Inbox and Outbox for incoming and outgoing mail. The messages contained in these folders appear on the right side of the window. You're ready to start sending and receiving mail!

Figure 6-11:
The
Microsoft
Exchange
Services
dialog box.

If Microsoft Exchange Server does *not* appear in the list, follow the remaining steps.

4. **To add Microsoft Exchange Server, click the A̲dd button to open the Add Service To Profile dialog box, as shown in Figure 6-13.**

5. **Select the Microsoft Exchange Server from the list of available services and click OK.**

The Microsoft Exchange Server dialog box appears, as shown in Figure 6-14.

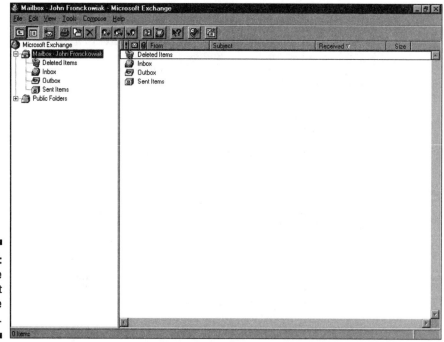

Figure 6-12:
The
Microsoft
Exchange
application.

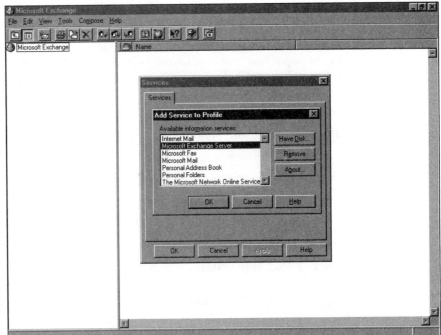

Figure 6-13:
The
Microsoft
Exchange
Add Service
To Profile
dialog box.

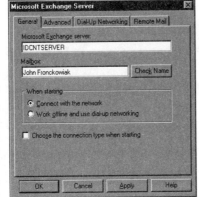

Figure 6-14:
The
Microsoft
Exchange
Server
dialog box.

6. Enter In the Microsoft Exchange Server text box the name of the Windows NT server where you installed the Microsoft Exchange Server.

Use the name of the server as you determined it in the steps in the section "Setting up Microsoft Exchange Server," earlier in this chapter. In my case, the Windows NT Server was called IDCNTSERVER, so I'd enter that name in the Microsoft Exchange Server edit box.

7. **Click the Chec_k_ Name button to make sure that you can access the Microsoft Exchange Server.**

8. **If an error message appears, make sure that you entered the right server name and that you actually created a mailbox for this user and then try again; if an error message doesn't appear, click OK to save your changes.**

   A dialog box appears telling you that you need to restart Exchange.

9. **Click OK to clear the dialog box.**

   You return to the Services dialog box.

10. **Click OK to close the Services dialog box.**

11. **Back in Exchange, choose _F_ile⇨E_x_it to close Exchange.**

    Now you're ready to re-start Microsoft Exchange.

12. **Click Start⇨_P_rograms⇨Microsoft Exchange⇨Microsoft Exchange.**

    Microsoft Exchange restarts.

Sending a message with Exchange

Sending a message in Exchange is easy — just follow these steps:

1. **In the Exchange window, choose Co_m_pose⇨_N_ew Message from the menu bar or click the New Message button (shown at left).**

   The New Message window appears, as shown in Figure 6-15.

2. **To enter a message recipient in the T_o_ text box, click the T_o_ button to open the Address book dialog box, as shown in Figure 6-16.**

3. **Select from the list the person to whom you want to send the message and then click the T_o_ button to move that person's name to the _M_essage Recipients list on the right.**

   If you want to send your message to more than one user, you can select additional recipients the same way. You can also use the Cc button to add people to your *Cc,* or Carbon Copy, list — these people simply receive a copy of the letter, so they're "in on the loop," so to speak. Cc recipients are not expected to respond to your mail.

4. **Click OK after you select all your recipients.**

   The names of the people you selected to receive your message now appear in the To and Cc text boxes of the New Message window.

5. **Enter a subject for the message in the Subject text box.**

6. **Type your message in the message area at the bottom of the New Message window.**

Message recipient   Message subject   Send message button

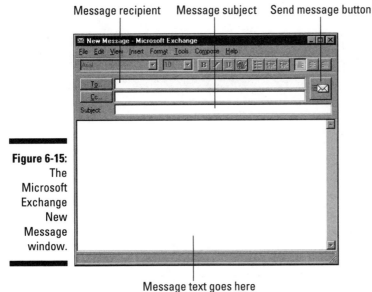

Figure 6-15:
The
Microsoft
Exchange
New
Message
window.

Message text goes here

Figure 6-16:
The
Address
Book
dialog box.

7. Choose File➪Send or click the Send Message button (shown at left) to send your message.

That's it — your message is sent!

Reading a message with Exchange

Reading your mail is even easier. To read a new message, click the Inbox folder on the left side of the Exchange window, as shown in Figure 6-17.

Message folders   New messages

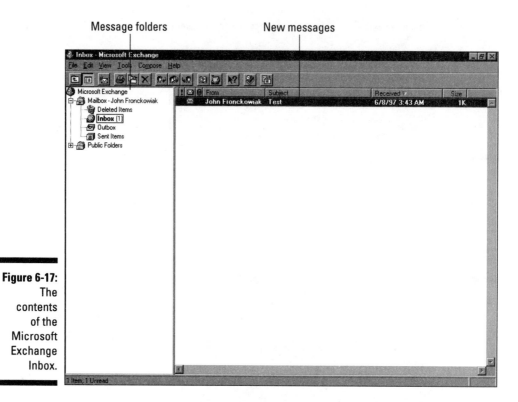

Figure 6-17:
The
contents
of the
Microsoft
Exchange
Inbox.

If the Inbox folder name appears in bold, you have new messages waiting (the number in parentheses after the Inbox folder name is the number of new unread messages). The messages in the Inbox folder are listed on the right side of the window — again, messages in bold are new, unread mail messages. Just double-click the name of any message in the list to read it.

If you need to answer a message, choose Compose⇨Reply To Sender from the menu bar of the window in which the message appears or click on the reply button on the toolbar. The New Message window appears, and the address for the person that sent you the message is automatically entered in the To text box. The original message also appears in the message area to remind the person you're replying to what the message is all about — it kind of keeps the conversation going. Just follow the rest of the numbered steps in the preceding section to send your reply.

Setting up a POP client — Eudora Light

Another very popular e-mail client is Eudora, by Qualcomm — a POP e-mail client. Eudora uses the POP mail protocol to communicate with an e-mail server, which means that you have no problem using Eudora with Microsoft

Where did they get the name Eudora?

The Eudora user documentation says that the name was dreamt up as the authors of the software were looking for a name for a new Post Office Protocol mail program. They recalled the title of a short story they once read called "Why I Live at the P.O." The author of the story is Eudora Welty — and the rest, as they say, is history.

Exchange Server. A big advantage of using Eudora Light as your e-mail client is that it's free, *free*, FREE! You can get it from the CD-ROM that comes with this book as well as from the Eudora Web site at: www.eudora.com

To get up and running with Eudora Light, follow these steps:

1. **Close any applications you have running (except Windows).**

2. **Start this application from the CD-ROM that comes with this book or download Eudora Light from the Eudora Web site.**

   Note: The current version of the Eudora Light installation program is called EUL301.EXE.

   The Eudora Light Welcome dialog box appears.

3. **Click the Next button to continue with the installation process.**

   The License Agreement dialog box appears.

4. **Click Yes to accept the license agreement and continue with the installation process.**

   The Choose Destination Location dialog box appears. The default directory, \EUDORA, that appears in the dialog box is fine for installing the program.

5. **Click Next to continue with the installation process.**

   The Installation Options dialog box appears next. You want to keep the recommended options and install the version of Eudora Light that's appropriate for your system.

6. **Click Next to continue.**

   The Start Copying Files dialog box appears.

7. **Review the options you selected and click Next to start installing the Eudora Light files.**

   Click the Back button if you need to make any changes.

   After the files are installed, you're asked whether you want to read the README file now.

8. **To read this file, click Yes; otherwise, click No.**

Don't worry — you're not missing anything exciting if you choose not to read the README.

That's it — you're ready to use Eudora Light!

Taking Eudora for a test drive

The next step is to test out your Eudora Light e-mail client to make sure that you can send and receive mail. You need to be at the computer of a user who already has a mailbox set up on the Exchange server; then follow these simple steps:

1. **Start the Eudora Light e-mail client by clicking Start⇨Programs⇨ Eudora Light.**

   The Eudora Light e-mail client appears, as shown in Figure 6-18. Notice that Eudora Light looks very similar to the Exchange client, with the mail folders on the left and the messages listed on the right.

2. **To configure Eudora Light so that the program can talk to your Exchange Server, choose Tools⇨Options to open the Options dialog box, as shown in Figure 6-19.**

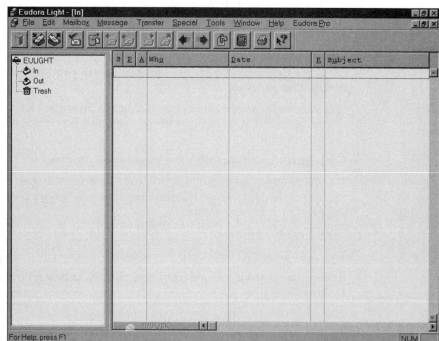

Figure 6-18:
The Eudora
Light
application.

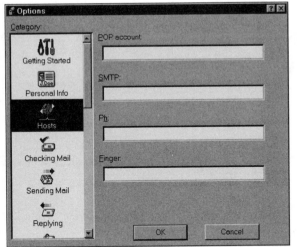

Figure 6-19:
The Eudora
Light
Options
dialog box.

3. **Select the Hosts item in the Category list box.**

4. **Enter the names of the POP Account and SMTP server in the appropriate text boxes.**

   Your POP account name is made up of the Exchange User Alias Name (the name that appears in the Properties dialog box as you set up a new user) and the name of the Windows NT Server where the e-mail server is running, separated by the @ symbol. An alias is just another name people can use for you when they send you mail.

   An account I created earlier had an alias of JohnF and my e-mail server is running on the Windows NT Server called IDCNTSERVER, so I enter **JohnF@IDCNTSERVER** in the POP Account text box. In the SMTP text box, I simply enter the name of the Windows NT Server where the e-mail server is running; so in my case, I simply enter the name **IDCNTSERVER**.

5. **Click OK to save these settings.**

That's it — you're ready to send and read mail.

Sending a message with Eudora Light

Sending a mail message with Eudora Light is very simple. Just follow these easy steps:

1. **Choose Message⇨New Message from the menu bar to open the New Message window, as shown in Figure 6-20.**

Message folders   Message recipient   Message subject

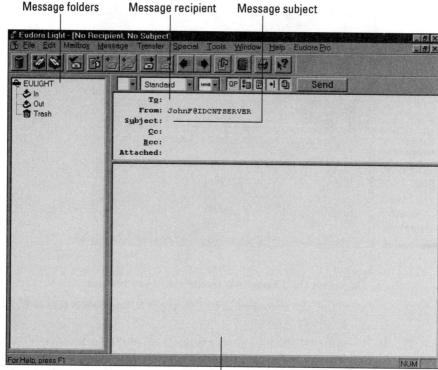

Figure 6-20:
The Eudora
Light New
Message
window.

Message text goes here

2. Enter the e-mail address of your message recipient in the in the area of the address box next to To.

Because you're using a POP mail client, you don't have direct access to the server address book as you do if you're using the Exchange client. The address book for Microsoft Exchange clients resides on the Microsoft Exchange Server system, but when you're using Eudora the address book resides on the client system (users' computer). This To address consists of the Exchange User Alias Name (the name that appears in the Properties dialog box as you set up a new user) and the name of the Windows NT Server where the e-mail server is running, separated by the @ symbol.

3. Enter a subject for the message in the Subject text box.

4. Enter your message in the message area in the bottom window.

5. After you finish entering your message, click the Send button to send it.

That's it — your message is sent into the electronic yonder!

Reading a message in Eudora Light

Reading your mail with Eudora Light is just as easy as sending a message; just follow these steps:

1. **To check for new messages, choose File⇨Check Mail.**

   The Enter password dialog box appears.

2. **Enter your password in the Password dialog box.**

   If you are connecting to Microsoft Exchange Server, the password is the same as the user's Window NT password. Eudora Light connects to the mail server and picks up any new mail messages. If the In folder name appears in bold on the right side of the window, you know that you have new messages waiting.

3. **Double-click the name of the message to read it.**

   The message appears in a separate window.

4. **If you need to answer the message, choose Message⇨Reply from the menu bar.**

   The New Message window appears, and you see that the person who sent you the message is automatically named in the To text box and that the original message appears in the message area. The original message is included to remind the person to whom you're replying what the message is about — kind of keeping the conversation going.

   Just follow the the message sending steps, starting at Step 4, to send your replies.

Now you know the basics of reading and sending mail with Eudora Light!

Using Outlook with Exchange

Microsoft Outlook is more than just an e-mail client. Outlook works in conjunction with Microsoft Exchange and enables you to do the usual stuff such as read, send, and sort out your mail. The big trick that Outlook has up its sleeve is a complete Personal Information Manager (PIM). Microsoft Outlook is part of Microsoft Office Professional and comes with many new computers. Check to see whether you have it on your machine: Click Start⇨Programs⇨Microsoft Outlook. Figure 6-21 shows the Outlook application in action.

Outlook provides the following features:

✔ Access to your Exchange mailbox.

✔ A calendar to help you manage your appointments.

✔ A contact manager for managing business contacts and personal information. This information is the kind of stuff that you put in your rolodex in the good old days.

✔ A task manager to help you manage lists of important things you need to get tasks done from day to day.

✔ A journal to help you keep track of how you spend your time everyday (playing computer solitaire, gabbing with all your new e-mail buddies, and so on).

✔ A place to keep little notes to yourself — kind of like an electronic version of stick-on notes.

When Bad Things Happen

After you begin to use your e-mail system, you quickly discover that it's one of the most mission-critical applications you can run on your intranet. Now, I didn't say *Mission Impossible* — that's something different. What I mean is that if e-mail isn't working, you're going to hear about it from your users — and fast!

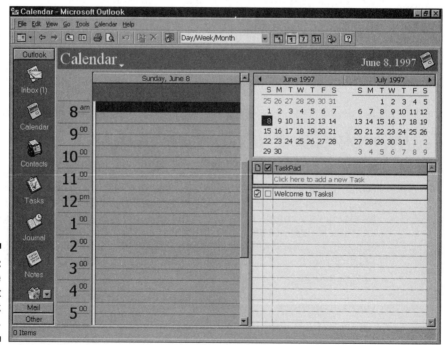

Figure 6-21:
The Microsoft Outlook application.

At the start of this chapter, I list the reasons e-mail is a better system than phone and fax, and believe me, your users no doubt agree — which means that you don't have any time to waste in getting your mail system back up and running. Microsoft Exchange Server provides two Web sites for support information on both the Exchange Server and the Exchange Mail client, located at the following addresses:

```
www.microsoft.com/exchange/pss.htm
```

```
www.exchangeserver.com
```

Eudora also provides a technical support Web site at the following Web address:

```
www.eudora.com/techsupport
```

Table 6-2 provides answers to some of the more common mail problems you may experience. Good luck and happy e-mailing!

Table 6-2	Common E-Mail Problems and Solutions
Problem	*Solutions*
I can't read or send any mail!	This situation can be caused by a number of problems. Make sure that your e-mail server is up and running. If your e-mail server is working, check to make sure that the user having problems is set up correctly in your mail server and that the e-mail client is configured correctly. If other users are having problems, your problem is likely to be a networking problem.
How do I send a file with a mail message?	This kind of file is called an *attachment*. See the table of terms in the "Cutting through the Technobabble" section. To send an attachment in Eudora Light, choose Message⇨Attach File as you write a message and then select the file you want to send with your message from the File Open dialog box that appears. To send an attachment in Exchange, choose Insert⇨ File and then select the file you want to send with your message from the File Open dialog box that appears.

(continued)

Table 6-2 *(continued)*

Problem	Solutions
How do I open an attachment?	If you read a mail message that contains an attachment, an icon representing the attachment usually appears in your message. Double-click the icon to open the attachment, and the file attachment should open in the associated application if that application's available. If, for example, you double-click a Word file attachment in a message, the file opens in Word; an Excel file opens in Excel and so on.

Chapter 7

Show Me the Database!

*I*n this chapter, I show you how to open your databases up to your intranet web. With your intranet, your data resources can become much more accessible than they ever were before because anyone with a web browser and access to your intranet can access database information. The primary idea behind building your intranet is to make information more accessible and improve communications. So what better to make available over your intranet than the informational gold locked up in your corporate databases?

Who Uses Web Databases, and Why Do You Want It?

Not really quite sure what a database is? No problem. A database is just a collection of information that, unlike my office, is organized so that you can find things easily. Here are some everyday examples of databases:

- ✔ Your appointment book
- ✔ The telephone book
- ✔ A set of encyclopedia books (you still remember when encyclopedias didn't come on CD-ROM, don't you?)
- ✔ The dictionary
- ✔ The Rolodex with information about the people you talk to everyday

Basically, a database is just a bunch of collected and organized information. A computer lets you organize and sort the information in a bunch of different ways.

A database typically begins with tables — just like a spreadsheet — with a number of rows and columns, each holding a different piece of information. For example, if you have a database table that contains addresses, you may include information like a first name, last name, street address, city, state, and zip code in the various columns. (In database lingo, these columns are called *fields*.) Then, you can imagine that each row in your spread sheet holds the fields that describe one person. (In database lingo, each row is called a *record*.)

The power of a database is that it keeps all this information organized. The beauty of computer databases is that you can quickly sort information based on particular fields and extract just the information you need. For example, in the example of the address database, you can pull out everyone with a last name that begins with an R, or everyone who lives on Essex Street, or any other criteria you want to apply. In most cases, you don't deal with an entire database directly. Instead, you use programs designed to specifically process and extract the information you have in your database.

An intranet web database takes the amazing power and utility of the information you have in a database and makes it available on your intranet web to all of your employees using the familiar web browser. Furthermore, putting database information, which is constantly changing (imagine a customer database with new additions every day — you hope) on your intranet means that everyone can get the latest information in one convenient place.

Do You Have the Right Stuff?

In this chapter I show you how to create a database of customer contact information, and make it available on your intranet using Microsoft Access. Microsoft Access is by no means the only database you can use on your web server. I focus on it in this chapter simply because it provides a nifty Web Publishing Wizard that completely automates the process of getting your database to your intranet users.

While I believe Access simplifies the process of creating truly interactive web/database applications, a number of other database applications provide web/database integration including:

> ✔ **DB2 from IBM:** www.software.ibm.com/data/db2
>
> ✔ **Visual FoxPro from Microsoft:** www.microsoft.com/vfoxpro

- **Interbase from Borland:** www.borland.com/interbase

- **Paradox from Borland:** www.borland.com/paradox

- **Open Ingres from Computer Associates:** www.cai.com/products/ingres.htm

- **Oracle from Oracle Corporation:** www.oracle.com

- **Informix from Informix Software:** www.informix.com

- **Sybase SQL Server from Sybase:** www.sybase.com

I have a few suggestion on how to choose the product that's right for you:

- **Which database applications are already being used in your company?** You probably have to work with what your company is already using. Check with your IS department before you attempt to deploy any database applications.

- **On what type of system will your database run?** Your choice of database solutions is also limited by the type of operating system you're using. If you use a UNIX based system, Microsoft Access is not an option.

- **Do you want to create highly customized applications?** You may opt for the more complex route of developing custom applications that run on your web server (usually in CGI script) to access your database. You probably need the help of your IS department if you need to do much of this kind of customization.

- **How much information and how many users do you expect to support?** If you're planning to create a database that supports a number of simultaneous users, or that needs to hold a large amount of information, you need to consider larger capacity databases like Oracle or SQL Server. These database servers are up to the task of handling multiple simultaneous users and large amounts of information. On the other hand, if you're only providing database access to automate tasks for a handful of users, applications like Microsoft Access and IBM DB2 are fine.

You probably already have most of what you need with Windows. If you have a database that you want to make available on your intranet web using Microsoft Access, you need at least one of the following:

- **Microsoft Access 97.** I explain how to publish information from other Office 97 software in Chapter 5, and Access 97 is part of Microsoft the Office 97 suite. For more information, try the Microsoft Access Web site at www.microsoft.com/access

✔ **Microsoft FrontPage 97.** I explain how to create your intranet web site using FrontPage 97 in Chapter 4. For more information, try the Microsoft FrontPage Web site at `www.microsoft.com/frontpage`

✔ **Microsoft SQL Server.** This program is Microsoft's *relational database server.* SQL stands for *Structured Query Language*, which is a way to look up information in a database. A relational database stores unique information in separate tables — SQL is commonly the language used to access information contained in relational databases. For more information, try the Microsoft SQL Server Web site at `www.microsoft.com/sqlserver`

✔ **Any other ODBC (Open Database Connectivity) compliant database.** Maybe you already use a database and you aren't ready to go through the major hassle of switching to new software. Check with your specific database to see if it can be accessed using ODBC — most popular databases can. If your database is ODBC compliant, then you are in business!

Cutting through the Technobabble

Databases have flourished with the servitude of their own specialists for quite along time, so you can expect the techno terms to get piled pretty deep. Throw web techology in for good measure, and you have a goulash of hideous jargon. When you decide to go to lunch with your database administrator, bring along Table 7-1.

Table 7-1	Database Administration Technical Terms Decoded for Non-database Administrators
Technobabble	*Decoded*
ADO	ADO stands for *ActiveX Database Objects* — a Microsoft-specific language that is used to access ODBC databases from within Active Server Pages.
ASP	Not your garden-variety Egyptian snake, ASP stands for *Active Server Pages*. Active Server Pages allow you to create programs that run on either your Internet Information or your Personal Web Server (see Chapter 1) each time they are accessed. (If you're familiar with VBScript, Active Server Pages work just like VBScript applications, except that they are executed by the web server instead of the web browser.)

Technobabble	Decoded
CGI	*Common Gateway Interface* is a way to develop programs that run on your web server. The CGI standard allows you to create programs that run when someone clicks on the appropriate link on your web page. When they run, they can produce web pages as their output. For example, you can write a CGI program that accesses the most current sales database information, and then delivers a web page to your users to display it.
Cursors	These are the people that are having problems with their computers. However, for the purposes of this chapter, a *cursor* is just like a pointer (for example, your computer mouse is a type of cursor). When you access a database table, a cursor points to a record to help you keep your place. You can usually move forward and backward through a table's records, and the cursor is there always pointing to the record you're currently visiting.
Database Server	A *database server* holds the actual database data and answers requests for data from your intranet users. Examples of database servers include Microsoft SQL Server and Oracle. Unlike stand-alone database applications, such as Microsoft Access, database servers are built to be used by many users at the same time.
Join	A *join* is like a marriage ceremony for database tables. Imagine that you have two database tables: In one table you have a product number and a description; in the other table you have a product number and the current quantity in stock. Say that you want to find out the current number in stock of each product along with the product description. Your solution is to join these two tables together to get the information you want. Table joins are created using table *keys* — in this case the table key is the product number, that is, the thing that both tables have in common. The result of a table join is, lo and behold, another table — in this example, the resulting table contains product number, product description, and current number is stock.

(continued)

Table 7-1 *(continued)*

Technobabble	*Decoded*
Keys	While database keys can't open your front door, they are very similar to the keys that can. Just like a door key, a database *key* is unique and only opens one lock — in this case, instead of a door, the lock is to a specific record in a database.
ODBC	*Open Database Connectivity* is a way for applications to connect to a database. Many databases and applications support ODBC, including Microsoft Access, Microsoft Excel, Lotus 123, SQL Server, and Oracle. For example, using an ODBC-compliant spreadsheet, you could go into a database containing customer names and ages and pull up the info to add total purchases from all of your customers under 30 years of age.
Relational Database	A *relational database* is simply a type of database system — almost every database used today falls into this catagory. All of the examples I give in this chapter are relational databases. You know that you have a relational database if your data is stored in tables. Microsoft Access, SQL Server, and Oracle are all relational databases.
SQL	Pronounced sequel — this isn't the follow up to Jurrasic Park. SQL stands for *Structured Query Language.* SQL is a language that the heavy programmers use to access database information (and give themselves job security). The database system interprets the SQL language and returns the data collected. SQL can be used to develop programs that access databases, or by anyone else that needs to get to data contained in a database.

Server Side Up!

Web databases begin with your servers — both your intranet web server and your database server. These two servers (which are really just programs that can be running on the same computer) work with each other to get your database information out to people on your intranet. In this chapter I focus on getting your database server up and running, and how to access your database information from your intranet web site without a stitch of programming!

Get your database ready!

The first step to getting your database ready for your intranet is to think about the information you're making available and make sure that you're not providing access to any sensitive data. You may find it necessary to work with your database administrator to set up the proper security for your database.

Some database servers, like Oracle, provide web servers that are closely tied to their database. While this type of setup can provide very efficient access to your database, it's not absolutely necessary in order to make your database available on your intranet.

Using FrontPage

Microsoft FrontPage 97 (see Chapter 4) provides a Web Page Wizard that allows you to access a database from your web page. However, the web pages that you can create with the FrontPage 97 Web Wizard are *static,* meaning that you have to specify a *query* (the request for data from the database) — your users can't come up with their own database searches. Each time someone accesses the web page containing the query, the query is executed and the latest data in the database is displayed. For some users, for instance a sales staff looking for the latest price list, this level of access may be perfectly adequate. For some other users, static queries may not be enough — they want to be able to move through a database table and query for a variety of items, which is where Active Server Pages come into play.

Using Active Server Pages

Active Server Pages (ASPs) are web pages that have built-in programs that run on the web server — you can identify them by the .ASP file extension. Each time you access an Active Server Page with your web browser, the built-in programs automatically run on the web server computer. The ASP programs can do a number of things, including provide access to a database. Microsoft has created the ActiveX Data Object (ADO) language to allow access to databases.

Microsoft Access provides a web publishing wizard that automatically generates an Active Server Page application — using Microsoft's ActiveX Data Object (ADO) language — to provide access to your database. Because Active Server Pages really work as applications, you have more control over the information you retrieve. Also, Active Server Pages aren't just for accessing databases — you can also use them to create *dynamic web pages* with content that changes based on a user's requests and actions.

Building a Customer Contact Database Using Access

Microsoft Access 97, like the other Office 97 applications I review in Chapter 6, provides a Web Publishing Wizard. The Microsoft Access Web Wizard guides you through the creation of an Active Server Page that you can use to access your database and display the results as an interactive web page. Sound complicated? It's not — it takes quite a few steps, but I explain everything.

Setting up Internet Information Server for your database

If you're using Internet Information Server, follow these steps to create a directory for your intranet database and web pages:

1. **Add a new directory to your web server for the database and Active Server Pages you want to create.**

   Your intranet web pages are stored in the `C:\InetPub\wwwroot` directory by default. You need to run the DOS Prompt or Windows NT Explorer to create a new sub-directory — in this example I created the `C:\InetPub\wwwroot\Database` sub-directory.

2. **Start the Internet Service Manager: Click Start⇨Programs⇨Microsoft Internet Server (Common)⇨Internet Server Manager.**

   The Internet Service Manager starts.

3. **Look in the Service column and click on the WWW service row to highlight it.**

4. **Choose Properties⇨Service Properties to display the WWW Service Properties dialog box.**

5. **Click the Directories tab to display the dialog box shown in Figure 7-1.**

6. **Click the Add button to display the Directory Properties dialog box as shown in Figure 7-2.**

7. **Enter the name of the sub-directory you created in Step 1 in the Directory edit box.**

8. **In the Alias dialog box, enter a web server alias such as** `Database`.

   You use the alias to quickly access the directory you created. For example, my intranet web server is named `idcntserver`. So I can access the Database directory using the URL `http://idcntserver/Database`.

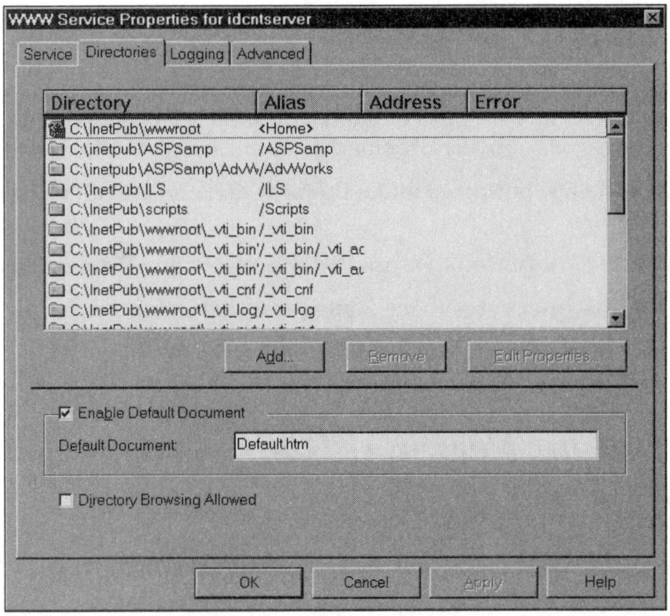

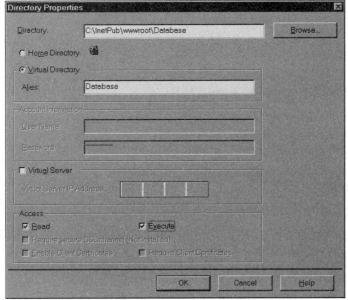

Figure 7-1:
The WWW
Service
Properties
dialog box.

Figure 7-2:
The
Directory
Properties
dialog box.

9. **Make sure that both the <u>R</u>ead and E<u>x</u>ecute access check boxes are checked.**

   The Execute access needs to be enabled because when a user accesses any Active Server Pages created by the Microsoft Access Web Wizard, the pages are actually executed as applications by the web server.

10. **Click the OK button to make the new directory available to your web server.**

11. **Click the OK button to close the WWW Service Properties dialog box.**

12. **Close the Internet Service Manager by selecting Properties⇨Exit.**

    You're done! You now have a directory ready for your intranet database.

Setting up Personal Web Server for your database

If you use Personal Web Server, follow these steps to create a directory for your intranet database and web pages:

1. **Run the MS-DOS Prompt or Windows Explorer to create a new sub-directory — in this example I created the** C:\WebShare\wwwroot\Database **sub-directory.**

   Your intranet web pages are stored in the C:\WebShare\wwwroot directory by default.

2. **Open the Personal Web Server applet from the Control Panel: Click Start⇨Settings⇨Control Panel.**

   The Control Panel pops up.

3. **Double-click the Personal Web Server icon to display the Personal Web Server Properties dialog box.**

4. **Click the Administration tab.**

5. **Click the Administration button to display the Internet Services Administrator web page.**

6. **Click the** WWW Administration **link to display the WWW Administration web page.**

7. **Click the Directories tab to display the WWW Administration - Directories web page, as shown in Figure 7-3.**

   I've scrolled down the web page a little in the figure.

8. **Click the Add link at the bottom of the Action column to display the WWW Administrator - Directory Add web page as shown in Figure 7-4.**

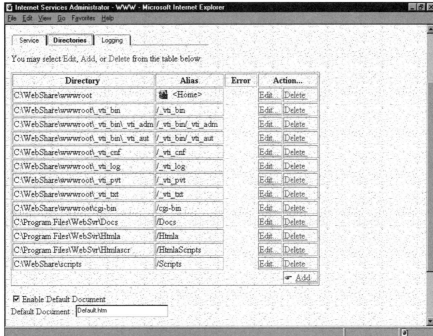

Figure 7-3:
The Internet
Services
Administrator
- WWW
web page.

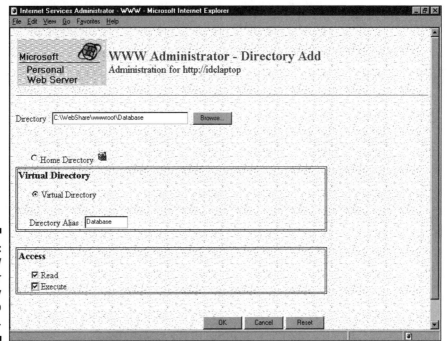

Figure 7-4:
The WWW
Administrator
- Directory
Add web
page.

9. **In the Directory edit box, enter the name of the sub-directory you created in Step 7.**

10. **In the Alias dialog box, enter a web server alias such as** `Database`**.**

   The alias name is used to quickly access this directory. For example, my intranet web server is named `idcntserver`. So I can access the Database directory using the URL `http://idcntserver/Database`.

11. **Make sure that both the Read and Execute access check boxes are checked.**

   The Execute access needs to be enabled (checked) because when you access any Active Server Pages created by the Microsoft Access Web Wizard, the pages are actually executed as applications by the web server.

12. **Click on the OK button to make the new directory available to your web server.**

   That's it! Now you have a directory on your Personal Web Server ready for your intranet database. You can now close your web browser and the Personal Web Server Properties dialog box.

Creating your database

Now to create a customer contact database with Microsoft Access, and then an Active Server Page to access your database from your intranet web server. The first step is to create a customer contact database using the mighty Database Wizard.

I can only cover the basics of Microsoft Access in this chapter. If you would like to find out more about Microsoft Access 97, *Access 97 for Windows For Dummies* by John Kaufield (IDG Books Worldwide, Inc.) is a great place to start.

1. **Click Start⇨Programs⇨Microsoft Access to open Microsoft Access.**

   When Microsoft Access starts, the Microsoft Access dialog box is displayed as shown in Figure 7-5.

2. **Select the Database Wizard radio button, and then click the OK button.**

   The New dialog box appears.

3. **Click the Databases tab to display the dialog box shown in Figure 7-6.**

4. **Select the Address book icon and click the OK button to continue.**

   The File New Database dialog box pops up, as shown in Figure 7-7.

Figure 7-5:
The
Microsoft
Access
dialog box.

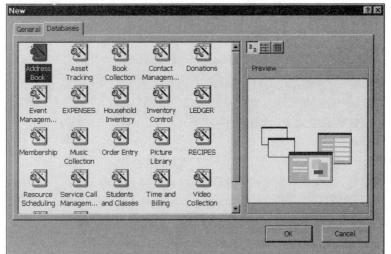

Figure 7-6:
The New
dialog box.

5. **Use the Save In combo box to select the directory you created for your database on your web server (see the previous two sections if you need more info).**

   By default, the database is named Address Book1.

6. **Click on the Create button to start creating your new database.**

   The mighty Database Wizard dialog box appears in a poof of smoke.

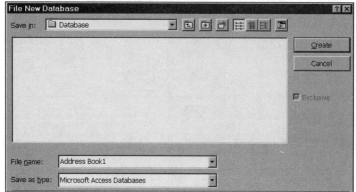

Figure 7-7:
The File
New
Database
dialog box.

7. Click the Next button.

The Database Wizard field selection dialog box appears as shown in Figure 7-8.

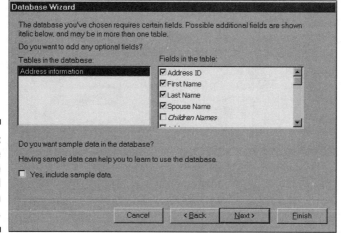

Figure 7-8:
The
Database
Wizard field
selection
dialog box.

8. Select the fields you want to include in your database — if you want to add any additional fields, place a check mark next to them in the Fields in the table list box.

The most commonly used fields are selected by default.

9. Click the Next button to continue.

10. You can make a series of choices about how your database forms and reports are displayed. The options you choose don't have any impact

on your intranet web pages, so you can accept the default options by simply clicking the Finish button.

The Main Switchboard dialog box appears. By creating a database, you also create a customized Access application along with it that you can use to manage your database.

11. **You want to make your database available on your Intranet, so just close this window for now.**

12. **Next, you need to create an Access form that you can use for your intranet web site: Double-click on the Address Book1: Database window.**

13. **Click the Forms tab.**

14. **Click the New button to display the New Form dialog box, as shown in Figure 7-9.**

15. **Select the Form Wizard in the list box, and then select the Addresses table in the combo box at the bottom of the New Form dialog box.**

16. **Click the OK button to continue.**

The Form Wizard dialog box pops up, as shown in Figure 7-10.

17. **Click the >> button to include all the table fields on the form.**

18. **Click the Next button to continue.**

The Form Wizard form layout dialog box appears.

19. **Click the Justified radio button — this layout looks the best when you convert it to a web page.**

20. **Next, you have a series of choices about how your form is displayed. Your choices don't have any impact on your intranet web pages, so accept the default options by simply clicking on the Finish button.**

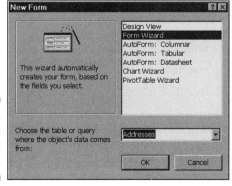

Figure 7-9:
The New
Form
dialog box.

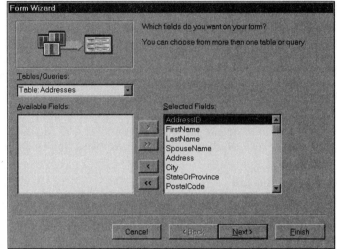

Figure 7-10:
The Form
Wizard
select fields
dialog box.

The Access form you just created — called Addresses1 — is displayed
in the Addresses1 window.

21. **Close the Addresses1 window.**

    Before you can convert the form you just created into an Active Server
    Web Page, you need to set up an ODBC (Open Database Connectivity —
    a way for programs to connect with your database) data source. The
    Active Server Page uses the ODBC data source to get to your database.

22. **Click Start➪Settings➪Control Panel.**

    The Control Panel pops up.

23. **Double-click the ODBC icon.**

    The ODBC Data Source Administrator dialog box appears.

24. **Click the System DSN tab to display the dialog box shown in
    Figure 7-11.**

    You need to add a new system data source.

25. **Click the Add button to continue.**

    The Create New Data Source dialog box pops up, as shown in
    Figure 7-12.

26. **Given that you are creating an ODBC data source for a Microsoft
    Access database, select the Microsoft Access driver from the list box,
    and click the Finish button.**

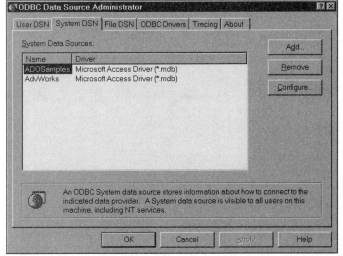

Figure 7-11:
The ODBC
Data
Source
Administrator
dialog box.

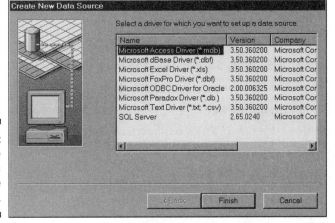

Figure 7-12:
The Create
New Data
Source
dialog box.

The ODBC Microsoft Access 97 Setup dialog box is displayed, as shown in Figure 7-13.

27. For the Data Source Name, type in a name like Address, or whatever name you want to give your database.

28. Click the Select button.

29. Select the database you created earlier.

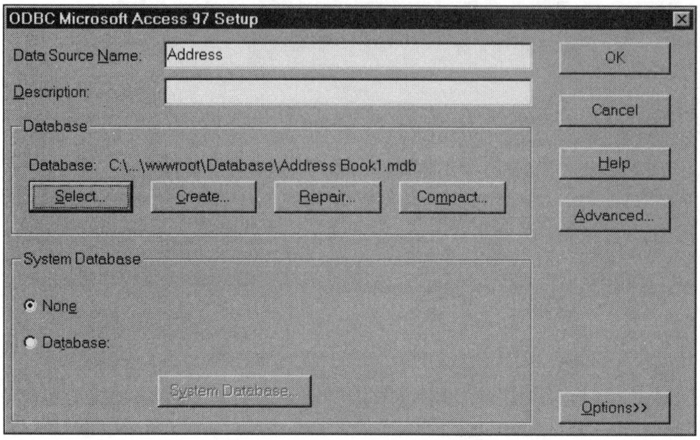

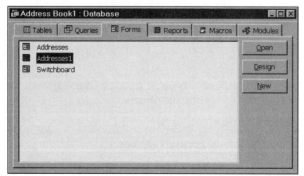

Figure 7-13:
The ODBC
Microsoft
Access 97
Setup
dialog box.

If you're using Internet Information Server and followed the steps earlier in this chapter, you find the database in the `C:\InetPub\wwwroot\Database` directory. If you're using Personal Web Server and followed the steps earlier in this chapter, you find the database in the `C:\WebShare\wwwroot\Database` directory.

30. **Click the OK button to save your ODBC data source.**

31. **Close the ODBC Data Source Administrator dialog box.**

32. **Return to the Microsoft Access application.**

33. **Select the Forms tab in the Address Book1: Database dialog box.**

34. **Select the Addresses1 form, as shown in Figure 7-14.**

35. **Choose File⇨Save As/Export.**

   The Save As dialog box pops up.

Figure 7-14:
The
Address
Book1:
Database
dialog box.

36. **Click the To an External File or Database radio button, and click the OK button.**

    The Save Form 'Addresses1' As dialog box appears, as shown in Figure 7-15.

37. **Select the Microsoft Active Server Pages in the Save as type combo box.**

    You need to save the Active Server Page in your web server directory — the same directory you selected from the Save in combo box way back in Step 5.

    If you're using Internet Information Server and followed the earlier example, select the `C:\InetPub\wwwroot\Database` directory. If you're using Personal Web Server and followed the earlier example, select the `C:\WebShare\wwwroot\Database` directory.

38. **Click on the Export button to continue.**

    The Microsoft Active Server Pages Output Options dialog box appears, as shown in Figure 7-16.

39. **In the Data Source Name edit box, enter the name of the ODBC data source you created in Step 27.**

40. **In the Server URL edit box enter the URL of the web directory you created in the Setting up Internet Information Server and Setting up Personal Web Server sections earlier — for my web server I use the URL** `http://idcntserver/Database`

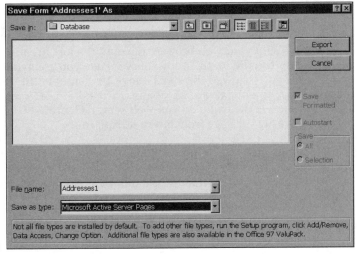

Figure 7-15:
The Save
Form
'Addresses1'
As dialog
box.

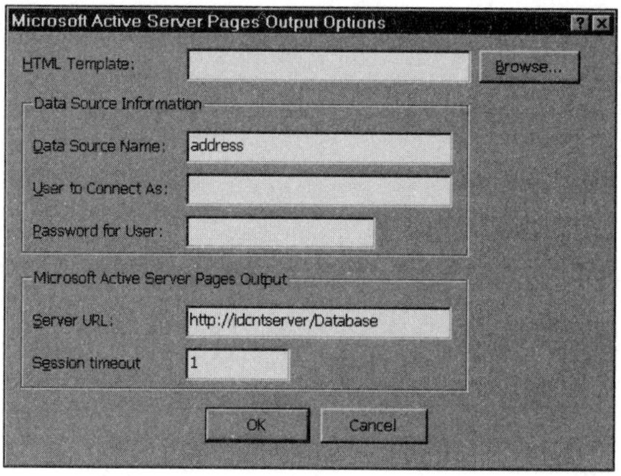

Figure 7-16:
The
Microsoft
Active
Server
Pages
Output
Options
dialog box.

Microsoft Active Server Pages Output Options

HTML Template: _____ Browse...

Data Source Information

Data Source Name: address

User to Connect As: _____

Password for User: _____

Microsoft Active Server Pages Output

Server URL: http://idcntserver/Database

Session timeout 1

OK   Cancel

41. **Finally, in the S̲ession timeout edit box, enter the number of minutes you want your database to stay open each time someone accesses it from your intranet — one to five minutes is fine for most users.**

42. **Click the OK button to save your Active Server Page.**

Believe it or not, that's it.

Getting to the Database from Your Intranet

Now that you have your intranet database ready to go, you probably wonder how to access it? With your web browser of course — just fire up your web browser and enter the URL of the Active Server Page you created in the previous steps. If you followed the steps above, you enter a URL something like `http://your_server_name/Database/Addresses1.asp` where `your_server_name` is the name of your web server. Figure 7-17 shows the Addresses1 Active Server Page from Internet Explorer.

Make sure that you close the database in Microsoft Access before you attempt to access it through your web browser. If you try to access your database Active Server pages while your database is open in Microsoft Access, you receive an error message.

You can use the arrow buttons at the bottom of the web page to move forward and backward through the Addresses1 table records. You can also add and delete new records using the Commit and Delete buttons. Use the Cancel button to abort any changes you make before they are added to the database. That's it! You can link this page to your web site, and now everyone on your intranet has access to your customer contact database!

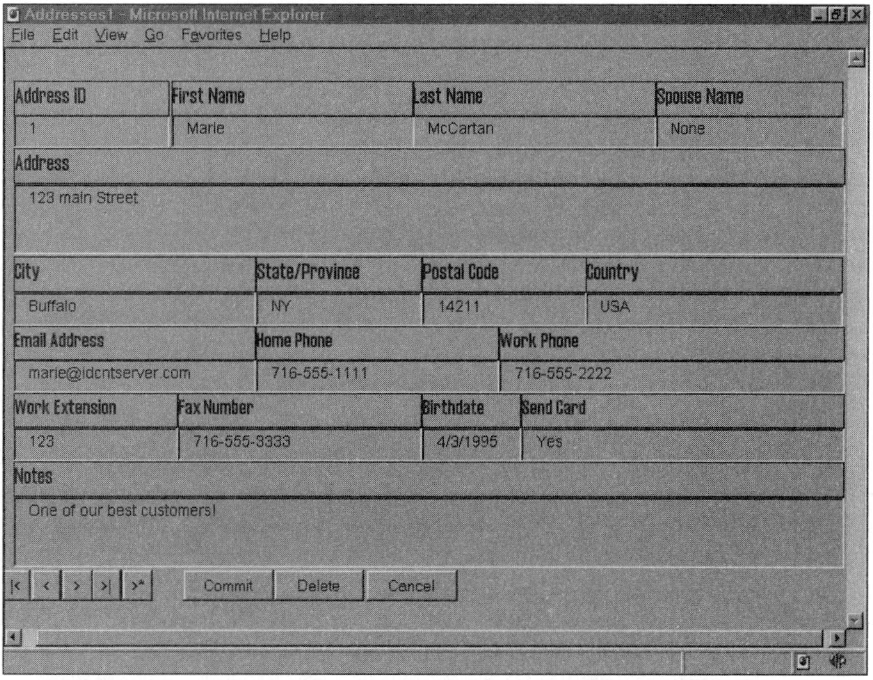

Figure 7-17:
The
Addresses1
Active
Server Page
when
accessed
from the
Microsoft
Internet
Explorer
web
browser.

General Web/Database Integration Recommendations

As you can tell by now, providing access from your intranet to your database can be quite an involved process. I've only presented one way this can be accomplished. In the mean time, I have a few general recommendations to help with your web/database integration projects:

- ✓ **Start small, think big.** This should be your main intranet mantra — start with small applications but keep in mind your bigger picture, and *scalability*, that is, the ability to expand your project. Small applications allow you to learn the potential pitfalls and problems you may encounter when working on web/database integration products.

- ✓ **Get the necessary help.** Don't be afraid to discuss your projects with your IS department — don't worry, they don't recruit people to wear a pocket protector and join their little club. They can let you know what and where current information is deployed, and they probably have a good understanding of the products that work with your system.

✔ **Select the right size database.** You need to select the database that can support your potential users and amount of information you intend to make available.

✔ **Stick with open standards.** Whenever possible use *open standards*, that is, languages and protocols that many applications understand such as SQL and ODBC, when developing your web/database applications. This ensures the greatest amount of portability and flexibility if you ever need to move or expand your applications, change your database, or change your web server.

When Bad Things Happen

Table 7-2 answers some of the more common problems you may encounter when you try to access your Access 97 database. The Microsoft Access 97 support web site at `www.microsoft.com/MSAccessSupport` is a great place to start answering the rest of your questions. You can also try the Microsoft Access Active Server Pages troubleshooter web site at `www.microsoft.com/support/tshoot/accessasp.htm` for any Active Server Page problems.

Table 7-2	Common Web Database Problems and Solutions
Problem	**Solutions**
An error message appears when I open the Active Server Page I created with the Access 97.	Make sure that you don't have your database open in Access 97. If your database is already open in Access 97, it's opened in what's called *exclusive mode*, meaning that other users aren't allowed to access the database.
I still get an error message when I try to access my Active Server Page.	Your web server directory may not be configured properly. Make sure that you have the Execute permissions enabled for the web directory — remember that an Active Server Page is actually a type of program that needs to be executed. Without execute permission, your Active Server Pages simply won't work.

Chapter 8

X Marks the Spot: Searching for Gold on Your Intranet

*I*f your intranet begins to feel about as organized as my desk, you're in need of some serious help. What good is building a great intranet and putting up a whole bunch of information unless you and your users can find what you want when you need it? The obvious answer is: Not much good at all — this is where *intranet search engines* enter the picture.

A search engine is like your intranet's own bloodhound. You give your electronic dog a sniff of what you're looking for, and in no time he leads you down the trail to your information goal. If you ever look for stuff on the Internet, you undoubtedly use one of the search engines out there. Though searching your corporate intranet is a much less daunting task then searching the entire scope of the World-Wide Web, you use the same basic equipment. In this chapter I show you how to get Microsoft Index Server up and running with Internet Information Server.

As your intranet site begins to grow, you may not always know exactly where to find the latest information. However, with a search engine on the scene, you can enter a keyword or words, and quickly search through the files on your intranet web server to return a list of files that contain the keyword or words you're looking for, as shown in Figure 8-1.

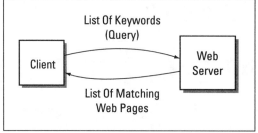

Figure 8-1:
How an intranet search engine works.

Microsoft Index Server

With most search engines, a user gives the search engine a list of words to search for, and the search engine examines each file on the intranet web server to determine if it contains the magic phrases, as shown in Figure 8-2. After the search engine finds the magic word or words, it churns out a web page showing the results. This method isn't too bad when your server has just a few files, but what if you have thousands of files on your intranet web server?

As shown in Figure 8-3, Microsoft Index Server takes a slightly different approach than many other search engines. Instead of searching through your intranet web server files when you start a search, it searches an *index*. Microsoft Index Server creates this index as a special, easily searchable file that contains information about all of your intranet files. Every time you add or change a file on your intranet web server, the index file is automatically updated with the keywords the new file contains.

Another major difference between traditional search engines and Index Server is the *type* of files that you can search. Most search engines just search through the HTML files. Index Server, on the other hand, can search through HTML files as well as the contents of Microsoft Word and Microsoft Excel files, which can be especially helpful on your intranet.

Figure 8-2:
How traditional intranet search engines get the job done.

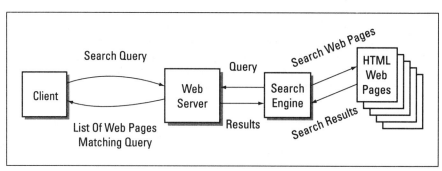

Figure 8-3:
How
Microsoft
Index
Server gets
the job
done.

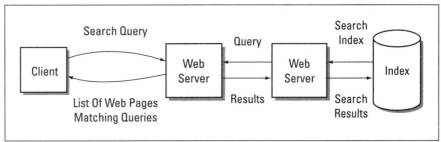

Do You Have the Right Stuff?

The most important thing to realize about Microsoft Index Server is that it only runs under Windows NT Server and works in conjunction with Internet Information Server. Here's the detailed lowdown on what you need in order to get started with Microsoft Index Server:

✓ **Windows NT Server or Workstation Version 4.0 or later.**

✓ **Internet Information Server Version 2.0 or later.** (Although I haven't talked about it, Microsoft Windows NT Workstation includes Peer Web Services, which is a scaled-down version of Internet Information Server. Though Index Server also works with Peer Web Services, Internet Information Server is the preferred web server.)

✓ **At least 32MB of RAM.** You definitely need more if you're running other services such as Microsoft Exchange Server, Microsoft SQL Server, or Internet Locator Server.

✓ **Finally, lots of disk space.** Remember how I said Index Server creates an index file that it uses to perform the actual searching? The size of the index file will be around 40 percent of the total size of the files that you want to index.

Where can I get a search engine?

Microsoft Index Server is a free download from the Microsoft Web site at www.microsoft.com/ntserver/search.

After you connect to the Index Server Web site, you see a button or some text that you click on to get to the download section. The Microsoft Web site download process is pretty painless. In order to download Index Server, you need to accept the licensing agreement and fill out an online registration form. Make sure that you note the name of the file you download.

Other search engines

While I focus on using Microsoft Index Server in this chapter, it's just one of your intranet web searching options. Some of the more popular Internet search engines provide the same proven technology for your intranet. If you want to find out more about these other intranet search engine options, take a look at the following Internet Web sites:

- ✔ **AltaVista Search Engine:** `altavista.software.digital.com/search/5/index.htm`
- ✔ **Excite Search Engine:** `www.excite.com/navigate`
- ✔ **Infoseek Search Engine:** `software.infoseek.com`
- ✔ **Open Text Search Engine:** `www.opentext.com`

When choosing a search engine, the most important thing to consider is whether the search engine works with your particular web server.

Cutting through the Technobabble

A good deal of the development of searching techniques is the work of real math and computer science eggheads that think an afternoon of fun includes discussing the merits of *context free grammars* and the efficiencies of *searching algorithms*. Unfortunately, some of this terminology has managed to make its way through. If you want to understand some of the more subtle issues of your intranet search engine, you may want to understand some of the terms I define in Table 8-1.

Table 8-1 Indexing and Searching Terms Defined for Those of Us Who Aren't Computer Science or Mathematics Researchers	
Technobabble	*Decoded*
Boolean Operators	These are special words you can use in your query, such as AND, OR, and NOT. You can use these operators between keywords, to fine tune your queries. For example, you may want to find all the files with information on research, but not on soap, and so you can enter: research NOT soap.
Catalog	A *catalog* is a directory that contains the indexes and other internal files used by Microsoft Index Server. Usually a catalog contains a number of different types of indexes.

Technobabble	Decoded
Free-text queries	With *free-text queries*, you can search for words with similar meanings. For example, if you search for the word search in a free-text query, any documents that contain keywords like search, searches, and searching are returned.
Indexing	*Indexing* is a process that pulls out the keywords from web files and creates a file with their locations in web documents. The index file you create works just like the index at the back of this book, only instead of a page number associated with each keyword, it associates web page addresses. Microsoft Index Server supports two types of indexing simultaneously: *content* and *full-text*. With content indexing, documents are indexed using document properties, such as the author's name or a brief description of the document. With full-text indexing, the actual text of the document is indexed.
Keyword	*Keywords* are the words you search for in your intranet documents.
Property-value queries	A *property-value query* uses the *content* type index as I explain in the "Indexing" entry in this table. Any documents that contain a property value you specify are returned. Table 8-4 lists and describes property values that are recognized by Microsoft Index Server.
Proximity operators	With the *proximity operator*, you can find keywords that appear close to each other — in Index Server, the proximity operator is NEAR. For example, to find all the documents where the words cheese and balls are close to each other, you can use the query: cheese NEAR balls. You can also use quotes to look for words that appear together. For example the query "cheese balls" grabs all the documents where the phrase *cheese balls* appears, though not documents that only mention *balls of cheese*.
Query	A *query* is just a question you ask your search engine — a typical query is made up of keywords.
Scanning	*Scanning* is the process performed by Microsoft Index Server to identify the files on your web server that have changed since the last index update.

(continued)

Table 8-1 (continued)

Technobabble	Decoded
Virtual root	A *virtual root* is simply another name for a directory on your web server. Sometimes a virtual root is also called a *virtual directory.*
Vector-space queries	Of all the types of queries, you're probably the most familiar with *vector-space queries.* A *vector* is "math speak" for a list, and a vector-space query is just a list of keywords. The search engine returns any documents that contain any or all of the keywords in the list.
Wildcards	A *wildcard* is a stand-in character for a piece of a query you either don't know, or don't want to specify. For instance, in Microsoft Index Server, if you specify a query such as cheese*, any documents that contained words that start with cheese, for example cheeseball, cheesey, and cheesecar are returned.
Word stemming	*Word stemming* works kind of like the wildcard operator, but it's a little more intelligent. You use it to match words that mean the same thing, but appear in a different word tense. For example, in Microsoft !ndex Server, if you specify the query throw**, then any documents containing the words throw, thrown, threw, throwing are returned.

Getting to Know Microsoft Index Server

Index Server is asleep much of the time you're running it, but anytime that you change files on your web server, a little alarm clock goes off and Index Server wakes up from its restful state. As shown in Figure 8-4, Index Server scans your web server files to determine which ones have changed. The changed files are then *filtered,* meaning that they are searched for keywords, and these keywords are then sorted and combined into an index. The resulting index file is what you actually search when you enter a query.

The filtering process recognizes what type of file is being indexed — whether it be HTML, a Word document, an Excel spreadsheet, or what have you — and pulls out the specific properties and their values (author name, date of file creation, and so on), as well as the actual text contained in the file. You can create (with the help of your trusty programmer pal) new filters for just about any type of document you want to index and search. Now creating filters isn't for everybody — you really need the expertise of a serious programmer to do this. However, it does mean that Microsoft and other companies can create filters for all kinds of files. Index Server comes with filters that can read Microsoft Word and Excel files.

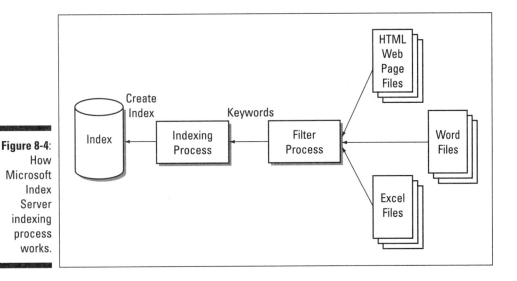

Figure 8-4:
How
Microsoft
Index
Server
indexing
process
works.

Getting Started with Microsoft Index Server

As always, before you install anything new on your server, make sure that you have a current backup. You may also want to perform any new installations during off hours, so that on the off chance you run into a problem, you aren't disrupting your users' work. With all of that in mind, you need to follow these steps to install Index Server:

1. **Log on to your Windows NT System as the Administrator, or another user with administrator access.**

2. **Go to the directory that contains the Index Server file you downloaded using Windows Explorer or the DOS prompt (for the golden oldies still out there), and run the file (either by double-clicking on the file in Explorer, or entering its name at the DOS prompt).**

   A dialog box asking you if you want to install Microsoft Index Server pops up.

3. **Click the Yes button to continue with the installation process.**

   That familiar old license agreement dialog box is displayed.

4. **Click the Yes button to submit to the powers that be, and continue with the installation process.**

   The Index Server files are unpacked — this takes just a second — and then the Setup dialog box appears.

5. **Click the Continue button to continue with the installation process.**

Your Internet Information Server stops for a brief moment while the Index Server files are installed, and your system files are updated. When the installation is complete, the installation complete dialog box shown in Figure 8-5 is displayed (surprise, surprise). A sample query form has been installed on a sample search web page — the URL of this web page is displayed in this dialog box. This default search web page URL is:

`http://yourservername/samples/search/query.htm` where `yourservername` is the name of your intranet web server.

6. **Click the Exit to Windows button to complete your Index Server installation process — you're done. Pretty simple, huh?**

Indexing your documents

Now that you have Index Server installed, you're probably thinking that managing it is going to take a lot of work. Well, this is your lucky day, because Index Server basically manages itself. As soon as you installed Index Server, it started to do its work. All of your intranet directories were automatically indexed. Every time you create a new directory, Index Server automatically adds it to the list of directories to search. (For more information on creating new directories for your intranet web files using Internet Information Server, see Chapter 7.)

Index Server provides an administrative web page that lets you:

- ✔ Choose which intranet web server directories to index for searches.

- ✔ View the intranet documents that could not be indexed (such as other word processing and database application files).

- ✔ View current indexing and search statistics, including the number of active queries, the number of query requests per minute, the number of documents indexed, and the size of the index file.

- ✔ Manually update the search index — important if you've recently added files to your web server and want to update your search indexes.

To access the Index Server Administration web page, click Start➪Programs➪Microsoft Index Server (Common)➪Index Server Administration. Your default web browser opens, and the Index Server Administration page is displayed as shown in Figure 8-6. You can use any web browser to perform these administration tasks.

To control which web server directories you want to include in the search index, click the View/Update Indexing Of Virtual Roots Start button. The web page in Figure 8-7 is displayed showing the web server directories for

your system. If the Index check box is checked for a directory, then it is included in the search index. To prevent directories from being indexed or to add new directories to the index:

1. **Click the corresponding Index check box to place a check in the Index check box for each directory you want to include, or click to remove the check for each directory you want to remove from the index.**

2. **Click the Submit Changes button to save your changes and update the search index to include only the directories you have selected.**

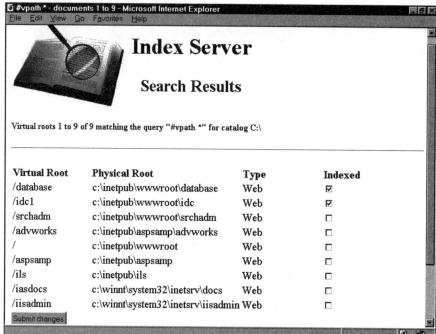

Figure 8-7:
The
Microsoft
Index
Server
Virtual Root
Indexing
web page.

To view the current index server statistics, click on the Index Statistics Start button to display the web page shown in Figure 8-8. You can review the statistics for queries. The search index statistics are also displayed, including the number of documents that have been indexed, the size of the search index, and the number of unique keywords that Index Server found.

To view the documents that have not been filtered, click the View Unfiltered Documents start button. Any documents that Index Server did not recognize are displayed.

To manually update the Index Server search index and to scan the web server directories for new or updated files for indexing, click the respective Start buttons.

That's Index Server administration in a nut shell! For the most part, you don't have much to worry about after you get Index Server set up — it's pretty much self-sufficient.

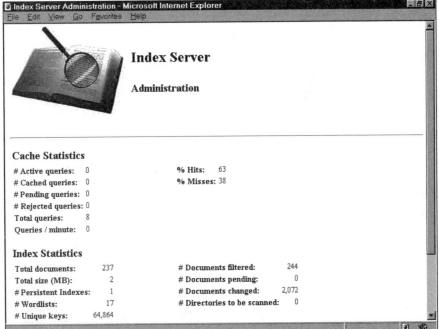

Making it go!

Okay, I know you want to run a search already, right? No problem — it's really easy. Index Server provides you with a default search web page at:

```
http://yourservername/samples/search/query.htm
```

where `yourservername` is the name of your intranet web server. The default search page, as shown in Figure 8-9, lets you perform simple queries.

For simple queries, all you need to do is enter the keyword or words you're looking for in the query edit box, and then click on the Execute Query button. The Index Server does its magic and then displays the query results page, as shown in Figure 8-10. The results page shows the title of each document that contains your keyword along with a brief abstract, and the total number of documents in the index that contain your keyword. You can click on the title of a document, or the URL listed at the end of the abstract to quickly jump to any of the documents that were returned by Index Server.

Figure 8-9:
The
Microsoft
Index
Server
Simple
Query
web page.

Figure 8-10:
The
Microsoft
Index
Server
Search
Results
web page.

Ten documents are displayed at a time — if more than ten documents are found, you can click on the Next 10 Documents button to see them. If you click on the New Query link, you return to the simple query web page where you can start another query. I show you how to create more complex queries a little later in this chapter.

Putting your own look on the results

Index Server uses three different types of files to perform its magic. You don't need to know the nitty gritty details of these files, but you do need to be aware of them:

- ✔ An HTML web page that contains the query form
- ✔ An Internet Data Query (.IDQ) file that accepts the query form data, and performs the actual query
- ✔ An HTML Extension (.HTX) file that controls how results are displayed

You can find a simple, usable query form web page and results HTML extension web page in your web server directory page, in the wwwroot\samples\search directory. You can find the Internet Data Query files in your web server directory page, in the wwwroot\samples\script directory. Unfortunately, if you want to customize the Internet Data Query (the query page) and HTML Extension files (results page), you need to be comfortable with HTML (or offer some chips and soda to someone who is). Web page editors like FrontPage don't work, but other editors like HotMetal and HotDog which work more closely at the HTML level do.

The Internet Data Query file is essentially a program that runs on your web server, so the directory it's stored in needs to have Execute privileges. I show you how to specify web server directory permissions, including giving directories Execute privilege, using Internet Information Server in Chapter 7.

To give your users the ability to search your intranet web site, you can simply link to the default search page, or you can import the simple query page into your web site. To import the simple query page into your web site using FrontPage 97, follow these steps:

1. **Select File⇨Import to display the Import File to FrontPage Web dialog box as shown in Figure 8-11.**

2. **Click the Add File button.**

3. **Select the Query web page.**

   When you're using Internet Information Server, the Query web page is in the C:\InetPub\wwwroot\samples\Search directory.

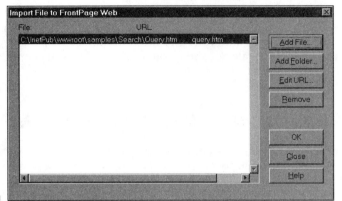

Figure 8-11:
The Import
File to
FrontPage
Web dialog
box.

4. Click the OK button to import the web page.

You can then link to this web page from you local intranet web. The HTML Extension and Internet Data Query files are accessed from their default locations.

Graduate level searching

Now that you have your intranet search engine installed, and you understand how to access it from your own intranet web site, you probably want to know how to use some of the cool search techniques. One very useful way to get more out of your searches is to make use of *Boolean operators.* Boolean operators are little words that you can add to your search keywords to help you to add focus to you searches. Table 8-2 lists and describes the Boolean operators recognized by Index Server, and shows some examples using the following four documents:

Document 1: I like to get cheese balls and coffee during Christmas time.

Document 2: If you like coffee, I suggest this fine Kona blend.

Document 3: Coffee is an excellent source of caffeine.

Document 4: Diane threw the cheese ball against the wall.

Table 8-2	Boolean Operators Recognized by Index Server		
Boolean Operator	**Description**	**Sample Query**	**Returns**
AND	Used to search for documents that contain two keywords. For example, `cheese AND balls`, only returns documents where the keywords cheese and balls appear in the document text.	cheese AND balls	Document 1, Document 4
OR	Used to search for documents that contain either keyword. For example, `coffee OR cheese`, returns documents where the keywords coffee or cheese appear in the document text.	coffee OR cheese	Document 1, Document 2, Document 3, Document 4
NOT	Used to exclude documents that contain certain keywords. For example, `NOT like`, returns only documents where the keyword like does not appear in the document text.	NOT like	Document 3, Document 4

When you use the Boolean operators, the keywords you're searching for can appear anywhere in the document. By default, the documents that match your query the closest are return first, the documents returned last match your query the least.

Another useful query command is the NEAR operator. When you use the NEAR operator, documents where the words you specify appear nearest each other are listed first. For example if you queried `like NEAR coffee`, using the four documents I list previously, both Documents 1 and 2 would be returned, however Document 2 would be listed first because the keywords *like* and *coffee* appear closer. You can use quotes anytime with Index Server to search for keywords that appear right next to each other. For example, the query "cheese balls" searches for the phrase *cheese balls,* which is where these two keywords appear next together.

I need to find something like this!

Imagine searching for something on your intranet that you only have a vague idea about — this is where *wildcards* and *word stemming* can really help out. As I explain near the beginning of this chapter in the "Cutting through the Technobabble" section, you can use a wildcard when you know the first few letters of a keyword, but you aren't sure how it ends, or at the beginning of a keyword if you're not sure how it begins.

Word stemming works the same as a wildcard, only with a bit of intelligence behind it — it can match words, such *run* and *ran*, that are related to each other. Table 8-3 shows some example queries (using the four documents I list in the previous section) that use wildcards, word stemming, and even Boolean operators for some extra fun. Remember that wildcards are specified using a single *, and word stemming uses **.

Table 8-3	Example Queries using Wildcards, Word Stemming, and Boolean Operators
Query Keywords	**Documents Returned**
chee*	Document 1, Document 4
throw** AND cheese	Document 4
ball*	Document 1, Document 4

Stupid search tricks

With you Microsoft Index Server, you can search your documents with more than just *free-text queries* (a fancy term for searches where you hunt for a given piece of text). *Property queries* can let you create queries based on document *property values*. When for example, when you use Word or Excel, you can specify document properties by choosing File⇨Properties, and then entering the your document properties in the Properties dialog box that pops up, as shown for Microsoft Word in Figure 8-12. You can then use Index Server to search for documents with particular properties, such as the author's name, the subject, and so on.

You can also search HTML documents using *META tags* (META tags are one type of the many HTML formatting tags that tell your web browser how to display certain elements of a web page). You can easily create META tags using the Microsoft FrontPage 97 editor:

1. **With the FrontPage 97 web page editor running, select File⇨Page Properties.**

   The Page Properties dialog box pops up.

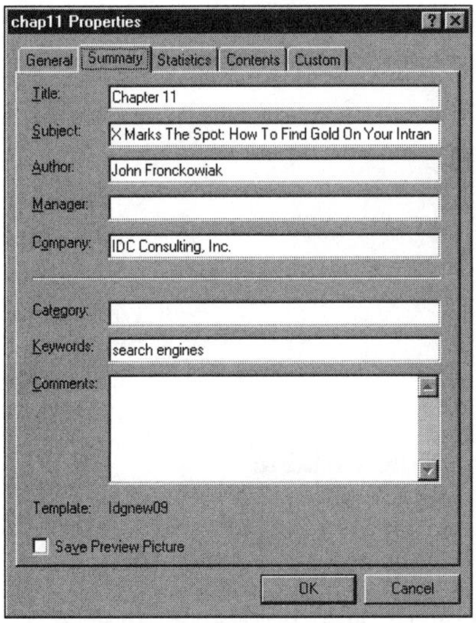

Figure 8-12:
The Word
document
property
dialog box.

2. Click the Custom tab to display the dialog box shown in Figure 8-13.

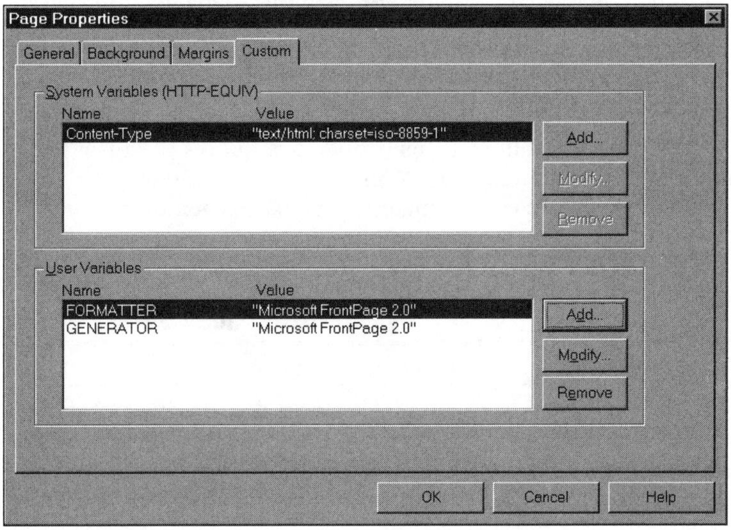

Figure 8-13:
The Word
document
property
dialog box.

3. **Click the Add button in the User Variables section to display the User Meta variable dialog box, as shown in Figure 8-14.**

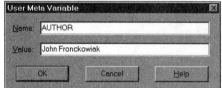

4. **Enter the <u>N</u>ame and <u>V</u>alue of the variable.**

A good entry for the <u>N</u>ame variable is Author, and then the <u>V</u>alue would be your name.

While you can create your own META tag property variables and values that you can then query with Index Server, Index Server already recognizes a few useful variables and values, as listed in Table 8-4. So, that leaves the $64,000 question: How do you query Index Server using these property values? All you need to do is specify the property name with a # before it, followed by the value you're searching for. For example, if you want to search for a document that I wrote, you can use the following query:

```
#Author "John Fronckowiak"
```

I've enclosed the value for this property in quotes because the value is made up of two words. You can use quotes anytime with Index Server to search for keywords that appear right next to each other.

Table 8-4	The Most Useful Property Names Recognized by Microsoft Index Server.
Property Name	**Description**
Access	The last date/time the document was retrieved
All	All property values are searched for the value you specify
Change	The last date/time the document was changed
Create	The date/time the document was created
DocAppName	The name of the application that was used to create the document
DocAuthor	The name of the document's author

Property Name	Description
DocCategory	The type of the document, for example a memo or a schedule
DocComments	Primarily used to search Microsoft Word and Excel file document comments
DocCompany	The name of the company that created the document
DocKeywords	Primarily used to search for the keywords specified when a Word or Excel file is created
DocLastAuthor	The name of the last person who edited the document, primarily used to search for the document author specified when a Word or Excel file is created
DocRevNumber	The current revision number of the document
DocSubject	Primarily used to search for the subject specified when a Word or Excel file is created
DocTitle	The title of the document
FileName	The actual name of the document file
HtmlRef	The text contained in an HTML HREF tag, used to create hyperlinks to other documents
HtmlHeading1-6	The text contained in an H1, H2, H3, H4, H5, or H6 tag. These tags are used to specify headers for document sections in HTML files
ShortFileName	The DOS-based (8.3 character) file name of the document

When Bad Things Happen

Having problems with Index Server? Table 8-5 lists and provides solutions to some common problems you may encounter. If you need more advanced help, try the Microsoft Index Server web site at www.microsoft.com/ntserver/search or the online web page help that is installed with Index Server (to access the online help, click Start⇨Programs⇨Microsoft Index Server (Common)⇨Index Server Online Documentation).

Table 8-5	Common Search Engine Problems and Solutions
Problem	*Solutions*
I can't search the directory I want to search!	You need to access the Index Server Administration web page: Click Start➪Programs➪ Microsoft Index Server (Common)➪Index Server Administration. This will load the Index Server administration page in your default web browser. Then click the View/Update Indexing Of Virtual Roots Start button. If the Included check box is checked for a directory, then it will be searched.
I can't find what I'm looking for!	Make sure that you spell the keywords in your query correctly (of course, they need to be spelled correctly in the documents as well). Try wildcards if you are unsure of spelling or think that the author who wrote the document may have incorrectly spelled the keyword you're looking for. You may also need to simplify your search — it's possible that no documents match your query the way you've defined it.

Chapter 9

Push It!

*W*hat do you get when you combine your intranet, the Internet, the latest business news, sports, weather, and your television set? A way to watch your favorite TV shows while you're at work? Hardly! You get a way to broadcast the latest breaking news and information to your employees — information that they can use to get their jobs done in a more informed and effective manner. This method of broadcasting information on an intranet or the Internet is called *push technology*.

Push technology is based on a really simple idea: Instead of having to search around for the information you want, you choose the kind of information you want to see, and the push program gives it to you — sometimes even before you know you want it. Push technology has been hyped as the next big intranet/Internet development — some say that it's going to put the nail in the Web coffin. In my opinion, and to paraphrase the immortal Mark Twain, "the death of the Web has been greatly exaggerated."

However, the hype surrounding push is likely to get even louder as the latest versions of Netscape Communicator and Internet Explorer are released. Both of these Web browsers have the ability to receive push technology *netcasts* (Inter**net** + broad**cast** = **netcast**) built in.

Who Wants It and Why?

While you may not be thrilled with the prospect of your employees reading and keeping up with the latest sports and entertainment news, the hard truth is that if your company has a connection to the Internet, and your employees know how to use a web browser, they're probably doing it already anyway. Now if you can pepper the sports and entertainment stuff with late-breaking news related to your business, you may just find a new way to help your employees get an edge on the competition.

You need two separate components to make push technology a part of your intranet: A *push server* and *client*. The push server is the program that spits out the information you want to "push" to your users. The push client is a lot like a web browser, only instead of displaying web pages, it displays the push content. Typically, push content comes from two places: your own internal corporate information, and external content providers. Push clients refresh their information on a periodic basis — from every few minutes to every few hours, and save the information they grab on your hard drive.

I show you how to get up and running with PointCast I-Server and PointCast, a popular push server and client, later in this chapter. PointCast displays information a lot like a 21st century, high-tech newspaper. It can even work as a screen saver and display information when you leave your computer for a specified time.

As you can imagine, if you have push clients all over your network requesting the same information over and over again, your network can quickly clog up. Using a push server takes care of this problem, as shown in Figure 9-1. The push server requests the information once from external data providers, and then the push clients on your intranet request information from your push server instead of having to contact the external provider each time they need an update.

The ultimate push client

So, what's the ultimate push client? E-mail of course — at least that's what I think. In spite of the latest technological developments, e-mail continues to be the most effective way to deliver important information targeted to just the people that need it. Unlike PointCast and other push clients however, e-mail can't bring you the latest news and information with much visual impact.

Upcoming versions of Netscape Communicator and Microsoft Internet Explorer integrate push technology, further blurring the line between the web (sometimes referred to as *pull technology*) and push clients. The one thing that's clear is that soon you'll have even more information to deal with — and sorting it out intelligently is going to be the next big intranet/Internet technology niche. In Appendix C, I offer a brief glimpse at this up and coming intelligent sorting technology with a discussion of *Intelligent Agents*.

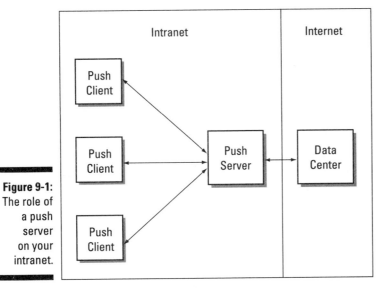

Figure 9-1:
The role of
a push
server
on your
intranet.

Note that PointCast is more than just a push client — it also provides access to information resources like Time and CNN. In addition, PointCast allows you to create your own corporate channels so that you can provide the latest company news and information.

Do You Have the Right Stuff?

The most critical requirement for PointCast I-Server and clients is access to the Internet from your intranet. If your network isn't connected to the Internet, you may want to jump ahead to Chapter 10 where I show you how to connect your corporate intranet to the Internet — this connection, where you connect your internal network (intranet) to an external network (Internet) is typically called an _extranet._

To install the PointCast I-Server, you need the following:

✔ **Windows NT Server 3.51 (with Service Pack 4 or later installed), or Windows NT Server 4.0.**

✔ **TCP/IP (Transmission Control Protocol/Internet Protocol) networking installed.** Refer to Chapter 1 for more information on checking if TCP/IP networking has been installed on your network.

✔ **A full-time dedicated connection to the Internet.** I discuss your Internet connection options in detail in Chapter 10.

✔ **Access to Internet mail.** You need to be able to receive a special mail message from PointCast that provides a code and other information that you need to complete the installation.

✔ **A web server to store your custom corporate articles.** Refer to Chapter 1 for more information about choosing and setting up your corporate web server.

✔ **A Pentium computer system.** PointCast recommends a 75 MHz Pentium system or faster.

✔ **At least 32MB of RAM.**

✔ **At least 10MB of free disk space to get started.** However, you need a lot more disk space as you start pulling down news and other information to your PointCast Server from the Internet — I recommend at least 100 to 200MB of additional disk space.

To install the intranet PointCast client, you need the following:

✔ **Microsoft Windows 95 or Windows 3.1.**

✔ **A computer with at least an 80486 33 MHz processor.** Realistically, a Pentium-based system gives you more reasonable performance.

✔ **A TCP/IP-based (Transmission Control Protocol/Internet Protocol) network connection.** Refer to Chapter 3 for more information on checking if your client systems are configured for TCP/IP networking.

✔ **At least 8MB of RAM.**

✔ **At least 10MB of free disk space.**

Where Can I Get It?

PointCast I-Server (in a free 30-day demo version — after the 30 days are up, you need to purchase the PointCast I-Server if you plan to continue using it), and the PointCast push client (which is a full-blown version) are available for free from the PointCast Web site at `www.pointcast.com`.

You need to use the PointCast push client that comes bundled with the PointCast I-Server because they are configured to work together. You may also want to download the useful online documentation from the PointCast Web site.

After you connect to the PointCast Web site, you see a button or some text that you can click to get to the download section. Be prepared to fill out an online registration form — you need to do this to obtain a *license key* through e-mail, so make sure that you have a valid Internet e-mail address before you get started. The license key works sort of like a password to let you install and use the software. Don't forget to note the name of the file you download.

I like to create a directory for Internet downloads on my hard drive, something like `C:\download`, and save the files I download from the Internet there so that I don't have to hunt around for them later.

PointCast is just one type of intranet push application, and other push applications are available, such as Castanet from Marimba (which I discuss in more detail in Appendix A). Intranet push software is still an emerging field, and you can expect to see more offerings in the near future. The newest version of Internet Explorer and Netscape Navigator also provide built-in push clients (I discuss these clients in more detail in Appendix A).

Cutting through the Technobabble

Time again for the technobabble to become technocool. Table 9-1 is your guide to the big terms of push technology.

Table 9-1	The Language of Push Technology Decoded
Technobabble	*Decoded*
Cache	The information PointCast I-Server saves from the external data center is put in a *cache* — cache is just a fancy name for a storage area on your hard drive.
Channel	Just like channels on your TV, PointCast offers different information *channels*, each with a different subject. You can tune in to just the information you want.
Data center	A PointCast *data center* works just like a television station transmitter, broadcasting the latest news and information. PointCast offers a number of these data centers on the Internet. When you install a PointCast I-Server, it connects to an Internet data center, stores the information, and in turn becomes the data center for the computers on your intranet.

(continued)

Table 9-1 *(continued)*

Technobabble	Decoded
Dynamic content	Most of the information you see on the Web is static content, meaning that once it's created, it basically doesn't change (or at least it doesn't change very often). PointCast clients offer *dynamic content*, meaning that the information is constantly being updated.
Network traffic	Just like the freeway enables automobile traffic to move around, your network is the freeway for your information traffic. Your network can get clogged up with *network traffic* just like the freeway at rush hour.
Proxy server	A *proxy server* is a system that communicates with an external network to reduce network traffic by saving information in a cache, and relaying it to the clients. PointCast I-Server works as a proxy server for your push clients. I talk more about proxy servers in Chapter 10.
Redirection	PointCast I-Servers are born to communicate with an actual PointCast data center. Having your push client communicate with your corporate I-Server instead of an external data center is called *redirection*.

Getting Ready with PointCast I-Server

Ready to push the latest information out over your intranet? Remember that you don't need PointCast I-Server to run PointCast push clients on your intranet — as long as your intranet is connected to the Internet, your users can go directly to PointCast data sites on the Internet for PointCast updates. However, beyond cutting down the amount of information that needs to be sent from Internet based PointCast data centers to your intranet, PointCast I-Server also lets you create your own corporate channels.

You can use a custom corporate channel to communicate all sorts of information to your employees in real time, such as meeting schedules, new policies, information about a big contract or sale, or even the current cafeteria menu (if your company is big enough to have its own cafeteria — otherwise you can update your employees on the latest shipment of dilly doos to the vending machine).

Setting up PointCast I-Server

As always, before you install anything new on your server, make sure that you have a current back up, and remember to perform any new installations during off hours so that you don't disrupt anyone's work.

The PointCast I-Server download file comes as a .ZIP archive. Take a look at Appendix C for information on how to extract the .ZIP archive so that you can install the PointCast program.

Now you're ready to start installing PointCast I-Server. But before you actually begin, you need to check your Internet e-mail. If you registered PointCast I-Server when you downloaded it from the PointCast Web site, a mail message was automatically sent to you with the CD key that you need in order to configure your PointCast I-Server. So check your e-mail for a message from isales@pointcast.com that looks something like the following:

```
Message-Id: <199706201539.IAA09490@www9.>
To: john@buffnet.net
From: isales@pointcast.com
Subject: I-Server CD Key for installation

Dear PointCast I-Server Customer,

... Message Text Removed ...

IMPORTANT INFORMATION FOR YOUR INSTALLATION
_____
To register your I-Server you will need the following CD
          Key:
CD Key: 999-9999999

... Remaining Message Text Removed ...
```

I highlighted the 10 digit CD Key you need in **bold**. If you didn't receive a mail message with the CD Key, you may need to return to the PointCast Web site at www.pointcast.com to register your I-Server 30-day trial version.

Now to install the PointCast server:

1. **Log on to your Windows NT system as the Administrator, or a user with administrator access.**

2. **Go to the directory that contains the Index Server file you down-loaded using Windows Explorer or the DOS prompt (for the golden oldies still out there), and run the Point Cast** SETUP.EXE **file (either by double-clicking on the file in Explorer, or entering its name at the DOS prompt).**

   The InstallShield Self-Extracting EXE dialog box appears. The installation process unpacks the files you need for the installation process — be patient.

3. **Click the Yes button to continue.**

   The PointCast I-Server setup dialog box pops up. Make sure that you close any applications other than Windows before you continue.

4. **Click the Next button to continue with the installation process.**

   The PointCast I-Server License Agreement dialog box appears.

5. **Click the Yes button to accept the legal license to use the PointCast software and continue with the installation process.**

   The Choose Directory Location dialog box graces your screen.

6. **Pick the directory for your PointCast I-Server — you shouldn't have any reason to change the default directory, so just click the Next button to continue.**

   The installation review dialog box appears. Review your installation choices — if you need to make any changes click the Back button and look at the appropriate steps in this list.

7. **Click the Next button to start installing the PointCast I-Server application.**

   Once the PointCast I-Server files have been installed, The ReadMe dialog box is displayed.

8. **Click the Yes button to review the current PointCast I-Server release notes, or click the No button to review them later.**

   The Setup Complete dialog box appears.

9. **You need to restart your system before you can use the PointCast I-Server — you can either restart it now, or do it later when nobody needs access to your network.**

   Remember that restarting your system makes it unavailable for a moment. If any of your users need to access any of the servers on the machine you are about to shut down, click the No radio button, and restart the system later when no one needs access.

10. **Click the Finish button to complete the installation process.**

After you restart your system, the PointCast I-Server group is added to your Start menu. That's it — after you restart your system, you're ready to begin configuring your PointCast I-Server.

Putting on your own show

After you have the PointCast I-Server application configured, you have to do hardly anything to maintain it. You can administer your PointCast I-Server and create your own information channels with the PointCast I-Server manager application.

Registering and starting your I-Server administration utility

1. **To start the PointCast I-Server Manager, click Start⇨Programs⇨ PointCast I-Server⇨I-Server Manager.**

At this point, you may want to review the README.TXT file you skipped during the installation process from the PointCast I-Server group — just go to Windows Explorer or the DOS prompt and open the file.

The first time you start the I-Server, the I-Server Registration dialog box appears, as shown in Figure 9-2.

2. **Click the Register Now button to display the Registration details dialog box, as shown in Figure 9-3.**

Remember that CD Key that came to you in an e-mail from isales@pointcast.com? Now's when you need it.

3. **Fill out the Registration details dialog box — the Administrator entry should be your name. Don't forget the all-important CD Key.**

After you fill out each field, the Register button is activated.

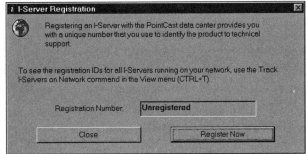

Figure 9-2:
The
I-Server
Registration
dialog box.

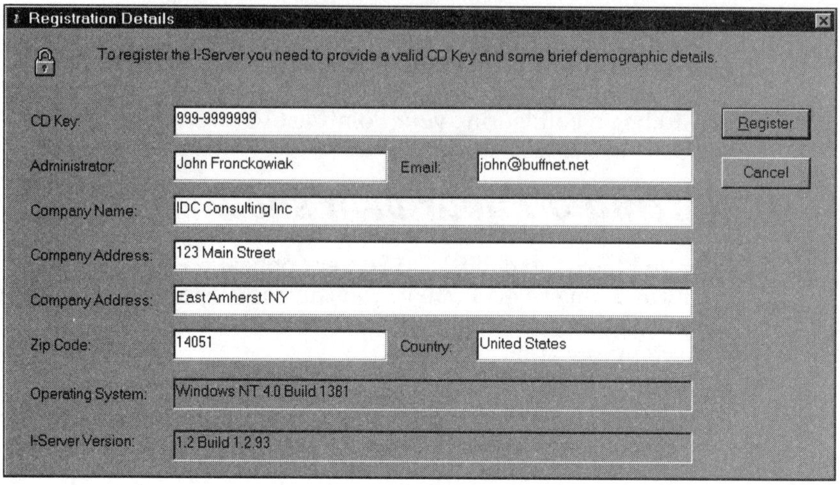

Figure 9-3:
The
Registration
Details
dialog box.

4. **Click the Register button to register your I-Server and begin your free 30-day trial period.**

   You are returned to the I-Server Registration dialog box, as shown in Figure 9-2, only now you have a coveted VRN (Valid Registration Number).

5. **Click the Close button to start the I-Server Manager, which appears next, as shown in Figure 9-4.**

   The I-Server Manager application is very similar to Internet Information Server Manager application in that it manages information access. To start or stop I-Server, choose I-Server⇨Stop Server.

Testing out your PointCast I-Server

The next thing to do is to test out your I-Server installation:

1. **Choose I-Server⇨Diagnostics.**

   The Diagnostics dialog box pops up, as shown in Figure 9-5. I-Server is already set up to run all of the necessary tests.

2. **Click the Run button to run through the various tests one at a time.**

   After all the tests have run and they check out, the text area at the bottom of the screen displays your results.

3. **Click the Help button if you have any problems.**

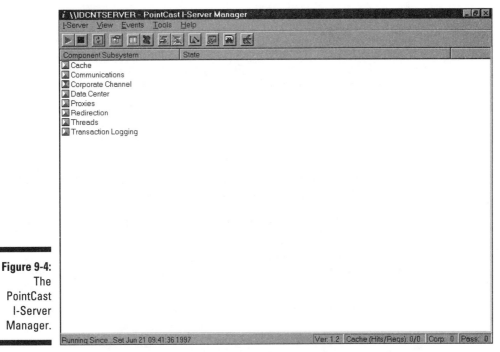

Figure 9-4:
The
PointCast
I-Server
Manager.

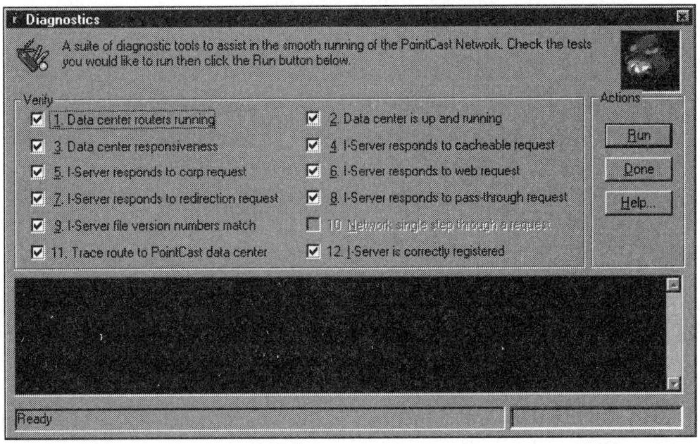

Figure 9-5:
The
Diagnostics
dialog box.

Pushing the Latest Corporate News

PointCast I-Server corporate channels let you send corporate news, announcements, and reminders directly to you employees. The first thing you need to do is enable your corporate channel. Here's how:

1. **Click Start⊃PointCast I-Server⊃I-Server Manager.**

   The PointCast I-Server Manager program starts.

2. **Choose I-Server⊃Properties to display the Properties dialog box.**

3. **Click the Corporate Channel tab to display the Corporate Channel Properties dialog box, as shown in Figure 9-6.**

4. **Enable your corporate channel by clicking (placing a check in) the Enabled check box.**

   Note the directory path in the Corporate Directory edit box — this is the directory where you need to put the content files for your corporate channel.

5. **Click the OK button to save your changes.**

Creating your channel

You can create your PointCast I-Server corporate channel, as well as manage I-Server using Internet Explorer, Netscape Navigator, or any other *Java*-enabled web browser. (Java is a programming language that's used on the Internet — it's special because it can run on pretty much any computer regardless of operating system or hardware):

1. **Fire up your favorite web browser, and enter the following URL:**

   ```
   http://yourservername:8070/admin/index.htm
   ```

   where `yourservername` is the name of the system where you installed the PointCast I-Server.

The number (8070) in the URL is something new — it specifies a *port*, which is just a special channel (just like a television channel or radio station channel) on the network. In this case, the port is a place that I-Server listens to for requests from clients and web browsers.

The Corporate Channel Utility web page appears, as shown in Figure 9-7. Because the corporate channel administration web pages are completely Java-based, you may have to wait a second or two before each web page is displayed. Try to contain your excitement as your web browser percolates the Java web application.

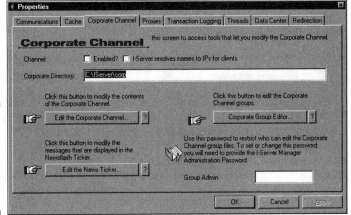

Figure 9-6:
The
Corporate
Channel
Properties
dialog box.

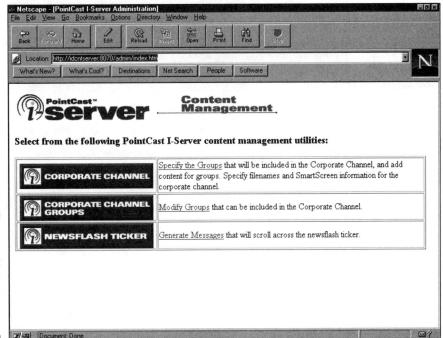

Figure 9-7:
The
PointCast
I-Server
Admini-
stration
web page.

2. **Click the Corporate Channel link.**

   The Corporate Channel web page appears.

3. **Click the Open Channel button to display the channel web page, as shown in Figure 9-8.**

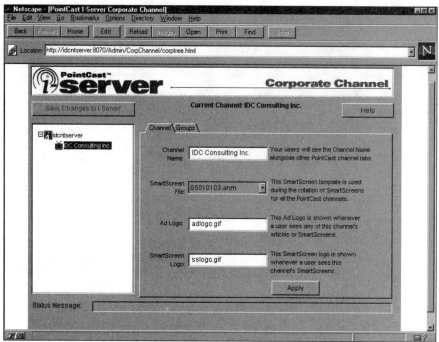

Figure 9-8:
The
Corporate
Channel
web page.

4. Enter the name of your channel in the channel name edit box.

You may notice that you can add images to your channel in the form of an Ad logo and a SmartScreen logo. If you have corporate logos in .GIF or .JPEG format, you may want to include them. However, PointCast has fairly strict limits for the size and colors — you need to refer to the Help file or README.TXT document for specific info.

5. Click the Apply button to save your changes.

Creating groups and adding articles

Channel groups are like sections of a newspaper — each channel contains a collection of related articles. To make things simple, try creating a Welcome group in the following set of steps:

1. Click the Group Tab to display the web page shown in Figure 9-9.

You can create as many channel groups as you like. You may want to create groups for each different department of your organization.

2. To create a new channel group, click the New Local Group button.

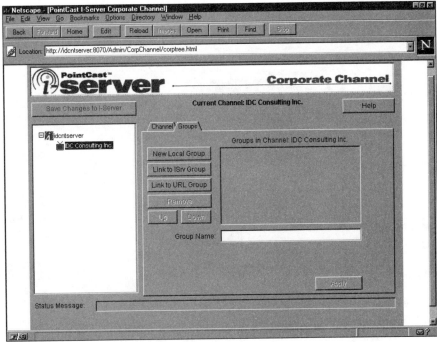

Figure 9-9:
The
Corporate
Channel
Group web
page.

3. **Enter** `Welcome` **in the Group Name edit box.**

4. **Click the Apply button.**

   On the left-hand side of the web page, you see a tree view of your corporate channel, similar to the way Windows Explorer shows directories. Your new Welcome channel appears as a folder icon.

5. **To start adding articles to your Welcome group, click your Welcome icon.**

   The Article web page appears, as shown in Figure 9-10. You can add up to 25 articles to each group.

6. **To add a new article to a group, click the New button, enter the article title and URL in the appropriate edit boxes, and then click the Apply button to save your addition.**

   PointCast *articles* are really web pages that you create and store on your web server — simply enter the title, something like **Welcome Page**, and the URL, for example, `http://server/welcome.html`, and you have a new article in your group. Check out Chapters 4 and 5 for info on creating web pages.

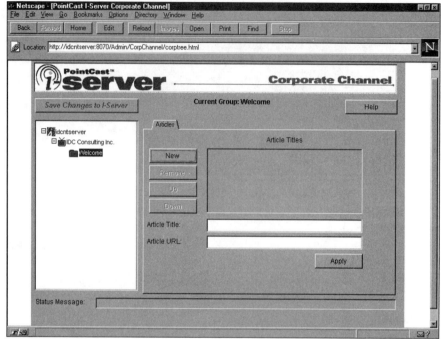

Figure 9-10:
The
Corporate
Channel
Article web
page.

7. **To make sure your channel changes and additions are saved to your I-Server, click the Save Changes To I-Server button.**

   Using the Up, Down, and Remove buttons, you can order and delete articles. You can continue to add new channel groups and articles, just make sure that you save your changes back to your PointCast I-Server when you're done.

8. **Close your web browser after you're done.**

If you're interested in building more complex PointCast corporate channel content, PointCast offers another product called PointCast Studio that lets you integrate animation effects and hot links into your channels. The beta version of the PointCast Studio application is available on the PointCast Web site at www.pointcast.com.

Installing the PointCast Push Client

So, you've got this great PointCast I-Server netcasting all the latest corporate gossip, and the Neilson ratings are decidedly low. Oh yeah — nobody has the client to view your PointCast channels yet!

Getting PointCast going

Make sure that the system on which you want to install PointCast meets the specifications for the PointCast push client that I outline in the "Do You Have the Right Stuff?" section in this chapter. You also need to have access to the PointCast push client installation file that you downloaded with the I-Server in the "Where Can I Get It?" section in this chapter. This installation file is called `PCNCORP.EXE`.

The PointCast push client installation file is too big to copy onto a single floppy disk, so you probably need to copy the file to a place on your network that's configured for sharing files — either a shared directory on another computer, or a shared-access server directory. After you have access to the installation file from the computer where you want to install the push client, you're ready to get started:

1. **Go to the directory that contains the PointCast push client file you downloaded (PCNCORP.EXE) using Windows Explorer or the DOS prompt (for the golden oldies still out there), and run the file (either by double-clicking the file in Explorer, or entering its name at the DOS prompt).**

   The Select Destination Directory dialog box pops up, as shown in Figure 9-11.

2. **Accept the default installation directory, and click the OK button to continue with the installation.**

   The client files are installed on your system. After the installation is complete, the PointCast Personalization dialog box appears with the option to either Personalize PointCast or Launch PointCast.

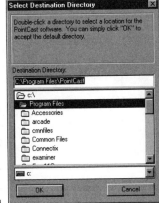

Figure 9-11:
The Select Destination Directory dialog box.

3. **Click the Launch PointCast button to start the PointCast application —
   you can personalize PointCast later, as I explain in the "Personalizing
   PointCast" section later in this chapter.**

   The PointCast License Agreement dialog box brightens your day.

4. **Click the Agreed button to accept the agreement and launch the
   PointCast application.**

   The Registration Information dialog box appears, as shown in
   Figure 9-12.

5. **Enter the user's e-mail address and other pertinent background
   demographic information.**

6. **Click the Continue button to continue.**

   The Internet dialog box is the next thing to show itself.

7. **Select the Direct connection option, as that is the way your users
   connect to the Internet, then click the OK button.**

   Now you're ready to begin tuning into the PointCast content. The
   Welcome To PointCast! dialog box appears.

8. **Click the Yes button to download your first batch of news.**

Tuning in to the broadcast

The PointCast push client is shown in Figure 9-13. You can change PointCast
channels with the Channel select buttons. Your corporate channel is automatically listed when it's configured. The Channel groups and article titles

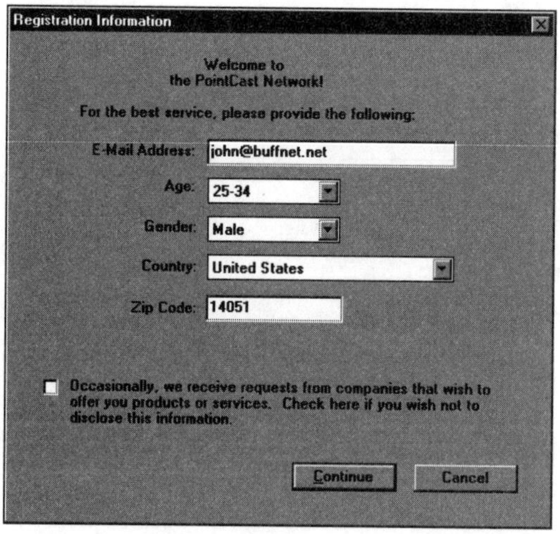

Figure 9-12:
The
PointCast
Registration
Information
dialog box.

Advertisements, or your corporate logo for corporate channels

Channel groups   Channel selector buttons   Articles

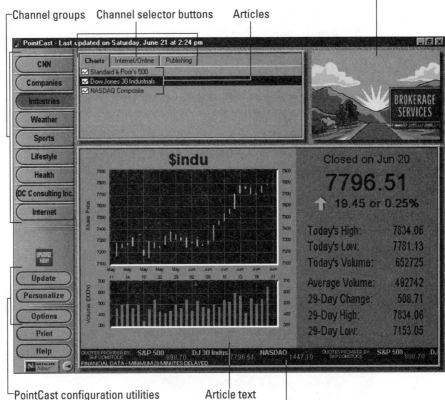

Figure 9-13:
The
PointCast
Push Client
Application.

PointCast configuration utilities   Article text

Scrolling tickertape displays continuously updated information

are displayed at the top of the screen. You can view any article by clicking it. You can print any article by clicking the Print button. The Help button gives you access to the online PointCast help.

PointCast as a screen saver

PointCast has also been installed as your default screen saver. Whenever your system is idle for a few minutes, the PointCast news and information appears on your desktop — hit the Enter key to clear the screen and return to work. If an article pops up in screen saver mode that you're interested in, just click it to get the details — simply moving your mouse no longer clears your screen saver. To modify the screen saver feature, follow these steps:

1. Click Start➪Settings➪Control Panel.

The Control Panel pops up.

2. Click the Display Icon.

The Display Properties dialog box appears.

3. Click the Screen Saver tab to get to a dialog box where you can select the screen saver you want, and the amount of time your system must be idle before the screen saver kicks in.

Personalizing PointCast

PointCast allows you to pick and choose which channels appear on your desktop. The only exception is the corporate channel, which always appears as long as it is available on the PointCast I-Server. To personalize PointCast:

1. Click the Personalize button.

The Personalize The PointCast Network dialog box appears, as shown in Figure 9-14.

2. Select the Channel tab.

Any channels or groups with a check mark next to them are displayed on your desktop. You can select up to 10 channels at a time. Use the Move Up and Move Down buttons to re-order channels or groups.

3. Select the channels you want to have available on your desktop and click OK.

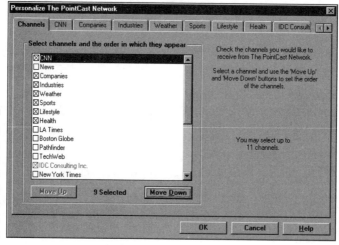

Figure 9-14:
The
Personalize
The
PointCast
Network
dialog box.

When Bad Things Happen

Table 9-2 solves some of the more frequent problems and questions you may have about PointCast push clients and the I-Server. If you need to call in the reinforcements, the PointCast web site is a good place to begin: `www.pointcast.com/support`.

Table 9-2	Common Web Database Problems and Solutions
Problem	*Solutions*
Do I really need dedicated Internet access to use PointCast I-Server?	Yes. PointCast I-Server stays in contact with the PointCast Data Center to access the latest news and information as it's requested by your PointCast clients. If a PointCast client can't get updates from a PointCast I-Server, it automatically tries to connect to a Data Center over the Internet instead.
I can't see my corporate channel.	You may have a problem with your network. You may need to consult with your local networking guru. Another step you can take is to check for the PointCast network file. In your PointCast push client directory (C:\Program FIles\PointCast by default), look for a file called 0.dc. Use the DOS edit command or the Windows NotePad editor to open this file. Look for a line that begins EnableCorpChannel, and make sure it has a -1 at the end like this: EnableCorpChannel-1. Save your changes to the 0.dc file; close your PointCast client; restart the PointCast client; and then click the Update button.

Chapter 10

Extra! Extra! Read All about Extranets!

In This Chapter

▶ Connecting your intranet to the Internet.

▶ Building extranets using Wide Area Networks (WANs).

▶ Securing your extranet from the sneaks, snoops, and hackers lurking on the Internet.

▶ Calling in the network plumber when your network pipes get clogged.

*T*he hottest trend in intranets today is hooking them up to wider networks, including the widest network of them all: the Internet. You may have offices across the country that want access to your now-famous intranet, or maybe you want to communicate more effectively with your customers and vendors.

Opening your intranet to a wider network requires some technical sleight of hand. Most well-developed and useful intranets contain a lot of proprietary information, and your intranet is probably no exception — you can't ignore the security issues. Securing your intranet when it's contained within the walls of your corporation is easy, but the stakes rise pretty quickly when you open it up to uninvited guests.

Who Wants an Extranet and Why?

Why would you consider hooking up your private corporate network to the Internet? I can think of a bunch of good reasons, including:

- ✔ To provide access to certain exclusive web pages for your customers, partners, and vendors
- ✔ To link offices in remote locations at minimal cost
- ✔ To provide a way for your employees to access your corporate intranet when they're on the road

At the core, creating an extranet is all about making the business of doing business easier and cheaper. Figure 10-1 illustrates a typical extranet business model: Customers and potential customers come to a company's Web site in search of information and to place orders; the company processes those orders and places orders for necessary supplies and materials with its suppliers; suppliers visit the company's Web site to pick up orders and provide up-to-date cost information.

This entire exchange happens over your network, and because your employees are already connected via your intranet, they have quick access to all this great information.

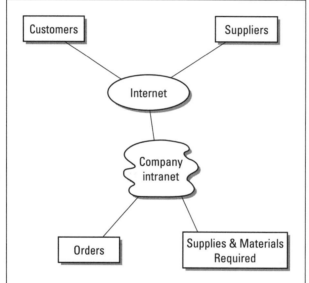

Figure 10-1:
How extranets improve the business model.

Do You Have the Right Stuff?

Here's a summary of the things you need to turn your intranet loose on the Internet:

✔ **A connection to the Internet through an Internet Service Provider.** You need to choose the type and speed of your connection to the Internet — in most cases, a modem isn't fast enough to support all your corporate users in addition to Internet visitors.

✔ **Additional networking hardware** to connect your intranet to the Internet.

✔ **A web server.** If you've already set up a web server on your intranet, you can use that as your Internet Web server also. However, depending on usage and security, you may want to set up another Web server just for Internet visitors, and offer links to just the relevant portions of your intranet web, such as product information and or inventory.

✔ **Extra security measures.** You may want to put up a protective *firewall* around your network — see the next section for an explanation.

Cutting through the Technobabble

Unless you're a networking plumber, you're probably not familiar with a lot of these technical terms. As your network gets bigger, so does the pile of jargon you have to wade through. Table 10-1 is your guide to some of the more common Wide Area Networking (WAN) and extranet technical terms.

Table 10-1	Wide Area Networking Jargon for Non-Plumbers
Technobabble	*Thank Goodness John's on the Scene to Explain Things!*
Bridges	Network *bridges* are typically hardware devices that link two different networks together so that they work together. Bridges act as traffic cops — making sure only the information destined for the other network is transmitted across.
Extranet	An extranet provides a door to your intranet through the public Internet. Wide Area Networks (WANs) are private networks that can be used to expand your intranet into multiple locations. Extranets provide this same type of extension of your intranet, but the Internet itself acts as your WAN.
Firewalls	A *firewall* is like a moat around a network. If you imagine a moat, the only way to get in the castle is over the drawbridge. Similarly, a firewall provides a single, defensible route into your network.
MultiLink	A *MultiLink* is a special type of modem connection protocol used by Windows NT Servers that allows the server to combine several modems into a single connection.
PPP and PPTP	Puh Puh Puh, Puh Puh Tuh Puh — Say it with me now! PPP, or *Point to Point Protocol* is used to network computers — over modems and other wide area networking devices — using TCP/IP-based networking standards (TCP/IP stands for Transmission Control Protocol/Internet Protocol — the core language of your intranet and the Internet). PPTP or *Point to*

(continued)

Table 10-1 *(continued)*

Technobabble	Thank Goodness John's on the Scene to Explain Things!
	Point Tunneling Protocol is used to network computers using something other than the TCP/IP protocol (like Netware's IPS, and Microsoft NetBEUI and NetBios) over the Internet in a secure fashion, meaning that only the sending and receiving computers can read the messages that are being sent. PPTP is used to provide a secure means of extending your internal network over the Internet.
Routers	A *router* works just like a *bridge*, only smarter. A router is typically a hardware device that can link two networks together, but can also figure out the best and fastest way to send information.
WAN	Wide Area Networks are just networks that are deployed over a wide area — pretty simple huh? With Local Area Networks (LANs) all the computers that are connected together are relatively close to each other — for instance, in the same building. With Wide Area Networks, the computers that are being connected together can be quite a distance away from each other — in other cities even. Of course, this means that you often can't just run your own cable between the computers on the WAN. I discuss the various WAN connectivity options later in this chapter.

Getting to Know WANs

A WAN, or *Wide Area Network*, is not that much different from your Local Area Network (LAN). In essence, they are both used to connect two or more computers together — the only difference is that in a Wide Area Network, the networked computers are typically far enough apart to make running new cable between them unrealistic.

So, given that the computers in a WAN are so far apart, you have a number of ways to overcome the distance. Your choice is ultimately a balance between *bandwidth* (just a fancy name for how quickly and how much information can travel) and cost. Not surprisingly, the faster your connection (more bandwidth), the more the connection usually costs. Wide Area Networks also present unique security challenges — I discuss how to secure your intranet using firewalls and proxy servers in the "Protecting Your Intranet with a Firewall" section later in this chapter. The following sections describe your connection options.

56K connection

The 56K connection has been the standard for Wide Area Network connections for a number of years, and it is one of the lowest cost ways to do it. A 56K connection is so named because of the amount of information it can send — A 56K connection can send 56,000 *bits* (that's 1's and 0's, the smallest pieces of information) each second. 56K connections are basically dedicated phone connections that you fix between two points. To access a 56K connection, you need a DSU (*Data Service Unit*). The DSU is a little box that connects the 56K line from the phone company to your network bridge or router (I talk about bridges and routers in more detail later in this chapter). Typically you can expect to spend a few hundred bucks a month for a dedicated 56K connection between two points.

ISDN

Integrated Services Digital Network has been touted forever by the telephone companies as the next big revolution in voice and data integration. However, the phone companies have taken such a long time putting in ISDN services, that by the time it actually started to roll out over the past few years, other technologies — even regular phone modems — are starting to approach similar speeds.

In any case, ISDN lines require a special connection from the telephone company. Unlike a dedicated 56K connection that is fixed between two points, you can use an ISDN line to dial any location that also has an ISDN connection. ISDN offers multiple channels, each up to 64 Kbps each (meaning you can send 64,000 bits, or 1's and 0's, each second). To use ISDN on your computer, you need an ISDN *adapter* (the ISDN equivalent of a modem) to connect the ISDN line to your computer. The typical ISDN adapter offers two 64 Kbps data channels and an additional voice channel. A single ISDN line is capable of supporting up to 23 separate 64 Kbps data channels, however, you need the proper ISDN adapter to support this many channels.

The cost of ISDN varies widely — anywhere from fifty to a couple of hundred bucks a month for a connection, plus possible per-minute usage charges. A hefty usage charge can quickly make an ISDN connection cost significantly more than a 56 Kbps connection. ISDN is offered through local phone companies — you need to get on the phone with them and discuss current ISDN rates.

T1

A T1 line is a digital connection that, like ISDN, is also made up of a group of channels. In the case of a T1 line, you have 24 separate 64 Kbps channels that are grouped together to form a 1.5 Mbps (yes, that's 1.5 million bits per second) connection. Some Internet Server Providers (ISPs) offer what are called *fractional T1 lines,* which simply means that you can purchase a portion of the 24 T1 channels for your connections. A full T1 line offers a connection that's comparable in speed to your Local Area Network. For many larger corporations, a T1 connection is more than adequate.

The typical T1 connection is a dedicated connection between two locations. To access a T1 connection, you need a CSU/DSU (*Channel Service Unit/Data Service Unit*) — a CSU/DSU is a magic little box that pulls together all the channels on the T1 line and links them to your network bridge or router. (I talk about bridges and routers in more detail later in this chapter.) Expect to pay a few thousand dollars a month for a T1 connection.

T3

T3 is the superstar of connectivity options. Like a T1 connection, a T3 is made up of a number of channels, but get this: it's 28 T1 lines grouped together to offer a whopping 45 Mbps (yep, it really is 45 million bits per second!). A T3 line isn't for your typical corporation — this is the type of connection Internet Service Providers use to connect up to the Internet.

Most T3 connections are delivered over fiber optic cable (these are cables made of glass that use light to transmit data) and require special adapters and networking hardware. If you want to surf the Internet at these super speeds, expect to pay several thousand bucks a month.

Cable modems

HBO and ESPN on your intranet? Not quite. Cable modems use the cable television networks that cable companies already have in place to provide a high speed connection to the Internet. Cable modems usually come as a small external box that connects to an Ethernet adapter in your computer. Cable is fast — many cable modems provide a full 10 Mbps (Megabits per second) connection to the Internet. This speed is generally referred to as *throughput* — how much information you can cram down the line over a certain amount of time. Think of the Coney Island hot dog eating champion — he can cram down about 20 hot dogs in 10 minutes — his hot dog eating throughput would be 2 hot dogs per minute (20 hot dogs divided by 10 minutes).

Though you don't actually see 10 Mbps level of throughput from cable modems — many cable modem providers slow things down to a few hundred kilobits per second — the potential for speed is really there. Also note that a couple of different types of cable modems exist. Some operate at full speed when requesting and retrieving information. Others operate only in this fast mode when retrieving information, and use slower modem speeds to send information out (such as requests and uploads). Check with your cable company to determine which type of cable modem is supported in your area. Only the full-featured cable modem — which operates at full speed for requests and retrievals — is powerful enough to consider as a Wide Area Networking alternative.

While a cable modem can be as fast as any of your other connection choices, they usually don't offer guaranteed connection speed (which can be bad for business). With the other connection options I mention — such as the 56K, ISDN, T1, and T3 — you can always be sure that your connection will be as fast as advertised.

Cable Internet service is a fairly new development, and it may not be available in your area. Where available though, cable Internet service can offer the highest networking bandwidth for the lowest cost (which hopefully will put pressure on other connection options to lower their costs a bit) — see the cost comparison table in the next section.

Making your choice

Choosing the best connection option for your company can be tough. Here are a couple of things to consider:

- ✔ **What's your budget?** Cost and budget for a given connection option is everyone's biggest limiting factor. You need to pick from the connection options that fit in your price range.

- ✔ **What type of information do you need to transmit?** If you only need to transmit mostly text-based web pages and e-mail, you don't need a high- speed connection.

- ✔ **How much information do you expect to transmit?** When you're first getting started, you may not have a quick answer to this question. How do you even measure your information volume? You may want to consult with your Internet Service Provider or other networking consultant to develop a plan that's right for your company. A service that provides a lot more capability than you're ready to use can be a waste of money.

- ✔ **What's available in your area?** Finally, not all options may be available in your area. Ask your Internet Service Provider, local telephone, or cable company to list your connectivity options.

Table 10-2 summarizes your connectivity options, speeds, and cost.

Table 10-2 Your Guide to Wide Area Network Connectivity Options			
Connection	*Speed (Bits Per Second)*	*Cost (Per Month)*	*Availability*
Modem	28,000 to 56,000	$100 to $200	Widely
56K (dedicated)	56,000	$200 to $500	Generally
ISDN	64,000 to 1.5 million	$50 to $150 or more, plus possible per-minute usage fees	Still somewhat limited
T1	64,000 to 1.5 million	$1,000 to $3,000	Generally
T3	1.5 million to 45 million	$5,000 and up	Generally
Cable Modem	10 million at the most	$50 to $150	Limited

Do You Have an ISP?

You need to contract with an Internet Service Provider to get access to the Internet. Besides your connection considerations, you also need to make sure that the Internet Service Providers you consider can handle your connection choice.

Internet Service Providers history

Not so long ago, no such thing existed as an Internet Service Provider. The only way to get access to the Internet in the early days was to have a special arrangement with a university, research institution, or a government organization that had Internet access. Then, in the 1980s, companies like UUNET and PSI started building their own Internet *backbone* connections, which slowly lead to businesses using the Internet more and more for commerce. (The Internet backbone is a set of very high speed network connections that provides the glue that keeps the Internet together. The bulk of information transmitted on the Internet travels through this backbone.)

In the past five years, the Internet has seen an explosion of Internet Service Providers — some people even say that there are too many, and that a consolidation will happen in the next few years. In any case, compared to a few years ago, you can get Internet access much more easily today, and at lower cost than ever before.

Yep! I'm all set with my ISP

Great! Now you need to determine how you're connected to your Internet Server Provider. Are you using a simple phone modem to connect? If you're trying to provide multi-user access to your network, a phone modem won't cut it. You need one of the dedicated Internet connection options I discuss in the previous section.

If you already have a dedicated Internet connection, then you're all set and you probably have most of the networking stuff I describe later in this chapter already up and working. You may want to jump ahead to where I discuss firewalls and other ways to ensure the security of your intranet.

Nope! Can you point me in the Internet direction?

You're not on the Internet yet? That's okay — in fact, in many ways it's good because it gives you the opportunity to make the right choices from the beginning. Here's a few things that you need to consider when hooking up with an Internet Service Provider:

✔ **How much do they charge?** Some ISPs charge based on the amount of data you transfer, while others may have flat rate costs for unlimited connections, while still others charge by the minute. You're likely to encounter as many billing options as vendors. Keep in mind that if you enter into a plan where you pay for your usage, either per minute or per quantity of data, make sure that you calculate your fees at your estimated usage — what initially seems like a good deal may turn out to cost much more than you planned.

✔ **What connection options do they offer?** Not all Internet Service providers support all the connectivity options. Make sure that you choose an ISP that supports the connectivity you want.

✔ **Do they have a good performance record?** Ask for references from other companies. Try to find out what other companies think about the service provider — have they experienced any service interruptions? How responsive is the provider to connection problems and questions?

✔ **Does the Internet Service Provider give you any help hooking up your intranet to the Internet?** Getting things configured and working requires a certain amount of cooperation between you and your ISP. Some providers may charge extra for this consultation — ask before you sign up.

✔ **How long does it take to get your company connected?** Getting the necessary connections installed and hardware in place may take a few weeks. Some ISPs may have close working relationships with connectivity and networking hardware suppliers. These relationships may be able to get your connection up off the ground more quickly when you're in the middle of a crunch, but like everything else, you may have to pay a bit more to move to the front of the line.

✔ **Shop around!** Take advantage of the fact that you have a number of options. See if you can't get a little bidding war going for the option to serve your company!

Where can I find an ISP?

Need some help finding an Internet Service Provider? While these lists can be rigged for obvious reasons, you may find them valuable resources nonetheless. If you can borrow a friend's Internet connection, or perhaps you're connected at home, here are a few Internet Service Provider directories worth checking out:

✔ C-Net Ultimate Guide to Internet Service Providers: `www.cnet.com/Content/Reviews/Compare/ISP`

✔ Yahoo!'s Guide To Internet Service Providers: `www.yahoo.com/Business_and_Economy/Companies/Internet_Services/Access_Providers`

✔ Boardwatch Magazine's Directory of Internet Service Providers: `www.boardwatch.com/isp/index.htm`

How badly am I going to get cleaned?

So, you may be wondering what kind of charges you're likely to find with the typical ISP. The simple answer is: No ISP is typical. However, to simplify your bill a bit, you may be able to get your ISP to roll all of these charges into one bill so at least your accounts payable people aren't pulling their hair out. Here's a summary of the charges you can expect:

✔ A fee from your ISP to get set up

✔ A charge from your ISP for services provided, either on a per-minute basis, flat rate for unlimited use basis, or as a function of the amount of data you transmit

✔ A setup fee from the local telephone company to install the communication line between your site and your ISP

✔ The monthly charge from the telephone company to keep your line active

Don't forget to factor in any additional hardware or software you need. The ISP you contract with may have specific hardware requirements, and you may be required to purchase the hardware from certain vendors to make sure that you don't run into compatibility problems.

Building Bridges to Your Intranet

A bridge is a piece of equipment that connects two networks together, as shown in Figure 10-2. You can use bridges to connect different types of networks together, but they're mainly used to connect smaller networks (like your intranet) with bigger ones (like the Internet).

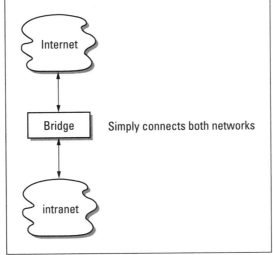

Figure 10-2:
How a bridge hooks your intranet up to the Internet.

In essence, a bridge listens to both networks that it links to figure out where each message needs to go, and then acts kind of like a network traffic cop, only letting through the messages that are intended for a computer on the other network. Some specialized bridges can also translate messages between different network types.

Rooting for routers

A router also connects two networks together just like a bridge, only routers are smarter. While bridges have to listen to the network to figure out the addresses of the devices on both sides of the network, routers know all this stuff constantly. Routers contain files — called *router tables* — that tell them where everything is located on the networks that they link. In order to always know what's what on both networks, the router tables need to be kept up to date. Fortunately, routers can communicate changes to one another, and for the most part maintain these tables themselves. However, even a simple mistake in the router tables can have disastrous effects for your network.

Routers can do one other thing a bridge can't do, and that is figure out the best way to send a message. If part of your network is clogged up or not working, routers can find a better pathway for network messages. This dynamic nature of router traffic cops keeps the Internet humming along even when parts of the Internet are loaded with traffic. Most companies use some sort of router in their connection to the Internet, as shown in Figure 10-3.

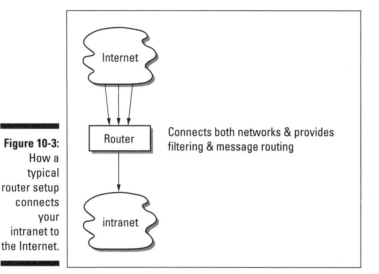

Figure 10-3:
How a typical router setup connects your intranet to the Internet.

Connects both networks & provides filtering & message routing

The Dirty Dozen Internet routers

Bet you didn't know that most of the Internet in North America is held together by a dozen or so routers scattered across the country. These routers keep the backbone of the Internet — which is a set of really fast fiber optic (FDDI) connections — functioning. Most of the traffic on the Internet winds up going through these routers at some point in its journey.

Crises do occur, and one or more of these routers can actually crash or have other sorts of problems from time to time. To date, other routers have been able to automatically pick up the slack, but every now and again, Internet service is lost in a few local areas due to router failure.

Have you ever had the urge to find out the current state of the Internet backbone? Probably not, but if you wake up in the middle of the night in a cold sweat wondering about it, I suggest that you stay away from your computer for a few days! If you're still curious, The NetStat Instant Internet Status Information Web site at www.netstat.net reports the current status of main Internet routers.

The difference between bridges and routers isn't all that clear, and it's getting more blurry — bridges are getting more and more sophisticated and approaching the function of routers. The real difference lies in *how* they actually operate and communicate on your network, the details of which are unimportant as long as you understand the function of both types of equipment.

Protecting Your Intranet with a Firewall

A *firewall* is an application that connects internal and external computer networks, as shown in a typical configuration in Figure 10-4. A firewall works similar to a router in that it examines all of the information that travels through your network (see the previous section for more info on routers). The main difference is that a firewall can prevent users on the external network from accessing certain internal resources, as well as control how users on the internal network gain access to the Internet.

To ensure the greatest degree of security for your internal network, you need to consider using a firewall. Without a firewall, every Tom, Dick, and Harry wandering on the Internet can access and explore your internal network, with potentially devastating results. Setting up a firewall can be a complex task, and you need to consult with the someone that's really familiar with networking and security issues to make sure that it's done correctly.

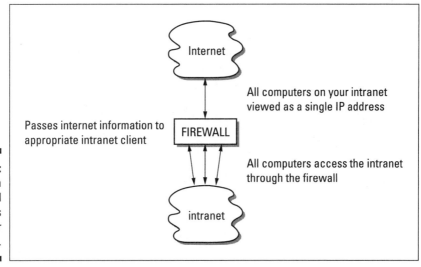

Figure 10-4:
How a firewall protects your intranet.

Firewalls and proxy servers

When it comes to firewalls, you have two different choices: a basic firewall, and a *proxy server*. A basic firewall is just a router that only lets computers with certain IP addresses pass through — if someone without a known address tries to communicate through the firewall, their requests are denied.

A more complex type of firewall, called a *proxy server,* works with specific applications, meaning that you can get proxy servers to work with web servers, mail servers, FTP servers, and any other Internet service you can think of. Proxy servers intercept information as it comes in through the Internet and only allow requests from computers with specific addresses to communicate with the internal network, as well as allowing only certain computers on the internal network access to certain Internet services. With a proxy server in place, the proxy server is what actually connects to the Internet — computers on the intranet or LAN then connect to the proxy server and pick up the Internet data.

While firewalls can protect your network, proxy servers can go a step further — they can actually improve the efficiency of your Wide Area Network. Proxy servers can store recently requested information, and when it's accessed again, the proxy server can return it from its local storage instead of having to access the Internet again.

Some of the newer proxy servers can communicate with each other in a secure manner, meaning that whenever they talk to each other, the information they send back and forth is encrypted. Using this mechanism, you can create secure private networks with the Internet as the connection between them.

Just because you open your network up to the Internet doesn't mean that you can't control access to your web server any longer. You can make your sensitive intranet web pages unavailable to unknown users by making the directories where your intranet web server lives a *secured directory.* Secured web server directories require users to supply a user name and password whenever they are accessed. In Chapter 11, I show you how to secure your web server directories and plan for other security issues.

Virus Inoculation

A computer *virus* is a program that is created by mean-spirited programmers to purposefully do something bad to your computer (such as erase your hard drive, or prevent your computer from starting up properly). And viruses are getting more and more sophisticated and more difficult to detect. Given that your NT Server and other corporate computers are connected to the Internet, you definitely want to protect yourself. Windows NT itself has various built-in security features that help to stop viruses, and, in fact, not many NT-specific viruses exist. *Boot-sector viruses,* however, can prevent your NT system from starting up. Windows NT and Windows 95 virus scanning software is available from the following companies:

- ✔ Carmel Anti-Virus for Windows 95 and NT: `www.carmel.co.il`
- ✔ InocuLAN for Windows 95 and NT Server: `www.cheyenne.com`
- ✔ Norton AntiVirus Scanner for Windows 95 and NT: `www.symantec.com`
- ✔ Dr. Solomon's Anti-Virus Toolkit for Windows 95 and NT: `www.drsolomon.com`
- ✔ NetShield for Windows 95 and NT Server: `www.mcafee.com`
- ✔ Sweep for Windows 95 and NT: `www.altcomp.com`

I have used a number of these virus protection applications, and they all basically work the same way. I prefer to use Norton AntiVirus for Windows 95 and NT because Norton provides updates that you can automatically download from the Internet, and that helps keep your system protected from the latest virus strains.

When Bad Things Happen

Table 10-2 answers some of the more common problems that you may encounter when you merge your intranet and the Internet. Security breaches have been on the rise lately, and the best way to prevent security problems is to stay informed — I discuss intranet security in more detail in Chapter 11. For now, here's a list of a few Internet Web sites that can help you stay up to date on the latest security issues:

- ✔ Microsoft Security Advisor: `www.microsoft.com/security`
- ✔ News.com: `www.news.com`
- ✔ ActiveXpress: `www.techweb.com/activexpress`
- ✔ C-Net's ActiveX Web Site: `www.activex.com`
- ✔ C-Net Central: `www.cnet.com`
- ✔ JavaWorld News: `www.javaworld.com/netnews.html`

Table 10-2	Common Wide Area Networking Problems and Solutions
Problem	*Solution*
How can I monitor my Internet traffic?	If you're using Windows NT for your web server, the Performance Monitor application is included. You can find it by clicking Start⇨Programs⇨ Administrative Tools (Common)⇨Performance Monitor. You can use the Performance Monitor to track a number of system, web server, and networking events.
How can I make sure certain files stay secure?	Once you open your system up to the Internet, you really have no way to be 100 percent sure that it's secure — sounds scary, huh? Usually, taking the necessary precautions such as securing your web server directories and erecting a firewall are good enough. If you have something that is really of vital importance, like the missile defense plan for the United States, the only way to ensure its security is to not put it on your network at all.
I can't access the Internet!	If you can't access the Internet from any of your local systems, check with your Internet Service Provider, perhaps they are having a problem, or one of their service providers is having a problem. Keep in mind that the Internet has recently experienced a few minor outages.

Part III

Intranet
Administration

"BETTER CALL MIS AND TELL THEM ONE OF OUR NETWORKS HAS GONE BAD."

In this part . . .

Now that you have your intranet up and running, you need to take care of it so that it can continue to flourish. In this part, I cover important intranet security issues, and show you how to keep nasty people from mucking around with your intranet. I also discuss planning for disasters (knock on simulated wood grain) and implementing virus scanners.

In addition, to help keep your intranet up and running smoothly, I cover feeding and caring for your intranet — monitoring intranet activity, planning for problems, and managing future upgrades.

Chapter 11

Keeping the Green Meanies Away: Securing Your Intranet

. . . .

In This Chapter

▶ Understanding the issues of intranet security

▶ Taking care of the server side security issues

▶ Planning for disasters, enemies, and other creepy things lurking around your intranet

▶ Taking care of the client side security issues

. . . .

Security is one of the most important issues for your intranet. Think about it: You don't leave the front door of your house unlocked when you leave for the day, and just the same, you need to make sure that the front and back doors of your computer systems are locked. Intranet security can be a balancing act between providing a useful, easy-to-use system for the people who need to use it, while preventing the people with bad intentions from getting in and mucking about. While you can never completely secure your intranet, you can take a number of measures to decrease the risks to a manageable level. The most important steps to take, and that ensure the most effective security for an intranet site, begin with how you build your intranet, and how you continually stay informed regarding potential new risks.

Security is an issue at both sides of your intranet: the server and the client. The server side, where your web server, mail server, push server, and/or your database server reside; and the client side, where your users actually use their web browsers, e-mail applications, and push clients both require security measures. In this chapter, I show you the ins and outs of security at both ends of your intranet, and how to make both sides as secure as they can be.

Know Thine Enemy

If your corporate intranet is also connected to the Internet, you need to be especially wary. When a computer system is connected to the Internet, it is open to attack by hackers, viruses, unauthorized internal users, and competitors from all over the world. A system connected to the Internet is potentially accessible to millions of people, some of whom may not have your best interests at heart.

However, just because your intranet isn't connected to the Internet doesn't mean you're off the hook. An intranet server can be just as open to attack from authorized users attempting to access unauthorized information. It may be even easier for an authorized user to exploit *backdoors* (undocumented methods used to access a system) or unnoticed security holes.

Sun Tzu was an ancient Chinese philosopher and military general. Many of Sun Tzu's ideas were used by corporate raiders in the 1980s to buy and dismantle companies, and corporate raiders and hackers are very similar — they don't have the best interests of your company or computer systems at heart. In Tzu's famous work, *The Art of War,* he wrote, "If you know your enemy and know yourself, you need not fear the result of a hundred battles." So, taking Sun Tzu's advice to heart, the most important thing is to think like a hacker: How can your intranet be broken into? Second, how can you stay informed and gain an advantage?

The Server Side

Server side security is the most important. Face it: Your web, database, and e-mail servers are where you store the bulk of your corporate information. All computer systems have an account which has complete access to all files and resources on your system — on UNIX systems that account is typically called *root*, on Windows NT systems that account is called *Administrator.* When you install Windows NT, it asks for a password for the Administrator account. To change the password of an account, you need to run the User Manager for domains application:

1. **Click Start⇨Programs⇨Administrative Tools (Common)⇨User Manager for Domains to start the User Manager for Domains application as shown in Figure 11-1.**

2. **Select the account for which you want to change the password in the list at the top of the window.**

   This list shows all of the user accounts that have been configured for your system.

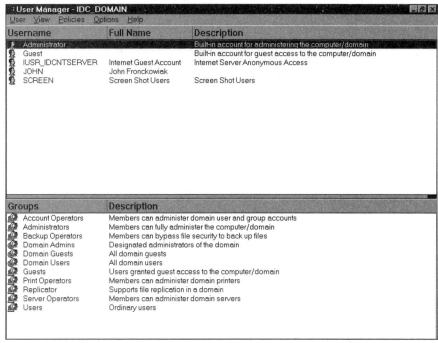

Figure 11-1:
The User
Manager
for Domains
application.

3. **Select the User⇨Properties to display the User Properties dialog box as shown in Figure 11-2.**

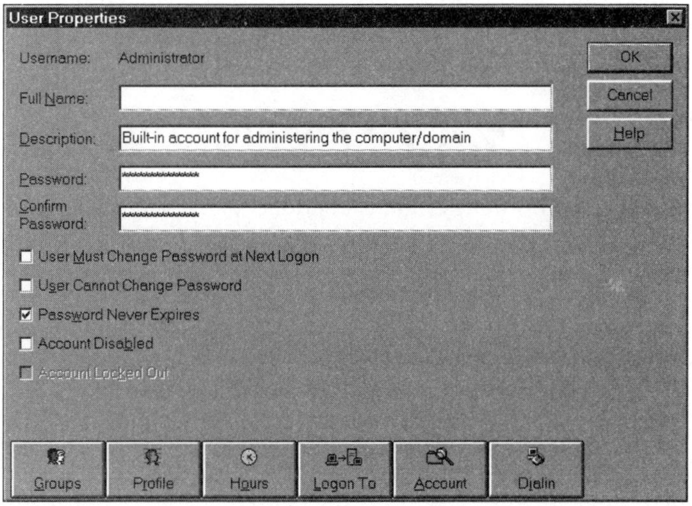

Figure 11-2:
The User
Properties
dialog box.

4. You need to enter the new password twice, once in the Password edit box and again in the Confirm Password edit box.

5. Click the OK button to save your changes.

The easiest way for a hacker to try to gain control over a system is by guessing the password of the Administrator — that's why you need to choose an appropriate (or maybe inappropriate, as the case may be) password. I have some simple suggestions you should try to follow when choosing a password for any account:

- ✔ Don't use your user name as the password.
- ✔ Don't use your name or nickname, or your spouse's, children's, or friend's name.
- ✔ Don't use your birthday or social security number.
- ✔ Don't use the server name.
- ✔ Don't use a repeated series of the same number or letter, for example, AAAAA or 11111.
- ✔ Don't use a single word that may appear in a dictionary (a common hacking technique is to use a dictionary of words for passwords when attempting to break into an account).
- ✔ Don't write your password down.
- ✔ Do use numbers and alphabetic characters (upper- and lowercase) in your password.

In Chapter 13, I show you how to create new users and groups using the Windows NT User Manager for Domains application.

Firewalls and Proxy Servers

A *firewall* is a computer system that connects a trusted and untrusted network together. A trusted network would be your intranet; an example of an untrusted network would be the Internet or perhaps another network in your organization. A firewall prevents unauthorized users on the outside of your trusted network from accessing the Local Area Network (LAN) and can restrict how internal users access the untrusted network, like the Internet.

Whenever you request information from a remote system, information that you may not want to be released can be exchanged, such as the network address of your computer system. A firewall alone can't prevent this information from being released, however, a *proxy server* can protect this information, and also help improve access to an external network. Instead of each user on your network connecting directly to an outside resource, such as an Internet web site, all requests are sent to the proxy server instead. The proxy server then requests the information for the user, and returns it to the user that requested it. The only system that the outside world can identify is the proxy server, which in turn protects any systems connected to the proxy server. Some proxy servers can also save the requested information to speed up subsequent requests for the same information. For example, if a user accesses a particular Internet web site, and then shortly afterwards another user accesses the same web site, the proxy server can spew out the stored information from the first request. A proxy server can also log user requests, which can be useful to track and detect attacks against your systems.

Setting up and configuring a firewall and proxy server can be a complex and time consuming process even for the experts. If you think that you would like to provide that level of security for your intranet, which can especially be important if your network is connected to the Internet, you need to consult with your local networking expert.

Keeping things locked up

The NT File System provides the ability to control access to files on a user-by-user, file-by-file basis. When you install Windows NT, you are asked to create an area on your disk, usually called a *partition,* to store Windows NT itself and all of your files. To make sure that you provide the highest level of security for your system, you need to make sure that you're using the NTFS (NT File System). To check if your disks are using the NTFS, you can run the Disk Administrator application: **Click Start⇨Programs⇨Administrative Tools (Common)⇨Disk Administrator**. The Disk Administrator application opens as shown in Figure 11-3.

As you can see, my C: drive is using the NTFS, while my D: drive is using the FAT (File Allocation Table) file system, a much older file system. You use the NT File System on the drive where your web server files are installed. To change a drive that's using the FAT file system to NTFS, you need to use the CONVERT command from the Command Prompt. For example, to convert the drive C: to NTFS, you enter the following command at the DOS command prompt:

```
CONVERT C: /FS:NTFS
```

You need to make sure that your drive isn't completely full before you run the conversion. If you try to convert the drive where your Windows NT system files are stored (usually the C: drive), a message is displayed telling you that the conversion can't be completed right now. You're asked if you would like to schedule the conversion for later. Respond by pressing Y (for Yes). The next time you restart your system, the files will be converted to the NT File System.

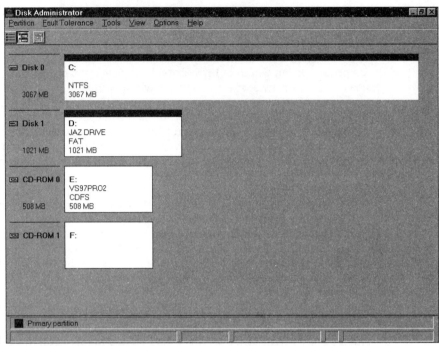

Figure 11-3:
The Disk
Administrator
dialog box.

Once you're using the NT File system, you can control user access to files and directories. To change and view a user's access to file or directory, follow these steps:

1. **Start the Windows NT Explorer application: Click Start⇨Programs⇨ Windows NT Explorer.**

2. **Click the file or directory you would like to change the permissions for.**

3. **Select File⇨Properties.**

   The Properties dialog box pops up.

4. **Click the Security tab.**

5. **Click the Permissions button to display the File Permissions dialog box shown in Figure 11-4.**

   The Name list box shows the users and groups that can access the file or directory you selected in Step 2.

6. **From the File Permissions dialog box you can specify permissions for new users by selecting an option in the Type of Access list box, and then clicking the Add button to add access, or clicking the Remove button to remove permissions for an existing user.**

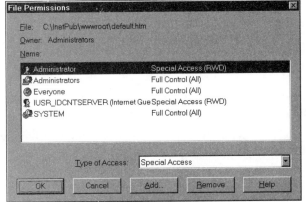

Figure 11-4:
The File
Permissions
dialog box.

7. **Once you have made your changes, click the OK button to save your changes and close the File Permissions dialog box.**

8. **Click the OK button to close the Properties dialog box.**

When a user tries to access a file or directory on your web server that doesn't allow access to the Internet Special Guest Account, he or she is asked to provide the name and password of a user that can access the web file before that file can be loaded in their web browser. The Internet Special Guest Account is usually called IUSR_YourServerName, where YourServerName is the name of your Windows NT Server. By default, all the files that are created in your web server directory are accessible by the Internet Special Guest Account user.

Auditing

Windows NT Auditing can track events performed by all users and can be a good way to find out if someone is doing something bad to your system. You can use The Windows NT Event Viewer to filter and view all such user events. The audit information is stored in files, typically called *log files*. Keep in mind that when you turn auditing on, performance decreases slightly and disk space is used quickly.

Windows NT can perform two types of auditing:

- ✔ **User Account Auditing** tracks and logs user-level security events.
- ✔ **File System Auditing** tracks and logs file system events.

User account auditing

User account auditing tracks when a user logs on or off, the files a user accesses, when the system is shut down and restarted, and the programs the user runs on your server computer. To turn on User Account auditing, follow these steps:

1. **Click Start⇨Programs⇨Administrative Tools (Common)⇨User Manager for Domains to start the User Manager for Domains.**

2. **Choose Policies⇨Audit to display the Audit Policy dialog box, as shown in Figure 11-5.**

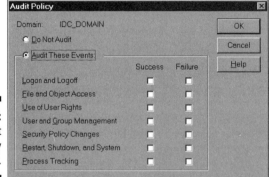

Figure 11-5: The Audit Policy dialog box.

3. **Click the Audit These Events radio button to turn on auditing.**

4. **Click the appropriate check boxes to track when an event occurs or is not permitted due to a user's lack of permission. You can track the following events:**

   • **Logon and Logoff** tracks when a user logs on, off, or connects to the server.

   • **File and Object Access** tracks when a user accesses a file, directory, or printer.

   • **Use of User Rights** tracks when a user exercises a user right, such as changing the system time or changing the ownership or permissions of a file.

   • **User and Group Management** tracks when a user account is created or changed.

   • **Security Policy Changes** tracks when a change was made to User Rights, Audit, or Trust Relationship policies.

   • **Restart, Shutdown, and System** tracks when a user restarts the system, shuts down the system, or an event occurs that affects system security.

> • **Process Tracking** tracks events such as starting and ending programs.

5. Click the OK button to save your changes.

File system auditing

To make sure that you implement the highest level of security for the files stored on your server, you need to make sure that all files are stored on an NT File Systems (NTFS) *partition*. A partition is an area on your hard drive that's used to store files — it's usually assigned its own drive letter. You can control access to files on a user-by-user, file-by-file basis only when you're using NTFS. File System Auditing can only be performed for NTFS file partitions. To turn on File System Auditing, follow these steps:

1. **Start the Windows NT Explorer: Click Start⇨Programs⇨Windows NT Explorer.**

2. **File System Auditing can be turned on for specific drives or directories. To enable File Systems Auditing for your web server directory, select the InetPub folder from the list of folders on the left-hand side of Windows Explorer.**

3. **Choose File⇨Properties menu items.**

   The InetPub Properties dialog box pops up.

4. **Click the Security tab.**

5. **Click the Auditing button to display the Directory Auditing dialog box, as shown in Figure 11-6.**

6. **To turn on auditing for all the files in the InetPub directory, and all of its subdirectories, make sure that both the Replace Auditing on Subdirectories and Replace Auditing on Existing Files check boxes are checked.**

7. **You can control which users or groups of users for whom you want to track file access: Click the Add button to display the Add Users or Groups dialog box as shown in Figure 11-7.**

   A special group — Everyone — is provided by default with your Windows NT system. The Everyone group is just what it says — it includes all system users.

8. **Select the Everyone item from the Names list box, to track the file access for *all* users.**

9. **Click the Add button to add the name to the Add Names list box at the bottom of the dialog box.**

10. **Click the OK button to return to the Directory Auditing dialog box — the Everyone group now appears in the Name list box.**

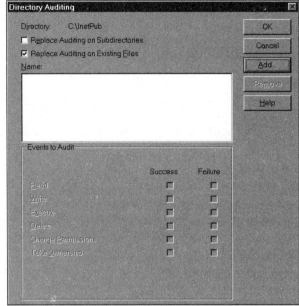

Figure 11-6:
The
Directory
Auditing
dialog box.

11. **Using the check boxes in the Events to Audit area of the Directory Auditing dialog box (see Figure 11-6), you can track when users have been able or not able to:**

   - **Read** files.

   - **Write** to files.

   - **Execute** a program file.

   - **Delete** a file.

   - **Change Permissions** for a file.

   - **Take Ownership** of a file.

12. **Once you select the file system events to audit, you can click the OK button to save your changes.**

   If you select the Replace Auditing on Subdirectories option, a dialog box appears asking you if you're sure that you want to apply the auditing to all files in the subdirectories.

13. **Click the Yes button to save your changes for all subdirectories.**

14. **Click the OK button to close the directory Properties dialog box.**

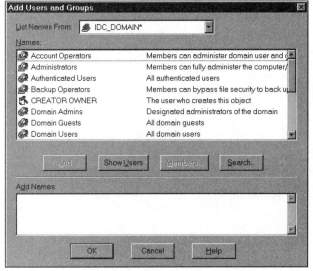

Figure 11-7:
The Add
Users or
Groups
dialog box.

If you're using a different operating system for your web server such as UNIX, you can also perform file auditing. Not all versions of UNIX provide this capability, so you need to check through your main pages to determine if your system supports file auditing. UNIX can also provide the same level of user and group file control as Windows NT. Actually much of the Windows NT NTFS (NT File System) is based on the UNIX file system.

If you decide to keep log files, make sure that you review them periodically. Like the moldy cheese in the back of the refrigerator, log files continue to grow every day. Make sure that you remove older log files as part of your regular system administration tasks.

Event viewing

Now that you know how to turn on all of this interesting auditing stuff, you're probably wondering how you can use the information you're collecting. Windows NT provides the Event Viewer application to view the auditing information you gather. To use the Event Viewer follow these steps:

1. **Click Start➪Programs➪Administrative Tools (Common)➪Event Viewer menu items to display the Event Viewer application.**

2. **A list of events is displayed in the Event Viewer window. To find out more information about any event, select an event from the list.**

3. **Choose View➪Detail to display the Event Detail dialog box, as shown in Figure 11-8.**

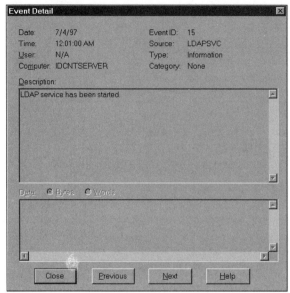

Figure 11-8:
The Event
Detail
dialog box.

4. **You can click the Next and Previous buttons to display the detail of the next and previous events in the list, or click the Close button to close the Event Detail dialog box.**

Your event log continues to grow over time, and you periodically need to clear out the event log information. You can do this by choosing **Log⇨Clear All** from the Event Viewer program. You are asked if you would like to save the log information in a separate file — you may want to click yes so that you can track system information over time.

Intruder alert! Disaster planning!

I can't say this enough: Make backups! Create a backup before you bring your system online, and continue to back up your system on a regular schedule afterwards — at least once a week. You also need to verify your backups — this step may take extra time, but you're better off knowing that your backup process is functioning properly before you need it. Make sure to keep permanent backups — ones that are not erased. You may not discover that your system has been broken into right away, and you may need to sift through your old permanent backups to figure out when your system was hacked. A permanent backup allows you to restore things to their appropriate state.

When Bad Things Happen

Hopefully, your system is never hacked — most never are. Nevertheless, you need a disaster recovery plan. This plan needs to include proper backups and plans to report a break-in to the appropriate authorities. You also need to run "fire drills" to test your recovery plan. If you make backups, make sure to verify them, and store them in a safe place. If you suspect a security compromise, follow these general steps:

1. **Disconnect the system from your network if possible.**

2. **Notify the proper authorities if you discover that your system has been broken into.**

A computer break-in is a very serious matter — legal and criminal issues may be involved. Determine whom you should contact before you need to contact them. CERT (Computer Emergency Response Team) may be able to use information about your break-in to help prevent other administrators from experiencing similar incidents. CERT was started in 1988 by the Defense Advanced Research Projects Agency, and they are charged with monitoring and taking proactive steps to ensure Internet/intranet security, and raise security issues and concerns. They are available 24 hours a day, to help respond to potential security threats. You can find the CERT web site at www.cert.org.

The Client Side

The client side is where everyone does the work they need to get done everyday. Making sure that your user's systems are secure is just as important as securing your servers. An important aspect of client security — all too often overlooked — is creating proper backups of each user's system. Many companies provide systems that can be used to back up all systems connected to your network.

Get a checkup with virus scanners

Computer *viruses* are one of the most critical security threats on the client side. A *virus* is a program that does bad things to your computer system, such as deleting files, preventing access to files or your system, or reducing your system performance. Recently, computer viruses have become quite sophisticated, and they are no longer limited to just programs. New varieties attach themselves to Word and Excel files and copy themselves to other document files. You need to obtain a third-party Windows 95 or NT-specific virus scanner to help ensure your system's integrity. Virus scanning software is available from the following sources:

- Carmel Anti-Virus for Windows 95 and NT: `www.carmel.co.il`
- Norton AntiVirus Scanner for Windows 95 and NT: `www.symantec.com`
- Sweep for Windows 95 and NT: `www.altcomp.com`
- Dr. Solomon's Anti-Virus Toolkit for Windows 95 and NT: `www.drsolomon.com`
- InocuLAN for Windows NT Server: `www.cheyenne.com`

What's Going On Out There?

The bad guys out there do their very best to stay informed regarding the potential security holes of every system, and you need to stay informed to stay a step ahead of them. A number of Web sites are available to help you stay up-to-date on the current security issues, including the following:

- Microsoft Security Advisor: `www.microsoft.com/security`
- Netscape: `www.netscape.com`
- World Wide Web Security FAQ: `www-genome.wi.mit.edu/WWW/faqs/www-security-faq.html`
- Computer Emergency Response Team: `www.cert.org`
- Forum of Incident Response and Security Teams: `www.first.org`
- Computer Incident Advisory Capability site: `ciac.llnl.gov`
- National Computer Security Association: `www.ncsa.com`
- NT Security Issues: `www.somarsoft.com/security.htm`
- Microsoft Proxy Server Web Site: `www.microsoft.com/proxy`
- C-Net's ActiveX Web Site: `www.activex.com`
- Javasoft Web Site: `www.javasoft.com/java.sun.com/sfaq/index.html`
- Yahoo!: `www.yahoo.com/Computers_and_Internet/Security_and_Encryption`
- World Wide Web Consortium: `www.w3.org`

Chapter 12

Feeding and Caring for Your Intranet

• •

In This Chapter

▶ Monitoring the use of your intranet

▶ Securing your intranet — using authentication and encryption

▶ Planning for potential intranet problems

▶ Managing hardware, software, and network upgrades without interrupting your users

• •

*M*onitoring intranet usage is important from two different perspectives: understanding which areas of your intranet are used the most, and checking for security threats. Every intranet web server provides the ability to keep a log of which web pages are accessed by your intranet web users, and when they are accessed. The intranet web master and IS support staff can monitor these logs to gain a better understanding of how the intranet is being utilized. While the specifics of logging usage differs for different intranet web servers, and you need to consult the manual for the particular server you are running, logging operations for different servers have many more similarities. In this chapter, I discuss logging in general, and quickly run through the process of enabling and viewing logs for the Microsoft Internet Information Server and Microsoft Personal Web Server.

Log Files

The log files generated by Internet Information Server and Personal Web Server and many other web servers provide a lot of useful information, as illustrated in Table 12-1. Both Internet Information Server and Personal Web Server generate standard log files — similar types of log files (containing essentially the same information) are generated by other web servers. Consult the documentation for the web server you're running to determine where these files are stored.

You can find your log files in the directory you specify when you configure logging properties for your web server — the files typically have a .LOG extension. You can open these files in any text editor such as Windows NotePad or WordPad, or you can import these files into your favorite database or spreadsheet application for a more organized way to display them. The log files are stored as *comma-separated value files,* meaning that each field in the log file is separated from the next field by a comma. The advantage of the comma-separated format is that most databases and spreadsheets can recognize it and import each comma-separated field as a new cell or field entry in the spreadsheet or database table.

You can examine your log files to determine which areas of your intranet are accessed by each user, and the date and time they were accessed. You may want to group users by their departments to determine if certain departments rely more heavily on specific areas of your intranet. Analyzing this information can be helpful in determining the peak and off peak hours for your intranet. The logs may also help you determine where to expand your intranet.

Storing this logging information in a database can help you better understand usage trends — you can create queries that return information on just specific users or specific time periods. You can also create queries which search for users that may seem suspicious — including log records with no user name, where the client's IP address isn't one that you assigned in your organization, or where the user name doesn't match one of the known user names on your system. Clearly having this logging information in a database lets you slice and dice this stuff up to determine what's really going on — this just isn't possible with a plain text file.

Table 12-1	Log File Contents		
Field Name	**Description**	**Data Type**	**Length**
ClientHost	Client IP address	Character	255
Username	Client user name	Character	255
LogTime	Time of access	Date/Time	
Service	Service accessed	Character	255
Machine	Name of the server	Character	255
ServerIP	IP address of server	Character	50
ProcessingTime	Time to process request (in milliseconds)	Integer	
BytesRecvd	Bytes received from the client	Integer	
BytesSent	Bytes sent to the client	Integer	
ServiceStatus	Service status code	Integer	

Field Name	Description	Data Type	Length
Win32Status	Windows NT status code	Integer	
Operation	Name of the operation	Character	255
Target	Target of the operation	Character	255
Parameters	Operation parameters	Character	255

Internet Information Server logging

Internet Information Server can store access logs in a simple text file (TXT) or in an SQL (Structured Query Language) database. As your intranet becomes larger, you may want to consider storing your logging information in a database rather than as a text file. Storing your log file in a database has some advantages: With a database, you can easily share the log information, create queries to examine the log files, and you can create custom reports to display log information in a meaningful way. If you decide to store your logging information in a database, you need an ODBC-compatible (Open Database Connectivity) database, such as Microsoft Access, Microsoft SQL Server, or Oracle. You also need to configure an ODBC connection for your database, as I explain in Chapter 7.

However, when you're just beginning and your intranet is still relatively small, storing your log files in simple text files is sufficient. The text file format is actually a *comma separated value format,* meaning that you can easily import the text file into any spreadsheet or database application such as Microsoft Excel, Lotus 1-2-3, or Microsoft Access — you just open the text file from the database or spreadsheet application and the software prompts you for how to organize the separate fields in the text file.

To configure logging for Internet Information Server follow these steps:

1. **Start the Microsoft Internet Service Manager Application by clicking Start⇨Programs⇨Microsoft Internet Server (Common)⇨Internet Server Manager.**

   The Internet Information Server application pops up with the Internet services currently running displayed in the main window.

2. **Click the WWW service item.**

3. **Choose Properties⇨Service Properties.**

   The WWW Service properties dialog box appears.

4. **Click the Logging tab to display the WWW Logging Properties dialog box, as shown in Figure 12-1.**

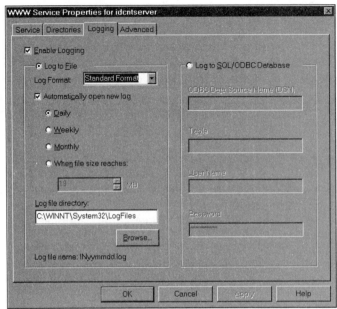

5. **To turn on logging, make sure that the Enable Logging check box is checked.**

   You can send your log to a file or database, by selecting the appropriate radio button, as I describe earlier in this section.

6. **To send your web server log to a text file, click the Log To File radio button.**

7. **In the Log File Format combo box, specify the layout of your log file.**

   You also have some tools available that can help you to analyze your log file, and they may require a special format. Internet Information Server supports a standard format and the *NCSCA* (National Center for Super Computer Applications) format. The *NCSCA* format is a generic format used by a number of web servers.

8. **You can open new log files daily, weekly, monthly, or when your log file reaches a certain size by clicking on the Automatically Open New Log check box and selecting the appropriate radio button.**

9. **Finally, you can specify the location where the log files are stored. By default log files are stored in the** C:\WINNT\SYSTEM32\LOGFILES **directory.**

10. **Click the OK button to save your changes.**

Now, whenever users access your web pages managed by Internet Information Server, the log file is automatically updated.

Personal Web Server logging

Microsoft Personal Web Server can only store log files in a text-based format. Again, this is a comma-separated value format, which you can easily import into any spreadsheet or database application, such as Microsoft Excel or Microsoft Access. To configure logging for Personal Web Server follow these steps:

1. **Start the Control Panel application by clicking Start⇨ Settings⇨Control Panel.**

   The Control Panel pops up.

2. **Double-click the Personal Web Server icon.**

   The Personal Web Server Properties dialog box appears.

3. **Click the Administration tab.**

4. **Click the Administration button to launch your default web server — Personal Web Server uses your web browser to perform administration tasks, as I explain in Chapter 1.**

5. **The Internet Services Administrator web page appears — click the WWW Administration link.**

6. **The Internet Services Administrator - WWW web page appears — click the Logging tab.**

   The Internet Services Administrator - Logging web page is displayed, as shown in Figure 12-2.

7. **To turn on logging, make sure that the Enable Logging check box is checked.**

8. **You can open new log files daily, weekly, monthly, or when your log file reaches a certain size by clicking on the Automatically Open New Log check box and selecting the appropriate radio button.**

9. **You can specify the location where the log files are stored. By default, log files are stored in the** C:\WINDOWS **directory.**

10. **Click the OK button to save your changes.**

As users access the web pages managed by Personal Server, the log file is automatically updated.

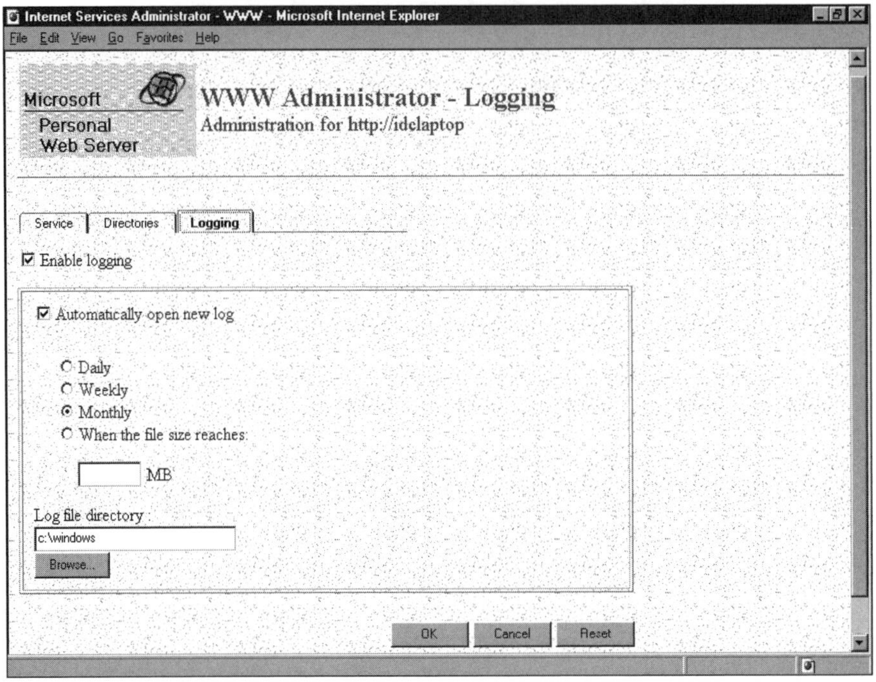

Figure 12-2:
The Internet
Services
Administra-
tor - Logging
web page.

Security

I discuss most of the specific intranet security issues in Chapter 11. However, you need to be aware of a few general web server security issues:
authentication mechanisms and *transmission security.* Web server authentication requires users to supply a username and password to access certain
web pages.

Authentication is necessary if you have sensitive information on your
intranet — for example, confidential executive, payroll, or human resources
information. No system is foolproof however — just because your web page
requires authentication doesn't mean a really smart hacker can't weasel a
way in. The bottom line is that you need to make sure that you don't make
anything available on your intranet that's so important you couldn't with-
stand someone else getting their hands on it. In the "Authentication" section
later in this chapter, I review how web server authentication works.

Transmission security can help you protect certain intranet web content
from getting into the hands of evildoers. For example, when a client web
browser is communicating with a web server, the information transmitted back
and forth is not encrypted in any way. If an individual gains access to your

network, that individual could conceivably listen in and intercept the information that is being sent back and forth. Many web servers support the encryption of this information. In the "Transmission security" section later in this chapter, I discuss how transmission security works.

Authentication

Many web servers allow authenticated client access, meaning that users must supply a valid username and password to access system resources. The basic authentication mechanisms provided by most web servers (including Internet Information Server and Personal Web Server) do not encrypt the username and password when they are sent to the web server. An evildoer with access to your network can easily intercept and decode the user name and password. This point is important: Once someone has access to a valid user name and password, it's a snap for them to get into your systems, and very, very, difficult to detect because they appear just like any other valid system user.

Internet Information Server and Personal Web Server support the Challenge/ Response encrypted password transmission mechanism. The Challenge/ Response feature uses encryption to scramble the username and password sent for authentication purposes. This can be a vital feature, especially if you open your intranet to the Internet as I discuss in Chapter 10. I show you how to configure Internet Information Server and Personal Web Server to use the Challenge/Response mechanism in the next section. Note that this feature is only available when you use either Internet Information Server or Personal Web Server in conjunction with Internet Explorer.

Configuring Challenge/Response encryption for IIS

To configure the Challenge/Response mode for Internet Information Server follow these steps:

1. **Start the Microsoft Internet Service Manager Application by clicking Start⇨Programs⇨Microsoft Internet Server (Common)⇨Internet Server Manager.**

   Internet Service Manager pops up with the Internet services currently running displayed in the main window.

2. **Click the WWW service item.**

3. **Select the Properties⇨Service Properties menu items.**

   The WWW Service properties dialog box is displayed.

4. **Click the Service tab to display the dialog box shown in Figure 12-3.**

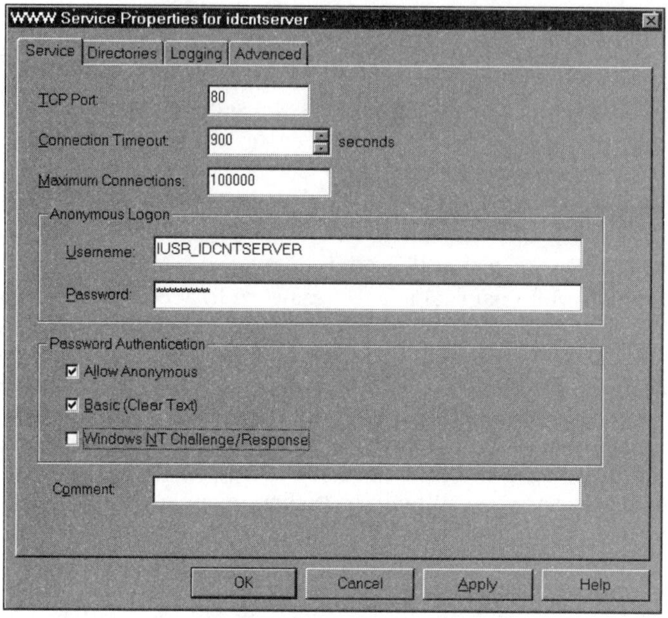

Figure 12-3:
The WWW
Service
Properties
dialog box.

5. **Check the Windows NT Challenge/Response check box.**

6. **Click the OK button to save your changes.**

Configuring Challenge/Response encryption for PWS

To configure the Challenge/Response mode for Personal Web Server, follow these steps:

1. **Start the Control Panel application by clicking Start➪ Settings➪Control Panel.**

   The Control Panel pops up.

2. **Double-click the Personal Web Server icon.**

   The Personal Web Server Properties dialog box appears.

3. **Click the Administration tab.**

4. **Click the Administration button to launch your default web server — recall that Personal Web Server uses your web browser to perform its administration tasks, as I explain in Chapter 1.**

5. **The Internet Services Administrator web page opens — click the WWW Administration link.**

6. **The Internet Services Administrator - WWW web page opens — click the Service tab to display the Internet Services Administrator web page, as shown in Figure 12-4.**

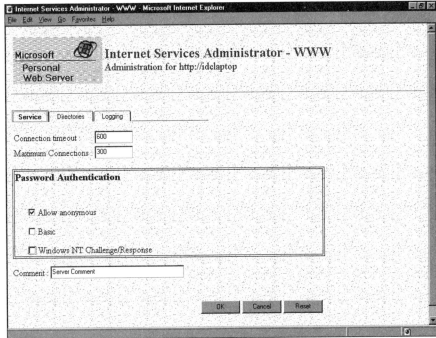

Internet Services Administrator - WWW - Microsoft Internet Explorer

Figure 12-4:
The Internet
Services
Administra-
tor-Service
web page.

7. **Check the Windows NT Challenge/Response check box.**

8. **Click the OK button to save your changes.**

The only web browser client that supports Windows NT Server authentication is the Microsoft Internet Explorer for Windows 95. With the combination
of Windows NT Server authentication and Internet Explorer, access to
secured web pages is only allowed when the user supplies a valid user name
and password. In Chapter 11, I review how to change file access permissions
on web page files so that they require authentication before they can be
accessed.

Transmission security

If you've ever used a cellular phone, or even just heard about them on TV,
you probably know that someone using a simple radio scanner can eaves-
drop on your telephone conversations. Your phone conversation comes
through clear as a bell with the right scanning equipment because your conversation isn't *scrambled* or *encrypted* in any way. However, if your conversation is scrambled or encrypted, even someone with the best scanner to
listen in only hears garbage.

Similarly, with your intranet, transmission security is about making sure that transmissions between two systems, for example your web browser and web server, can only be *interpreted* by the sender and receiver. Many people can try to "listen in" and intercept your encrypted web pages, but viewing them in a meaningful way is darn near impossible.

Many currently available web servers support Secured Sockets Layer (SSL) encryption, which encrypts the transmissions between the web browser and web server so that they are secure. Anyone intercepting your data gets a screen full of nothing.

The Secured Sockets Layer is kind of like a lock and key — the server creates a unique key which it passes to the web browser. This key opens a special lock on the web server. Every time the web browser communicates with the web server, it scrambles the transmission using that special key. When the web server gets this scrambled transmission, it uses the key it sent to the web browser to reconstruct the information. Each time a web browser and web server use the Secured Sockets mechanism, the web server generates another unique key.

All my warnings aside, it takes some sophisticated equipment to actually intercept network transmissions. Don't underestimate the abilities of someone trying to break into your network, but remember that breaking in is quite an undertaking. If your network contains information that's highly valued by someone unscrupulous, the motive to either obtain the appropriate equipment or the individuals with the appropriate expertise is certainly there — just take a look at the ads in the back of Hacker of Fortune for the mercenaries that are currently hawking their services.

What's the right level of security?

In the end, security is always a balancing act between ease of use and the appropriate level of protection. Though I hesitate to say that you can achieve too much security, security may at times appear to your users to get in the way of convenience.

If your intranet network is connected to another outside network such as the Internet, you obviously need to provide a greater level of security than if your network is completely self-contained. You need to analyze the potential threat to your intranet and its content, and select the security mechanisms that are appropriate for your company and applications. If you're aiming for the highest level of security for your intranet, using authentication to access your intranet web pages and using Secured Sockets Layer (SSL) to encrypt transmissions between the web browser and web server provides you with some of the best security currently available.

However, remember that in the end, nothing is completely secure. If someone wants to break in badly enough, a way can no doubt be found. New ways to work around current security mechanisms are discovered every day. Remember to visit the web sites I list in Chapter 11 to keep up with the most current intranet security developments.

Disaster Plans

Your intranet faces threats from internal and external hackers, hardware failures, software bugs, and simple diet cola in the disk drive-type accidents. Part of your intranet development plan needs to include planning for these and other disasters. The most important element in your disaster recovery plan is to ensure that you have the appropriate backup mechanisms in place.

Make backups! Make a backup before you bring your system online, and make backups continually afterward at regular intervals. You need to be vigilant with your backup plan and back up on schedule, as well as verify each backup you make to be sure that it can do the job if it needs to. Verifying backups can take extra time, but you are better off knowing that your backup process is functioning properly before you need it.

Be sure to keep permanent backups as well. A permanent backup is a backup that you store permanently in a safe place, unlike regular backups which you can recycle periodically to save money on disks. You may not discover a security compromise until many weeks after it happened, and you may need to sift through your permanent backups to discover when a breach occurred so that you can restore things to their proper state.

Managing Your Intranet

Managing your intranet can be a complex process. You need to coordinate the hardware and software upgrades, the integration of new content and applications, and network upgrades. As you wind your way through this process, don't forget to keep your intranet users in mind. As users come to rely on your intranet, they will demand and expect reliable intranet access. In order to keep your users behind your intranet project, perform your upgrades during off-peak hours.

You also need to ensure that as you build up your intranet content, you maintain a level of consistency. Make sure web pages provide a similar look and feel so that users can begin using new content without having to figure out a new format every time.

Whenever you perform any hardware or software upgrades to your intranet, follow these simple rules to help minimize unnecessary problems or interruptions:

✔ Make sure that you have a current backup of your entire system.

✔ If possible, attempt to put any new software applications through a test phase before you move to deployment across your entire intranet.

✔ The Internet has made new and beta versions of software available as it has never been before. Be very careful of deploying and relying on beta software — they often are not fully tested and may have devastating bugs. Notable examples include security holes found in recent web browser beta releases.

✔ Be sure to perform any upgrades during off peak periods — such as evenings and weekends — so you don't disrupt your users.

Part IV
Intranet Groundwork

The 5th Wave   By Rich Tennant

"For further thoughts on that subject, I'm going to download Leviticus from the church intranet and go through the menu to Job, chapter 2, verse 6, file 'J'. It reads..."

In this part . . .

If you're new to intranets, you may want to know what they are and how they work. I know I do (just kidding).

This part offers an easy-to-understand chapter on putting together your intranet construction and management team so that you can build things right. And for those that still need to convince their boss that this intranet stuff is a good idea, I give you a chapter dedicated to the purpose — how to answer all of your boss's key questions about the intranet, and how to make the case that it's a great idea without groveling.

Chapter 13

Go Team! Creating Your Intranet Management Team

- -

In This Chapter

▶ Bringing the right people together to build your intranet

▶ Creating a plan for the development of your intranet

▶ Keeping the needs of your users in mind

- -

*H*ave you ever seen some of those old black and white *Little Rascals* movies where the whole gang gets together to put on a show to raise money for some sort of cause? Well, building your intranet is a lot like bringing together a gang to put on the big show. And while the people (your cast) are important, having a script to direct your show is important too.

The Cast

Your cast and crew is what makes your intranet show happen. For your intranet to work, you have many different roles that need to be filled. You don't need a separate person for each part — in fact if you're building an intranet for a small company, you may have to fill all of the roles yourself. Whatever your situation, you need to understand what to expect of your intranet development team as you build your intranet, and make sure that every member of the team understands their role.

Management

Direct support from your corporate management for your intranet certainly enhances your chances of success. However, you also need to realize that management support isn't an absolute necessity. Blasphemy you say? Well, perhaps, but many intranets begin as pet projects of specific departments and slowly grow into an organization-wide project — this can be a good thing. You may be able to use your fledgling intranet to show management an example of how intranet technologies can be used to improve communications and get your job done better.

To move your intranet into a role as a resource for your entire organization, however, you absolutely need the support of corporate management, as I discuss in "The Show" later in this chapter. Corporate management can be a big asset in setting the overall goals and tone of your intranet — they undoubtedly have certain goals to meet with an intranet. However, you and they both need to realize that the greatest utilization and guidance for where the intranet needs to go comes from employees.

To be successful, intranets need to fit your management style. The attributes of the management style that work best with intranet environments include:

✔ The ability to trust, appreciate, and reward high-performing employees, while taking the time to coach the employees that need extra help.

✔ The ability to work with employees to create measurable goals and objectives.

✔ The ability to lead by example and feel comfortable with the delegation of large tasks. This also requires the ability to trust workers to make decisions on their own, and to support their decisions even if management may have solved the problem differently.

The best way to sell an intranet to your corporate management is by showing them how it will save them money. These savings come in the form of:

✔ **Reduced meeting times.** More information is readily available on your intranet, and so you have to spend less time distributing it verbally.

✔ **Reduced training costs.** Once users understand how to access your intranet, they can easily understand how to access any new information that you publish there.

✔ **Cheaper and faster information.** Intranets get the important information out to the decision makers faster and easier than ever before.

Web master

The director of the show is the web master. The web master is charged with keeping the overall continuity for your intranet web site. While intranets can truly become an organization-wide collaborative effort, someone needs to have the task of keeping a common look and feel. The major benefit of an intranet comes from its ease of use, and your intranet web site needs to provide web pages that are consistent to realize this benefit.

Some individual users no doubt want to develop their own web pages. While their creativity shouldn't be stifled, it does need to be kept under control. One good way to do this is to provide a special area on your intranet web for your individual users, but keep the bulk of your web site under the direction of your web master. If individual users develop useful web pages or applications, the web master can integrate them into your larger intranet and at the same time act as a filter so that the new pages match the same ease of use that employees have come to expect.

Your web master should be selected by and have the support of corporate management so that their concerns for an intranet that meets company goals is met. In addition, the skill level of your intranet web master is critical to the success of your intranet — he or she should have the following skills:

- ✔ **Technically enlightened.** Your intranet web master needs to understand the technical details behind your intranet so that he or she can communicate what is and isn't possible. A firm understanding of intranet technologies — such as HTML, TCP/IP, web page editors, and web browsers — helps your web master work closely with Information Systems support staff to monitor and manage your intranet. Web masters need to be continually on the lookout for new technological developments.

- ✔ **Close attention to detail.** Building an intranet web site can be a complex task (they don't call them *web* sites for nothing). The web master needs to design web pages that are consistent and easy to use. As your intranet web site grows, web pages will be added, removed, and changed, and the web master needs to pay close attention to keep the various links between pages up-to-date. A web site development tool like Microsoft FrontPage, Sausage Software HotDog, or Claris Home Page, can help to identify links that have changed and help to automate the update process.

- ✔ **Able to communicate with others.** The web master is the key intranet administrator and needs to be able to communicate what the intranet is doing with management and users. Your web master must be able to explain how the intranet functions in easy-to-understand terms. A good web master is open to suggestions from users and other administrators and can understand and respond to their needs.

- ✔ **Must be adaptable.** Intranet technologies change faster than the weather and your web master has to adapt to new technologies as they emerge. In addition to staying abreast of new technologies, a good web master must be able integrate them into your intranet as they benefit your intranet project.

Department heads — content creators

As with any good show, someone needs to create a script, or in the case of an intranet, a plan — a good plan lets you specify where you want to go with your intranet and how you're going to get there. Department and division heads are responsible for gathering together the information relevant to their areas. They may also consider gathering suggestions for web pages and intranet-based applications that they and their employees would like to see deployed. These department and division heads can then relay their suggestions to the web master for implementation.

Information to make available on your intranet may include:

- ✔ Departmental reports
- ✔ Departmental financial information
- ✔ Personnel information
- ✔ Employee handbooks and benefits information
- ✔ Product information
- ✔ Any other relevant information that needs to be shared with other departments

Special effects crew

If your company is big enough, you may have an art department where you can offload the development of your intranet web site graphics. If you're working for a smaller company, you made need to be your own special effects department. While the graphically-based special effects are not at all critical to the success of your intranet, they can bring a level of sophistication and polish to your project. Furthermore, if you expect that some day parts of your intranet may go public, that is, become an *extranet* (I discuss extranets in more detail in Chapter 10), you may want to invest a little time in a good look and feel for your intranet web site.

IS support staff

While the IS (Information Systems) support staff can sometimes be hidden behind the scenes, they are the individuals charged with keeping your intranet running and answering user questions. If your users can't access or don't understand how to use your intranet, it isn't useful to your organization. Support staff needs to be easily available and willing to help users work out their difficulties.

Technical support staff must understand the technical details of your intranet and be able to assist users in working out their individual problems. The support staff becomes an extension of the web master, communicating with users to understand what they like and dislike about your intranet and communicating those needs back to the web master so they can be incorporated into the design. Support staff, web masters, and department/division heads need to have regularly scheduled meetings where they discuss current user issues and plan for future intranet developments.

Information Systems support staff may be relied on to perform other intranet related tasks such as:

- ✔ **User account management.** Creating new accounts, removing old accounts, and user password management.

- ✔ **E-mail account management.** Creating new e-mail accounts and removing old e-mail accounts.

- ✔ **System maintenance.** Backups, user related equipment problems, and other routine tasks.

- ✔ **Network management.** Troubleshooting and monitoring your intranet network.

The Show

Once you assemble your intranet development team, you're ready to start formulating your intranet plan. While formulating a plan is an easy step to overlook in the process — especially when you're raring to go forward with the cool stuff — you really help your project if you spend time to go through the planning process before beginning real hands-on work. Many corporate intranets are started as departmental or divisional projects with more of an unplanned, guerrilla attitude. However, as your company decides to scale your intranet to corporate-wide use, you absolutely need to develop a plan or you end up with a revolution and an overthrown intranet every other week.

Creating a plan

Once you have your intranet team assembled, you're ready to start planning your intranet. In essence, your plan needs to outline your goals for your intranet, both short- and long-term. You may find it useful to have an initial meeting with management to discuss the larger, long-term goals for your intranet, and then once you define those goals, begin to include your users in the process. Users are the people who ultimately receive the most benefit from your intranet, and so may also end up being the most integral part of your intranet planning process and offering the most useful suggestions for where your intranet should go. They have their own ideas regarding the type of information they need and their own goals for what the intranet should be able to do.

As you develop your intranet plan, you need to get a *buy in* of the concept from management and employees. By buy in, I'm talking about not just support and approval, but the desire to contribute and support your intranet *actively*. Once both sides pledge to contribute to, work with to make it better, and use your intranet, as well as know that this high level of support comes from both management and employees, then you are poised for success.

You also need to make sure that you include your web master and other appropriate technical staff to ensure that your plan is technically feasible.

An important part of your intranet plan is the justification of your intranet investment. Some of your primary costs include:

- ✔ The costs for the software required to implement your intranet (luckily much of this stuff is free or comes with the Windows 95 operating system)

- ✔ The cost for the hardware required to run your web server and other intranet applications

- ✔ The cost of intranet development tools

- ✔ The costs of developing and maintaining intranet content

- ✔ The costs of personnel to support and maintain your intranet

Some of these costs pop up only during the initial deployment of your intranet, while others continue to be an issue as your intranet grows. In the "Management" section earlier in this chapter I review how intranets provide a return on this investment.

Carry it out

Once you have an intranet plan figured out, you are ready to start the implementation process. However, one piece of advice — stick to your plan. Of course, sticking to your plan means building a plan you can stick to — the best way is by starting small.

Begin with a small group within your company that can benefit from an intranet-based application. Focus on solving their needs first. A small group plan is a great way to begin to get your feet wet and start to gain a deeper understanding of what it takes to scale up your intranet. Working with a small group gives you the highest chance for success with the lowest risk — success and risk being important considerations as you begin the learning process.

Once you deploy your first small-scale application, you can start to grow your intranet around an even larger group that can benefit from the same application. Always remember to keep your larger, long-term goals in mind as you begin to scale up and reach your smaller short-term goals. In addition, don't forget to maintain the same look and feel as you build.

While your employees should find your intranet relatively easy to use — after all, they are probably already familiar with the technology (the web browser) — you still need to plan training sessions for your intranet users. Employees may need a chance to become familiar with the layout of your intranet site and how best to use it. Of course, one big benefit of an intranet is that you don't have to create paper documentation — you can develop an online help section right on your intranet to provide an overview, a guide to frequently asked questions (FAQ), and even a way to submit requests and questions to your intranet support staff.

Standard Operating Procedures (SOP)

The trick here is to create a set of Standard Operating Procedures without stifling the creativity that needs to be part of your intranet. Nonetheless, creativity needs structure and guidance to succeed. In corporations, structure comes in the form of Standard Operating Procedures — they may include:

- **Planning on things changing often.** Your business is dynamic and your intranet will most likely reflect that dynamic nature. The ability to deliver timely information is the key to your intranet, and so as the information you need to deliver changes, you need to have key people in place to keep the information in their areas current.

- **Maintaining a consistent look and feel.** You don't want to stifle creativity, but if every page on your intranet web site looks different, people have a harder time finding what they want and knowing what they're doing. In addition, a consistent interface helps decrease training costs by allowing people to use any new intranet features just by being familiar with the old features.

- **Choosing the right tools for the job.** If you already have information in Word or Excel documents, then you have no need to turn those into web pages if everyone has access to Word and Excel.

- **Including intranet content standards as a part of training.** Make sure employees understand your intranet goals, and understand what you expect. An intranet opens up a new freedom to express information, make sure you set some limits on what is and isn't acceptable to publish.

- **Standardizing your intranet.** Unlike the Internet, you have total control over the tools your employees use to create and view intranet content. By standardizing your web browsers, web content creation tools, and building your intranet around these tools, you can help keep your intranet consistent and simple.

The Audience

Don't forget about your audience — without them and their support, your intranet show is going to close after opening night. Audiences can be a fickle bunch, but if you include them early in your planning process your intranet has more of a chance to gain blockbuster status.

Involving your users early in the planning process is what can make or break your intranet project. Involve users early and often as you begin to develop new applications and areas of your intranet web site — they can tell you what will and won't work for them. You may want to provide an area for user feedback on your intranet web site, or even a mail account for routing requests. Your intranet needs to help break down the barriers to communications, and that includes communications about the quality or usefulness of your intranet. Facilitating the participation of users in the development and planning stages of your intranet is a great place to begin breaking down those barriers.

Where to Next?

Once you assemble your intranet management team, and you create your intranet development plan, you're ready to begin putting your intranet in place. I believe that the following four key considerations can help you implement a solid intranet:

✔ **Mission.** A clear mission is the cornerstone of any successful project, but even more so when it comes to intranets. The most important mission-related questions include: For whom is the intranet being developed and what is its primary purpose? A clear mission for your intranet sends your development efforts in the right direction from the start.

✔ **Standards.** Selecting intranet standards can be like wading through a mine field. Each set of standards has its individual strengths and weaknesses. Remember that one advantage of an intranet is that you can exercise control over every user's desktop and decide which of these standards you will and will not use. My best advice is to choose conservatively and stick to the choice that you make.

✔ **Start Small.** You can't rule the world in a single day, and completely developing your intranet into everything that you want in a single day isn't possible either. Intranets are well suited to incremental development. You make small steps forward, all the while keeping your bigger mission in mind.

✔ **Security.** While Internet security always seems to be a high profile issue, intranet security is just as important, if not more so. Intranet security is probably the most overlooked aspect of the planning, design, and development stages. You need to make sure that your web server and databases are secure. You also need to be sure that each user has access only to the information that they need. While security issues can be tedious, be careful not to underestimate their importance.

Chapter 14

Convincing Your Boss to Build an Intranet

. . . .

In This Chapter

▶ Understanding how the Internet, groupware, and intranets work

▶ Getting to know the differences between intranets and traditional approaches

▶ Building a team-oriented approach using intranets — the management issues

▶ Factoring costs into your intranet decision

. . . .

*I*ntranets offer a number of advantages to corporations that other technologies just can't bring. The intranet advantages include bringing together a number of proven technologies to improve corporate communications, providing better and faster access to new and existing information resources, and providing a single unified environment for access. You can use your intranet to:

- ✔ **Publish corporate information,** such as the latest product information, human resource handbooks, reports, marketing information, and even corporate telephone directories.

- ✔ **Conduct virtual meetings** — running advanced video conferencing applications on your intranet.

- ✔ **Provide access to electronic mail.**

- ✔ **Broadcast the latest corporate news and information to all corporate computers at the same time.**

- ✔ **Provide an easy way to access centralized databases.**

Remember that an intranet is more than any one of these applications — it's the sum of these applications working together to help an organization communicate more efficiently and effectively.

Building a Team

Intranets facilitate the team building process by simplifying the communications you need to keep a team together. Many recent trends in management, such as *Management by Objective* and *Total Quality Management,* support the idea of team and consensus building as the cornerstone of successful corporations.

Each division or department within your company may have its own set of goals and objectives it needs to achieve within the organization. At the same time, the company at large may have its own set of goals and objectives. When divisions, departments, and employees tend to lose track of these larger corporate goals, how do you bring everyone together again? The answer is not the mission statement that's engraved on a plaque collecting dust somewhere in the office of the corporate president or CEO. That stuff is usually just a lot of hot air that makes a company look good, and few people bother to pay it much attention. What I am talking about are the goals that really make a company successful: earn the trust of customers, keep the customers happy, outmarket your competitors, offer something of value to the world at large. In the rush to complete the myriad tasks that come up each and every day, it's easy to lose track of these core values and goals.

The corporate intranet can help by communicating these goals more effectively than ever before. An intranet helps employees stay in touch with the larger mission of the corporation, and keep up to date with the latest internal developments. An informed employee who knows where the company stands in terms of goals, and who can measure and participate in the effort to reach those goals, can accomplish their job with more success than the uninformed employee who works in a vacuum and may at times wonder why they even need to bother.

In Chapter 12, I discuss the need for management to buy into the intranet as a way to reach common corporate goals. A management that believes in a system certainly makes it easier for employees to do the same. I'm not saying that intranets create any radical new corporate management philosophies — improved communications are a part of just about every management plan. Intranets just allow the communication to operate faster and easier than ever before, and at the same time may even bring about some communication that you never even knew you missed.

Better/faster information access

Business processes are successful when they are built around a simple premise: better, faster, cheaper — an intranet is a great way to get there by providing:

✔ **Better information access.** Intranets can provide access to information, such as the latest trends in the marketplace or late-breaking corporate news, that was difficult or impossible to access previously.

✔ **Faster information access.** Once information is updated on your intranet, it is instantly accessible by your entire corporation. Many companies provide employee directories or reports in print, and by the time they reach each employee's desk, the information they contain is already out of date — not so with an intranet.

✔ **Cheaper access to information.** You can build an intranet around proven technologies that many companies already have in place. Many companies already have a Local Area Network (LAN) and a computer on every desktop, and all you need to do is add a few pieces of software and you are off and running. Because intranets are based on proven Internet technologies (the web browser) that many employees are already comfortable with, your training costs are relatively low as well.

Integrated environment

Your corporate intranet can be made up of more than just an internal web site. However, your internal web site is what ultimately provides the framework for a single unified interface for all the reports, manuals, and corporate directories you eventually publish on your intranet. So what if you already have a computer system in place, and you want to integrate it with your new intranet in order to reap the benefits of the intranet's ease?

Many larger companies may have centralized applications that are deployed on centralized computers such as IBM mainframes and AS/400 systems. These applications typically require specialized *terminals* (user computers) or *terminal emulation applications* (software that makes one computer behave like another in order to connect to a picky server) to be installed to use these applications. These specialized terminals and terminal emulation applications can be a support burden.

To solve the problem, many third-party providers have created Java- and ActiveX-based terminal emulators that can be embedded in Web pages, and thus allowing the integration of older computer systems with your intranet. Java is designed to provide the highest level of security, and as part of this security, does not allow direct access to *client hardware* (the user's computer). Due to this limitation, Java emulators generally cannot provide file transfer or print services. ActiveX emulators, on the other hand, do not have these limitations. Third-party companies providing Web-based 3270/5250 terminal emulators include these:

✔ **RUMBA 95/NT for the AS/400.** An ActiveX 3270 terminal emulator. www.walldata.com

✔ **OC://WebConnect.** A Java-based 3270 terminal emulator. www.oc.com

Intranets and Groupware

Out of the many *groupware* products commercially available, the most well-known is Lotus Notes. Groupware applications are designed to be used in a confined location as a way to exchange information within an organization — obviously quite similar to the goals of an intranet. The main differences between groupware applications and intranets include:

- ✔ **Groupware applications require the same software on each client.** Typically this requires a greater level of processing power for each client (user's computer).

- ✔ **Where the data is processed.** Intranet data processing occurs on the server, and the results are displayed through the web browser which can run easily on just about any computer. Groupware processing, on the other hand, relies on the client (user's computer) for processing and updates are sent to the server for storage.

- ✔ **The protocols.** Intranets are built on *open standards,* meaning that because almost all computers can connect to the Internet, just about all computers can be hooked into an intranet. Groupware applications are more *proprietary,* meaning that the company that designs the software also designs the protocol (a closed standard), and require that each computer in the groupware environment is running the groupware application.

- ✔ **Integration with existing applications.** An intranet can provide web-based integration to *legacy systems* (older systems that have been working for your company for a while). The way they do this is by interacting with applications that reside on your web server to access these centralized systems, and return information in nicely formatted web pages. See the "Integrated environment" section earlier in this chapter for more info.

The Bottom Line

If you can prove to management that an intranet can and will save money, then you're more than halfway home. Recent studies by International Data Corporation (home.netscape.com/comprod/accounce/idc/summary.html) have concluded that the average ROI (Return On Investment) for intranets has been above 1000 percent, and that these returns are being seen in *weeks,* not the typical months or years that it takes for a return on typical investments in technologies! (I need to catch my breath — if that doesn't fulfill the goal of this chapter, I don't know what will.) The keys to this high rate of return are that intranets allow you to:

✔ **Use existing technologies and systems in new ways.**

✔ **Lower user training costs because users are already familiar with how to use web browsers.** They train themselves when they surf the Web at home!

✔ **Increased gains in productivity, because information becomes more accessible.** An intranet eliminates the lag time in all work projects by providing immediate answers.

What's it going to cost?

How can you estimate the cost of building your intranet? Well, as with any project, you have two basic types of costs you need to estimate: the visible costs and the hidden costs. The visible costs include the things that you can easily anticipate and estimate, such as hardware and software. Hidden costs are tougher to identify and relate to a dollar amount — they include the cost of creating and maintaining intranet content, training your users to use your intranet, and network support costs.

Visible costs

You may find that your company has already made many of the visible investments you need to get your intranet up and running. If you already have a LAN (Local Area Network) in place, you cut your visible costs by (very) roughly 30 percent or more. When you sit down to outline the cost plan for your intranet, you need to remember to define these costs of course, but you also need to remember to show how much of your network infrastructure is already in place. The five basic types of visible costs you should plan for with regard to your intranet are:

✔ **Server.** You need a computer to run your web server application, and other server-side applications. As I discuss in Chapter 1, your web server is the heart of your intranet. You may also need to purchase dedicated computer systems for other applications such as e-mail — discussed in Chapter 6; push servers, discussed in Chapter 9; and databases, discussed in Chapter 7. You need to identify the technologies that you plan on deploying on your intranet and make sure that you have the right equipment in place to support your intranet infrastructure.

✔ **Network.** Your network is the backbone of your intranet. If your company doesn't already have a local area network (LAN) in place, you face the prospect of installing a network from the ground up. This includes installing wiring, routers and hubs, network adapters, and drivers, and can be a complex process requiring not just materials, but professional installation technicians as well. Unless you work at a really small company, you may want to seriously consider *outsourcing* (contracting out) this task to a qualified consultant. An outside consultant has the proper tools to install, configure, and monitor your intranet networking environment. They can also help you to estimate the appropriate equipment for the amount of information that you need to transfer over your intranet.

✔ **Client.** Client costs include the costs of deploying the appropriate equipment (computer, monitor, browser, network card, and so on) for each user. In Chapter 3, I discuss a typical and ideal configuration for your users' desktops. Hardware costs are constantly changing, and the good news is that you can get more and more processing power for less and less money. Hardware isn't the only client side cost however, you also need to make sure that you have the appropriate licenses for the software installed on each of your clients. Many applications such as database and e-mail systems have a fee for each user. Don't overlook or underestimate the number of users and the software they require.

With some software applications you may need to purchase a *per copy license,* with others you may be able to purchase a *site license*. With a per copy license, you need to purchase a license for each user that needs to use the application, just as if you bought a copy for each user at the computer store. With site licenses, you pay a one-time fee for use of the application throughout your organization, and they are sometimes based on the total number of users in your organization, or that you expect to use the application at the same time. You need to closely evaluate both options to determine which is the most cost effective for your company.

✔ **Application development.** Developing custom applications for your intranet comes with a price tag as well. You may have to spend your own salary budget on internal efforts, or put together special budgets to contract with outside resources. If you decide to use consultants for your development efforts, make sure that you clearly identify the requirements for the applications you need so that their job is clearly outlined and you don't end up spending a lot of money on fluff. Also, make sure that your outside consultant has previous experience in building intranet-enabled applications, and be sure to ask for references. Any reputable consultant is more than happy to provide references — if they truly do a good job, their references are their best advertisement. Whenever you decide to use a consultant for the first time, if you can, you may want to start working with them on small, simple projects to determine how you work together before moving on to bigger and more ambitious projects.

✔ **Support staff.** Finally, you need to make sure that you have the right personnel in place to deploy and support your intranet as it takes shape. When hiring new employees, if possible, include relevant experience in creating and managing intranet applications as part of your criteria. While Internet skills are directly transferable to your intranet, experience with only the older legacy systems, such as older mainframe applications or older strictly DOS-based applications, usually doesn't transfer to intranets that well. For example, I wouldn't hire someone that's been a mainframe COBOL and APL programmer for the past 10 years and expect them to become the corporate web master. Remember that personnel costs and experience can vary widely by geographical location. You can determine the going rate for support staff salaries by discussing it with your human resources department (if your company has one), scanning the local help wanted ads, or asking any people you know in the local industry.

Hidden costs

The biggest hidden intranet cost is that of creating and maintaining your intranet content. Face it — the fuel for your intranet is its content. Once your intranet is running and your users are realizing its benefits, you still need to maintain good and consistent content. Over time, your publishing efforts will be the largest cost associated with your intranet. Content development and maintenance costs are made up of primarily five different types of costs:

✔ **The conversion of existing documents and information.** This includes the costs of labor and tools to convert your current content so that it's accessible on your intranet. In Chapter 5, I show you how to convert existing word processing, spread sheet, and other documents from a vast array of applications into a form (HTML) that's directly accessible on your intranet. While much of this process is pretty simple, it takes some manipulation to get your documents to appear just right, and then to integrate them into your web site.

✔ **The management of your intranet web site.** Maintaining your corporate web site can be a complex task. Making sure that links are kept up to date and that content remains fresh can take quite a bit of time. Many web development tools now also include web site management capabilities as part of their list of features.

✔ **The coordination of intranet web site content.** Coordinating content submissions from different departments and getting them into the standard look and feel established by your webmaster can be a big project. Consider developing a Standard Operating Procedure (SOP) to help minimize costs. Departments and divisions can then provide information in an accepted format and style established by the SOP before it is integrated into your intranet.

✔ **Taking areas of your intranet public.** As your intranet develops, you may identify areas and functions that are ideal for the use of business clients, business partners, or suppliers, and you may decide to connect your intranet to the Internet, also called an *extranet* — I review extranets in Chapter 10. You may need to redevelop these areas so that they are more friendly to the public. You may also need to invest in more hardware as the usage of your web server and network increases with public traffic.

✔ **Training and support costs.** The cost of training and supporting your users is sometimes easy to overlook, but it is crucial to the success of your intranet. Plan for an initial training session to introduce your users to the intranet and to give them an idea of the type of information and resources it provides. And because your intranet is likely to always be a work in progress, you may want to have short introductory courses every few months to introduce employees to new features and web pages. Also, don't overlook the process of training new employees on your intranet.

These choices lead to the classic business question: Should I do all this myself or should I hire an outside consultant to do this for me? I believe that your intranet has the best chance of succeeding if you develop it completely in house, or if you have a blend of in-house personnel and consultants. You need to determine if you have the right personnel available in house to build your intranet, and whether the costs of using in-house personnel is a better bargain than simply hiring a consultant to do it for you. I believe that in most cases, keeping things in house is more cost effective and provides better control over your project in the long run.

Consultants are certainly useful in helping get your intranet off the ground — a successful blend between a consultant and your own personnel may even provide training to your in-house staff as they put your intranet together. Be wary of consultants that come in and set everything up and then leave. Chapter 12 provides a bit more info on the type of personnel and support you need to develop and manage your intranet.

How will it pay for itself?

So, enough about costs — what about the benefits? Intranets provide a number of tangible and intangible benefits. The tangible benefits of intranets include:

✔ **Reduced paper costs.** Instead of printing and distributing material, it can be placed on your intranet for immediate, cheap electronic access.

✔ **Lower support and training costs than other similar technologies.** Remember that the web browser is already a popular home tool for computer users, so much of your training is already done. In addition, as you add new features to your intranet, for the most part, they run through the same web browser and so only minimal additional training is necessary.

✔ **Less time required to develop meaningful applications.** HTML is so easy that you can have new web pages to meet new needs in a matter of days.

The intangible benefits of intranets include:

✔ **Improved communications between employees and management.** On an intranet, everyone is connected and communicating with everyone else.

✔ **Increased employee productivity.** Information and the tools to process it and make decisions are available in an instant on your intranet.

✔ **Better informed and motivated employees.** Information can bring a sense of empowerment. Corporate intranets bring information to employees that may not have been easy to obtain previously. Information has become an increasingly important tool in today's business environment. Employees that feel they have the right tools to do their jobs feel like they can make better decisions and accomplish more.

Finally, you need to remember to protect your intranet investments:

✔ **Make conservative technology choices.** Intranet technologies change rapidly — what seems like a hot new technology poised to take over the world may not actually pan out. Unless a hot new technology provides an immediate, pressing, and tangible benefit to your company, I advise you to wait until the technology works itself out. New software often has a bug problem and you can't really rely on it until the first revision or two have passed. Furthermore, new technology may not be accepted in the marketplace when it first arrives, and the latest software may not work well with the rest of your intranet components.

✔ **Protect your personnel investment.** Some companies can view employees as cogs in the machine, blindly plugging in new employees when old employees leave. Don't underestimate the value of your intranet development team's experience and knowledge of your company's structure — new employees can take six months before they have even the introductory knowledge level of your company's procedures and policies.

✔ **Make sure that your corporate culture fits the intranet experience.** I know that I've mentioned this a few times already, but it's a very important concept: Unless your company's structure supports the team building and shared goals approach an intranet can bring, your intranet won't realize its fullest potential.

Intranet deployment tips

The Meta Group, www.meta.com, recently completed an analysis of the Return On Investment (ROI) experienced by companies that recently started intranets. The Meta Group's analysis concluded that a number of things they found are worth sharing to help other companies succeed with an intranet project:

✔ The most successful intranet applications are those that coincide with business goals.

✔ The technologies you use to deploy your intranet have less of an impact than the applications you put in place on your intranet.

✔ It doesn't take a lot of money to deploy successful intranet applications.

✔ Your return is not necessarily based on the size of the intranet. Departmental or divisional scale intranets can also provide benefits.

Begging!

If your dream of an intranet really begins to fizzle, you can always beg your boss — well, maybe you don't need to resort to that. You can always let your boss borrow this book so that he or she can get a better understanding of how intranets can work for your company. Of course, you can always pick a small application on your own, and develop a localized pilot project intranet around that. A pilot project can provide you with a concrete example to demonstrate to your boss, and also give you some relevant intranet building experience that you can use to impress your boss and give you a realistic idea of how long larger projects are going to take.

Part V
The Part of Tens

The 5th Wave — **By Rich Tennant**

The computer virus crept silently from network to network, until it found its way into the cafeteria vending machines.

In this part . . .

The traditional ...For Dummies Part of the Tens is not forgotten! In this part, I include a chapter answering the top ten most frequently asked questions about intranets. I also give you the ten ways your intranet differs from the Internet, and ten ideas for utilizing your intranet in new and exciting ways.

Chapter 15

Ten (Or So) Frequently Asked Questions about Intranets

. . . .

*I*ntranets are a new technology and everyone still has questions — hopefully I answer many of these questions elsewhere in this book. For those of you who cheated and jumped here to get the skinny on intranets, and for others that just want a quick reference to some intranet answers (either for themselves or to show their boss), this chapter is for you.

What Exactly Is an Intranet?

An intranet is a network of computers that are connected together and talk to each other using the same protocols used on the Internet (TCP/IP and HTTP). Intranets are private networks that are setup for exclusive use by a company. So, what's the big deal? Intranets are more than just Local Area Networks (LANs), in fact they are being used to transform the way companies communicate and deploy information systems.

Intranets provide a framework for making a company's information and information systems available and easily accessible. They do this through a universal application: the web browser. And because web browsers are available on multiple platforms (Mac, PC, UNIX and so on), and the intranet works on an *open standard,* meaning that the way you connect computers to it is available for all manufacturers and computer types, an intranet breaks down the old computer network barriers. With an intranet, everyone in your company can share information with everyone else.

Do Intranets Cost a Lot?

Of course, it depends on what you mean by a lot. While one million dollars could be virtually nothing for a large company, it could be a king's ransom to smaller companies. Generally intranets are fairly inexpensive, because they rely on many of the technologies companies already have in place. In addition, a good deal of the necessary software for an intranet is free.

Intranets certainly do sound exciting, and they can certainly increase corporate communications, but how can you convince your boss that they are a good idea? There's an old saying that goes: To get to the root of something, follow the money. With intranets, the money comes in the form of ROI (Return on Investment). If you can prove to the powers that be that intranets can and will save money, you're more than halfway home. Recent studies by the META Group, Inc., `www.microsoft.com.intranet/articles/META.htm`, show that 80 percent of the companies they surveyed generated a positive ROI from their intranet investment. The average ROI for these companies was 38 percent — and the even bigger news is that these returns are being seen in weeks, not the typical months or years with typical investments in technologies. A few keys to this high rate of return are:

 ✔ Use of existing technologies in new ways

 ✔ Increased gains in productivity because information becomes more accessible

 ✔ Lower end-user training costs — most users are already familiar with how to use a web browser

Just What Can I Do with an Intranet?

You can use an intranet to:

 ✔ **Publish corporate information.** The latest product information, human resource handbooks, reports, marketing information, and even corporate telephone directories are all candidates.

 ✔ **Provide access to electronic mail.**

 ✔ **Conduct virtual meetings.** An intranet allows you to run advanced video conferencing applications to connect users across distances.

 ✔ **Provide an easy way to access centralized databases.** This includes asking questions (making *queries*) of the database and displaying the answers in nicely formatted web pages that any computer running a web browser can display.

 ✔ **Broadcast the latest corporate news and information to all computers at the same time.**

Remember that an intranet is more than any one of these applications — it's the sum of these Internet-proven applications working together to help an organization to communicate more effectively and efficiently.

How Big Can an Intranet Be?

Your intranet can be as big as you want. Remember: Intranets are designed around Internet technologies, and the Internet spans the entire world. As your intranet scales up, however, you may need to consider faster computers for your intranet web server, or even multiple web servers. An organization can have one or hundreds of web servers running and still be considered an intranet. Size doesn't so much determine an intranet as the fact that it's intended for private, internal use.

Does My Intranet Require a Web Server?

The web server is what lets you publish information on your intranet in a centralized location. Technically, you can have an intranet without a web server, but it would be kind of like Independence day without fireworks — just not the same. While many of your intranet applications can and do run without requiring a web server, it's the web server that makes the exchange of information easier.

Netscape Navigator or Internet Explorer?

I'm not trying to cop out here, but this is just a matter of personal preference. Both Netscape Navigator and Microsoft Internet Explorer bring different features to your intranet. If you're planning on using ActiveX controls on your intranet, then Internet Explorer is clearly the better choice. If you have many different computer platforms (Mac, PC, UNIX, and so on) on your network and want to support a single web browser, then Netscape Navigator is the better choice. The newest versions of Netscape Navigator, now called Communicator, and Internet Explorer will be even more intertwined with your operating system and the way that you do all of your work.

Ideally, your intranet should support both web browsers. However, if you're looking to take advantage of some of the latest features of one or the other, or are interested in providing the best possible look and feel to your intranet, you're better off picking one and sticking with it. Unlike the Internet, you have complete control over your intranet, how people access it, and the browser they use. Picking one web browser can help keep your support and development costs down.

Do I Need to Run TCP/IP to Create My Intranet?

Simply: yes and no. Web servers only work with the TCP/IP (Transmission Control Protocol/Internet Protocol) networking protocol. Without getting into the nitty gritty technical details, you *can* run a network in a Netware-based environment using the IPX protocol, by running applications that convert the networking protocols to the Internet protocols (TCP/IP, HTTP). Sound complicated? It is. This really is an area for the networking experts in your company; my advice though is to avoid setups that don't use TCP/IP if at all possible.

How Are the Internet and My Intranet Alike?

Intranets are based on the same technologies that built the Internet. Intranets are basically a mini version of the Internet that for the most part is private. Unless you choose to allow public Internet access to your intranet, only the people in your office building, or that work for your company are allowed to access the computers that are connected to it. An intranet is kind of like having your own private party — anyone in the world can eat chips and drink beer, but you only share *your* beer and chips with people at your party.

How Are Intranets and Groupware Different?

Intranets and groupware solutions such as Lotus notes are built on the same design philosophies — enabling groups of people to work together and exchange information more efficiently. The difference is in the way that they accomplish the task. Intranets are built on *open standards* (such as TCP/IP and HTTP), and many vendors out there are developing solutions using these standards. Groupware, on the other hand, is *proprietary* — using specialized, vendor-specific servers and clients to access the information they store. Intranets can connect seamlessly to the Internet because they are based on the same technologies. It takes some extra magic and money to connect groupware-based solutions to the Internet.

How Are Intranets and Client/Server Systems Alike?

Intranets pull together the best aspects of the client server solution — file oriented application deployment and multitiered data access. The biggest innovation of intranet technology is that it delivers corporate information in a familiar manner that's standard across different types of computers — a web browser. Users can access the web server from their web browser to display standard HTML files, just like traditional file-based client/server systems. Using web server-side applications, with CGI or other server-side applications, you can develop applications that access a server-side database, return the requested data to the web server for processing, and display the results in a user's web browser — just like multitiered client/server models.

How Do I Assign IP Addresses for My Intranet?

Internic is the provider of domain name registration services. They assign a name to an IP (Internet Protocol) address so you can enter an address like www.dummies.com in your web browser and you don't need to know its actual IP address (which looks like a bunch of numbers with periods). Internic provides a document that describes the conventions you should follow when assigning IP addresses for your intranet computers at www.internic.net/rfc/rfc1597.txt.

Chapter 16

Ten Differences between the Internet and an Intranet

• •

*I*nternet? Intranet? It all gets confusing doesn't it? Just what really is the difference? This chapter is here to help sort out the mess with the ten most important differences between the Internet and intranets.

About a Zillion Computers

The Internet is used to connect together millions of computers, while intranets connect fewer computers. True, your intranet has no limit to the number of computers it can support, and no one's going to stop you from creating an intranet as big as the Internet, but it's unlikely that anyone has the money to build an intranet that big. Unless of course, you own a software company and have a ton of money like someone you may have heard about.

The Internet Reaches Out across the World

The Internet reaches out over the entire world, while intranets usually function within the walls of your company. With an intranet, you can use a private Wide Area Network (WAN), or even piggy back on the Internet, using proxy servers and encryption to keep your communications private as they cruise through public Internet networks. However, unlike the Internet, your intranet is designed for the private, exclusive use of your company and requires authorization. In Chapter 10, I cover how to bring your intranet outside the walls of your corporation and on to the Internet. If you stop to think about it, the Internet is really just a big intranet for the private use of the planet earth — no space aliens allowed without proper authorization, please.

Your Intranet Is Faster

A completely local intranet is hundreds of times faster than the Internet. Inside the walls of your company, computers are connected to form your intranet using a Local Area Network (LAN). Depending on the type of network hardware you use, your LAN can transfer information from any-where between 10 and 100 million bits per second (Mbps). A bit is just a 1 or 0, and 10 to 100 Mbps is *a lot of information*. By comparison, typical connections to the Internet are anywhere between 28 and 256 thousand bits per second — not nearly as fast as your LAN.

Another factor that makes intranets faster is simply the number of users. Think of driving down your local freeway during rush hour versus at 2 a.m. It probably takes a lot less time to get to where you want to go at 2 a.m. than during the peak of rush hour. The Internet usually functions at the peak of rush hour all the time, while your intranet is more like taking a drive at 2 a.m.

Intranets Help You Work

If your boss had the choice of letting you cruise around the Internet for a couple of hours or cruise around your corporate intranet, I'm sure that he or she would choose the intranet every time. The Internet is full of all sorts of information — from the latest news, sports, and weather to the *Gumby on the Web* web site (`www.emsphone.com/gumby` if you're interested). True, you can find a lot of useful information on the Internet, but there's a lot of silly time-wasting stuff out there too. Hey, I've got nothing against silly stuff and wasting time — it's just that your boss may have something against it while you're supposed to be at work.

Your intranet, on the other hand, is full of company-specific information. So, the next time your boss catches you using your web browser, you can say, "It's not what you think — I'm cruising the intranet!" Then you can explain the whole intranet thing to him (bosses are always the last to know about this stuff) and look really smart in the process!

No Telephone Companies or ISPs Required

When you're building a basic intranet, you don't need to set up service with an ISP (Internet Service Provider) or telephone company. The connectivity of your intranet is provided by your local area network. However, you can connect your intranet to the Internet (called an *extranet*) as I explain in Chapter 10 — if you go that route, you need an ISP and some sort of service from a telephone company.

Intranets Are Changing the Face of Internal Corporate Communications

Intranets make it easier, faster, and cheaper for organizations to distribute information. Instead of spending thousands of dollars to create and print corporate telephone directories and employee manuals that are probably already out of date by the time they reach an employee's desk, you can use your intranet to instantly release changes and updates to corporate information. Your intranet can ensure that everyone in your organization has the latest information available when they need it.

The Internet Is Public and Intranets Are Private

Everyone and your grandmother is on the Internet these days — millions of computers all across the world are connected. Intranets, on the other hand, are a private thing — basically there for the exclusive use of your company. Even if your company's network is connected to the Internet, your intranet can remain a little private and exclusive party.

You Can Be in Complete Control over Your Entire Intranet

Everyone at one time or another has a desire to be in complete control of things — your corporate intranet is your chance. The Internet is built on the cooperation of thousands of individuals all working together to keep their computers linked together. Sometimes this cooperation or some other equipment fails, and the Internet experiences a brief outage.

With your intranet, you're in complete control. However, with independence comes responsibility: If you control it, you have to fix it when things go wrong. May your intranet experience smooth sailing!

Tastes Great/Less Filling

Okay, it's an old argument but it applies to the Internet and intranets as well. The Internet is on the tastes great side — it offers tons of information from all around the world. You can literally find information in seconds that would have taken hours to uncover (if you ever got to it) previously.

The intranet is on the less filling side of this argument. While your corporate intranet can't store the breadth of information found on the Internet, it has a lot more depth focused on your company. The ideal solution is a combination of the Internet and your corporate intranet. Push applications like PointCast and those found in the latest versions of Internet Explorer and Netscape Communicator can help bring more focused external Internet information to your employees, while the intranet brings depth to the internal organization information. The combination can give employees the most current information available on all fronts.

A Big I and a Little i!

Did you ever wonder why the Internet uses a capital I and intranet uses a lower case i? If so, then you may want to consider getting away on a vacation for a few — I think you're spending too much time with your computer. Since there is only one Internet, "Internet" is a proper name like Tom, Dick, or Harry, and it gets the big I and the proper introduction at parties.

The world has literally thousands of intranets, so just like apples and oranges it gets the little i. However, just because it has a little i doesn't mean that it shouldn't get its proper respect.

Chapter 17

Ten Ways to Use an Intranet to Achieve World Peace, Save the Whales, and Become a Millionaire!

· ·

*O*kay, I guess that I'm exaggerating a little. I can't show you how to achieve world peace, save the whales, or become a millionaire. Maybe I'm just getting a little giddy since this is the last chapter. In any case, I want to leave you with ten quick tips that can help to ensure the success of your intranet project.

Make Sure Your Intranet Fits with Your Corporate Structure

Does your company have an open management structure? If yes, then an intranet will probably work well within your organization. Intranets help workers share information faster than ever before possible, and this helps workers make decisions on their own. If your company is supportive of the team-building concepts and the ability of employees to make their own decisions with the information sharing that intranets can bring to an organization, then an intranet should be a good fit for your company.

Set Your Goals Early and Stick to Them

A clear mission is the cornerstone of any successful project, but even more so with intranets. The most important mission-related questions include: For whom are you developing the intranet, and what is its primary purpose?

Having a clear idea of the mission of your intranet can direct your development efforts and keep everything cool. Once you agree to a plan for your intranet, you need to stick to it. Take notes as you go and use them to revamp the plan for the next phase of your intranet project.

Content Is the Key

The most critical aspect of an intranet is content. Without content, your intranet is a wasteland and totally useless for employees. The four basic principles to follow when you develop and maintain the content of your intranet are:

✓ **Relevance.** Provide information that's relevant for your users — stuff that helps them get their jobs done. Without relevant information, your intranet web can quickly turn into a cob web.

✓ **Timeliness.** Make sure that your intranet functions quickly. If users find that they can obtain information more quickly using other channels, then that's the way they'll go. The path of least resistance is the one people follow.

✓ **Up to date.** Setting up your intranet is only the beginning. Make sure that your intranet provides the most up-to-date information. The advantages of intranets can only be realized when they are continually kept up to date.

✓ **Easy to access.** Make sure that all your users can access your intranet web site easily and quickly. If access proves too difficult, users will simply find another easier way to get the job done (or not get the job done at all). This tip also applies to the design of your intranet site — make sure that you design a site that's easy to use and allows users to quickly get to the information they want and need.

Use Open Standards

Open standards (TCP/IP — the Internet protocols) are the key to intranets. Always try to steer clear of products that are proprietary in nature. With all the maneuvering between Microsoft, Netscape, and Sun, determining whose standards will be the winner is nearly impossible until a winner is actually declared. You need to keep up to date with the latest developments (in Appendix B, I list a number of Internet Web sites, news groups, magazines, and newsletters dedicated to discussing intranets and keeping you informed).

Consider the Big Picture

Don't force your intranet to live in a vacuum. Look at ways to share information between different departments and divisions. Sharing information requires that departments and divisions coordinate amongst themselves, but it also requires that you create a format for your intranet that ensures that collaboration and department projects still meet the overall design guidelines of your intranet.

Experience Is Important

Don't underestimate the value of experience. If your company doesn't have the time or ability to get your intranet off the ground, look to the outside for help. Look to companies that can help you to get started, and that provide the proper training so your organization can maintain your intranet when the initial deployment is completed. This approach may cost more up front, but a good foundation saves a lot of money in the long run.

Maintenance!

Make sure that you have the proper backup and security systems in place. Users will learn to rely on your intranet more and more the longer it is up and running. You need to provide a level of safety behind their blind faith by implementing appropriate security measures and making backups at regular intervals.

Be sure to plan upgrades to your intranet during off hours. While that can be difficult for the individuals that are performing the updates, it provides the continuous and timely service your users will come to expect and demand.

Remember Your Users

Make sure you involve your intranet users in the development and direction of your intranet. Many applications look great on paper, but then in practice, users find that they can't stand them. Make sure your employees have the training and ability to update areas of your intranet on their own — intranets work best as a collaborative effort.

Start Small and Let It Grow

Intranets are well suited to incremental development. Even though your initial development efforts may start small, don't forget to keep your bigger mission in mind. As employees begin to see the benefits of an intranet, they bring new ideas to the table which help you grow your intranet into a tool that's tailored to the needs of your company.

Monitor Progress

You can't plant a seed without watering it and you can't start building your intranet without monitoring its progress either. Make sure that you take the time to review the current content on your intranet, and update it as stuff goes out of date. Keep in touch with your users and make sure that your intranet is continuing to meet their needs and expectations. The most successful intranets are those that are grown from the ground up by the people that use and depend on them.

Part VI
Appendixes

In this part . . .

*B*uilding an Intranet For Dummies wraps up with this here reference guide. I include references to help you stay on top of the future of intranets and intranet technology. I also provide a guide to where you can find out more about intranets. Finally, I include information on intranet tools you can get for free, those that are commercially available, and intranet-related Web sites, newsgroups, magazines and newsletters that you may find helpful as you build, maintain, and look toward the future of your intranet.

Appendix A

Beam Me Up!
Intranets: The Next Generation

. . . .

In This Appendix

▶ Looking where intranet technology is headed

▶ Keeping an eye on new software

▶ Making sure that your intranet is up to date without being on the "bleeding edge"

. . . .

*T*o really stay on top of your intranet, you need to understand where intranet technology is headed. No, I don't have a crystal ball, and I can't tell you exactly where intranets will be 1, 5, or 10 years from now. However, I can give you an overview of technologies and applications on the near horizon that will undoubtedly play key roles in the future of intranets. Will all of these technologies and applications succeed? Probably not, but that's the fun of predicting the future — you never know where you're going to wind up.

Next generation web browsers

Microsoft and Netscape are already in the marketplace with preview versions of their latest web browsers. The big news on this front is that web browsers are likely to become a permanent part of your computer desktop. These latest browsers make the intranet argument even more compelling, because they promise to make the web browser the common interface to not only the Internet and intranets, but also to other applications running on the user's computer such as word processor and spreadsheet software.

Netscape Communicator

Netscape Communicator, the newest intranet/Internet application suite from Netscape Communications Corporation, provides the following features:

- ✔ **The latest version of Netscape Navigator.** Shown in Figure A-1, the latest version of Navigator supports the most recent HTML specification, authentication of plug-ins, enhanced Java support, built-in support for VRML (*Virtual Reality Modeling Language*), and improved support for Secured Sockets Layer security (SSL).

- ✔ **Netscape Messenger.** Shown in Figure A-2, Netscape Messenger is a full-featured e-mail client with the ability to send and receive encrypted messages. Netscape Messenger supports all the Internet-based mail standards, including MIME (*Multipurpose Internet Mail Extensions*), SMTP (*Simple Mail Transfer Protocol*), and POP (*Point of Presence*). Netscape Messenger also provides access to LDAP (*Lightweight Directory Access Protocol*) services.

- ✔ **Netscape Collabra,** which provides bulletin board-type discussion groups.

- ✔ **Netscape Composer,** which provides the ability to edit HTML-based web pages.

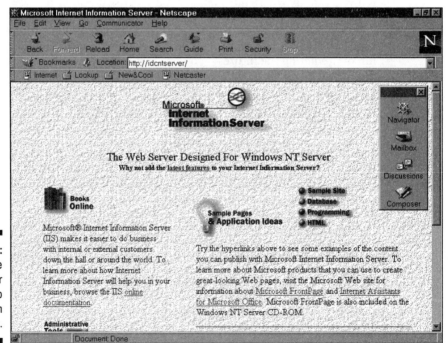

Figure A-1: Netscape Navigator web browser in action.

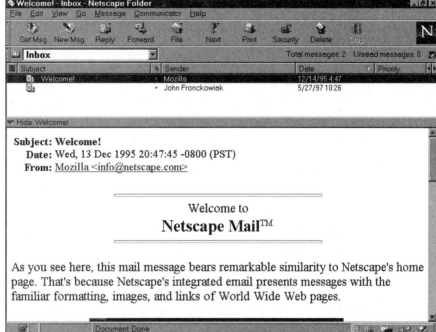

Figure A-2:
Netscape
Messenger
mail client
in action.

✔ **Netscape Netcaster,** which provides the ability to access push-based content.

✔ **Netscape Conference,** which provides the ability for real-time voice communication and document collaboration.

The Professional version of Netscape Communicator provides the following additional features:

✔ **Netscape AutoAdmin** with centralized administration capabilities for the product suite.

✔ **Netscape Calendar,** which provides group scheduling.

✔ **Netscape IBM Host On-Demand,** which provides Java-based IBM 3270 terminal emulation over the Internet or your intranet.

For more information about the Netscape Communicator product suite, visit the Netscape Web site at `www.netscape.com`.

Internet Explorer

Internet Explorer Version 4.0, shown in Figure A-3, provides the following new features:

- ✔ **An updated web browser** with improved security, support for Dynamic HTML, and the latest Java, ActiveX, and HTML standards.

- ✔ **The Active Desktop,** which allows you to place web pages that update at regularly scheduled times right on your desktop.

- ✔ **Microsoft Outlook Express e-mail client** with the ability to send and receive encrypted messages. Outlook Express e-mail supports all the Internet-based messaging standards, including MIME (*Multipurpose Internet Mail Extensions*), SMTP (*Simple Mail Transfer Protocol*), and POP (*Point of Presence*). Outlook Express also provides access to LDAP (*Light Weight Directory Access Protocol*) services.

- ✔ **Microsoft NetMeeting 2.0,** which provides real-time voice, video, and application sharing.

- ✔ **Microsoft NetShow,** which provides access to live Internet and intranet video and voice broadcasts, similar to RealAudio and RealVideo

- ✔ **Microsoft FrontPad,** which provides web page editing capabilities.

To find out more about the latest version of Internet Explorer, check out the Microsoft Web site at `www.microsoft.com/ie`.

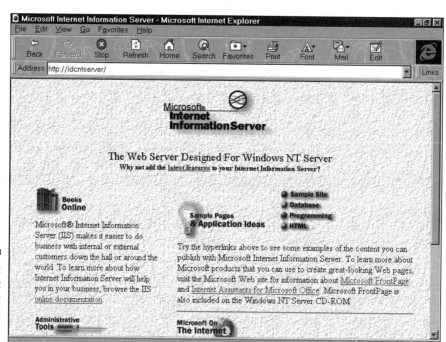

Figure A-3:
Internet
Explorer
Version 4.0
in action.

Smart card authentication

Similar to a an automatic teller machine card, smart cards are credit card-sized devices that help identify authorized network users. Client computers need devices to read the cards, each of which contains information such as user ID, work hours, address — anything that may be useful to your network administrator for network security. Unlike current credit cards that have a simple magnetic strip designed to hold limited, read-only information, smart cards can contain a variety of information that can be read *and* written. Companies that currently provide smart card technology include:

- Bull: www.bull.com
- DataCard: www.cardshow.com/industry/DataCard/about.html
- Circuit Link Inc.: www.circuitlink.com
- Innovonics Inc.: www.innovonics.com

Interested in finding out more about smart card technologies? The following Internet Web sites contain useful information about this technology:

- American Bankers Association: www.aba.com
- Card Technology Magazine: cardtech.faulkergray.com
- MasterCard International: www.mastercard.com
- PCMCIA (Personal Computer Memory Card Interface Association): www.pc-card.com
- Smart Card Resource Center: www.smart-card.com

VRML

VRML, or *Virtual Reality Modeling Language,* brings 3-D virtual reality to the Web. As shown in Figure A-4, VRML files can be viewed from your web browser. Although VRML has been around for a couple of years, it really hasn't taken off as expected. The three reasons for its slow growth are:

- **Extra downloads.** Before you can view a VRML file, you need to download and install special web browser plug-ins. While this isn't a very complex task, it's tedious enough to prevent many people and organizations from going through the trouble. Some of these VRML web browser add-ons are free, while others require a licensing fee.

- **Lack of simple editing tools.** Creating VRML worlds is a complex and tedious process. While it's recently become easier, it's still a lot simpler to learn how to create web pages.

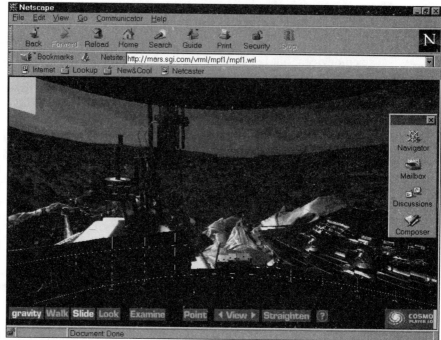

Figure A-4:
VRML
panoramic
view of the
Mars
landscape
from the
Carl Sagan
Memorial
station.

✔ **No "killer" application.** VRML is lacking the "killer" application that will turn it into a star, and it's hard to say if that application will ever arrive. Some research has been done to create 3-D virtual library and filing rooms, which would allow you to move through and examine documents. The applications, however, haven't been useful enough to truly take off.

If you're interested in developing your own 3-D worlds, the following companies offer VRML authoring tools:

✔ Caligari Pioneer: www.caligari.com

✔ PhotoModeler: www.photomodeler.com

✔ OpenInventor: www.sd.tgs.com/Products/openinv.html

✔ Strata Studio Pro: www.strata3d.com

After you construct your 3-D worlds, you need the appropriate browser plug-ins to view them. These plug-ins can be found at the following Web sites:

✔ VR Scout: www.chaco.com/vrscout

✔ Live3D: www.netscape.com/comprod/products/navigator/live3d/index.html

- ✔ WebFX: `www.paperinc.com`
- ✔ Microsoft VRML Viewer: `www.microsoft.com/vrml/toolbar`

The following Web sites provide even more information on VRML:

- ✔ Virtual Reality Center: `www.newtype.com/NewType/vr/index.htm`
- ✔ VRML Forum: `vrml.wired.com`
- ✔ VRML Site Magazine: `www.vrmlsite.com`
- ✔ VRML Repository: `www.sdsc.edu/vrml`
- ✔ Microsoft VRML: `www.microsoft.com/vrml`

Intelligent agents

Intelligent agents merge the areas of artificial intelligence and web-based searching to create smart applications that can anticipate the type of information that you're looking for and then, retrieve it (sometimes even before you know you need it). Intelligent agent technology is already apparent in applications like Office 97, which attempts to offer you application help when it senses that you're trying to perform certain operations. Intelligent agents can visit the areas of your intranet that other employees frequent and create summaries of the information found there, with the idea that people probably hit (and return to) places where they find important information. *Want to find out more about Intelligent Agents?* The following Internet Web sites offer more detailed information:

- ✔ Intelligent Agents at Carnegie Mellon University: `www.cs.cmu.edu/~softagents/`
- ✔ NetBots: `www.printerport.com/klephacks/netbots.html`

Next generation networks

Many next-generation network components are already available. These new networks promise to provide faster, cheaper, and easier-to-deploy networking solutions. These components include:

- ✔ **100 MBPS (Megabits per second) Ethernet.** These networks can transmit data at 10 times the speed of traditional Ethernet-based networks. Be aware of the more stringent specifications for cabling, and the need for newer client-side network cards in 100 MBPS systems. These *Fast Ethernet* networks are usually deployed today to connect servers together (as a *backbone* or *trunk*, as server-to-server connections are called). In the future, you may see 100 MBPS Ethernet networks throughout organizations connecting clients to the server — a big boon for video and conferencing applications.

✔ **Ethernet switching.** When information is transferred over a traditional Ethernet network, bottlenecks can cause slowdowns. Ethernet switching reduces these bottlenecks and allows your network to function closer to its 10 MBPS limit by routing data *packets* to their destinations via the least trafficked route. Ethernet switching offers the advantage of not having to update your cabling and networking cards, as you would need to do to move up to 100 MBPS Ethernet.

✔ **Cable modems.** These modems connect to existing cable television lines and provide fast (up to 10 MBPS) connection to the Internet at lower costs than traditional telecommunications solutions.

✔ **Wireless networks.** Wireless systems provide access to the corporate network along with complete mobility for users within a given space. Wireless networks are currently more expensive then traditional wire-based networks, but are easier to expand because you don't need to run cables each time you add a system to your network. These networks work great in campus-style work environments where users have notebook computers and may work in one building on a project today, and another building on a different project next week.

Interested in finding out more about the latest developments in networking? The following Internet Web sites can help you stay up-to-date with the latest information:

✔ C-Net Daily News: `www.cnet.com`

✔ LAN Magaizine: `www.lanmag.com`

✔ LAN Times: `www.lantimes.com`

✔ NEI Networking References: `www.netevolve.com/lazar/`

✔ Network World: `www.nwfusion.com`

✔ Yahoo! Daily Networking News: `biz.yahoo.com/news/networking.html`

Thinning clients

Thin clients are computers that provide just enough functionality to access the Internet or your intranet. Thin clients provide minimum hard disk storage space, and obtain most of their functionality and software from your web server. If they ever have a chance of succeeding, it will be because of the boom in the Internet and intranets on which they rely. Standards for these devices are still emerging, and opinions on their actual cost savings vary widely.

Currently, you find two competing thin client standards. One is supported by a group composed of Oracle, Sun, and IBM, with an eye toward clients that have hardware specifically designed to run Java applications. The other group is led by a group primarily made up of Intel and Microsoft, with the focus on clients that use the same basic design you find in many PCs today. The Intel/Microsoft thin client is really a scaled-down version of computers found in most homes and businesses.

The thin client concept recalls the older days when LANs (Local Area Networks) were introduced. At that time, there was a rush to deploy low-powered PCs on the desktop and let the bigger servers do the processing. In spite of all the hype surrounding thin clients, they seem more like a repackaging of old "dumb terminal" ideas that people abandoned for the Personal Computer (PC).

Although a compelling argument can be made for thin clients, I'm still not sold on the concept. In the long run, I don't expect thin clients to have a large impact of the enterprise, unless they can break the $500 per unit barrier and offer usable performance.

Castanet

Marimba was founded by some of the developers of the Java programming language. They set out to create a new product that takes the concept of push technologies (see Chapter 9) to new levels — that product is Castanet. Castanet creates *push channels* that deliver the latest information and applications. Castanet's three primary components are:

- ✔ **Castanet Channels.** Similar to channels on your television, each channel contains various applications or information that's transmitted across an intranet or the Internet by the Castanet Transmitter.

- ✔ **Castanet Transmitter.** This componet is a server side application that delivers and manages channel information.

- ✔ **Castanet Tuner.** The tuner is a client side application that's used to receive channel information sent by Castanet Transmitters.

Castanet also provides the Bongo application for creating channel content. Both Microsoft and Netscape have announced support for Castanet channels in the latest versions of their browsers. For more information about Castanet and Bongo, visit the Marimba Web site at www.marimba.com.

More . . .

New intranet technologies are continually emerging, and it's difficult to stay up-to-date with all this stuff, let alone pick the winning technologies of the future. In Appendix B, I present a list of Internet Web site and magazine resources that can help keep you informed about the latest intranet developments. With all this in mind, I have a few suggestions on planning for the future of your intranet:

- ✔ **Pick new technologies conservatively.** Stay away from 1.0 versions of applications, if possible. While I know that being on the bleeding edge of technology can be fun and exciting, it also comes with a lot of risks. If you feel that you can afford the risks of the technology becoming a flop, disappearing, or simply not working correctly (and the wrath of your users), then by all means head out to the edge — otherwise stay inside.

- ✔ **Be wary of radically new technologies.** Much of the future is a derivative of the past. If a new technology promises to revolutionize the world overnight, be skeptical. Ask questions, and dig in deeper before you rush to deploy any new technology in your organization.

- ✔ **Finally, always try to roll out new technologies in a limited test mode.** Remember to start small and think big!

Appendix B

How Can I Find Out More?
A Guide to Intranet Resources

- -

A Guide to Where You Can Get Stuff for FREE!

The Internet hosts a gold mine of intranet information, tools, and utilities available for free download. These cool sites include

- ✔ **Download.com:** www.download.com
- ✔ **HTML Editors:** yahoo.com/Computers_and_Internet/Software/ Internet/World_Wide_Web/HTML_Editors
- ✔ **Internet Download Top 20:** www.pi.net/~turr
- ✔ **Microsoft BackOffice Download and Trial Kits:** backoffice.micorosft.com/downtrial/default.asp
- ✔ **Microsoft Intranet Solutions Products:** www.microsoft.com/ intranet/misc/products-f.htm
- ✔ **Netscape Software Download and Product Overview:** www.netscape.com/download/index.html
- ✔ **Shareware.com:** www.shareware.com
- ✔ **Windows95.com:** www.windows95.com
- ✔ **Yahoo!/ZDNet Software Library:** headlines.yahoo.com/zddownload/ internet

A Field Guide to Intranet Resources

Keeping up to date on the latest developments in intranet technologies is crucial to the future success of your intranet. A number of Internet Web sites devote exclusive coverage to intranet-related issues. In addition, a number of magazines and periodicals offer sections that cover the latest intranet-related technological developments. The most important thing to realize is that much of this information is free! While some of the magazines are only available through a paid subscription, many offer a free subscriptions to qualified people (like you, after reading this book).

Web sites

The Internet has a number of Web sites that offer exclusive coverage of intranets:

- Building an Intranet from Fortune Magazine: `pathfinder.com/fortune/specials/intranets/index.html`
- A Guide to Intraprise-Wide Computing: `www.process.com/news/intrawp.com`
- Intranet Design Magazine: `www.innergy.com`
- The Intranet Information Page: `www.strom.com/pubwork/intranet.html`
- Intranet Journal: `www.intranetjournal.com`
- The Intranet Resource Center: `www.cio.com/WebMaster/wm_irc.html`
- Intranet Solutions: `home.netscape.com/comprod/at_work/index.html`
- Intranut: `www.intranut.com`
- The Complete Intranet Resource: `www.intrack.com/intranet`
- Intranet Research Links: `sd.znet.com/~zoro/is698/index.html`
- Microsoft Intranet Solutions Center: `www.microsoft.com/intranet`

Magazines

Many monthly and weekly computer industry magazines devote sections to the discussion of intranet-related issues and topics. Magazines are a great way to stay in touch with and on top of the constantly changing world of intranet technologies. Many of these magazines even offer free subscriptions to qualified individuals! And now that you've read this book and can consider yourself qualified, how can you turn down free information? Stop at the magazines' Web sites for more information. Some of the more popular magazines that devote coverage to intranet issues include

- **CIO.** Monthly guide to executive-level information technology issues: `www.cio.com`
- **Info World.** Regular coverage of networking and intranet-related issues: `www.infoworld.com`

✔ **Information Week.** Weekly in-depth coverage of technology-related issues for business and technology managers: www.informationweek.com

✔ **Inter@active Week.** Weekly coverage of the Internet, intranets, and networking technology: www.interactive-week.com

✔ **Internet Week.** Formerly known as *Communcations Week;* offers in-depth weekly coverage of networking and communications issues: www.comweek.com

✔ **Internet World.** Monthly coverage of Internet- and intranet-related issues: www.iw.com

✔ **Java Developers Journal.** In-depth monthly analysis of Java development issues: www.javadevelopersjournal.com

✔ **LANTimes.** Weekly coverage of Local Area Networking issues: www.lantimes.com

✔ **Microsoft Interactive Developer.** Monthly coverage of development issues using Microsoft-related tools and products: www.microsoft.com/mind

✔ **Network Computing.** Coverage of corporate networking issues: techweb.cmp.com/nc/docs

✔ **Network World.** Weekly coverage of networking and enterprise computing issues: www.nwfusion.com

✔ **PC Magazine.** Bi-weekly coverage of PC-related issues: www.pcmag.com

✔ **PC Week.** Weekly coverage of PC- and PC-related networking topics: www.pcweek.com

✔ **Web Master.** Monthly executive-level guide to the use of the Web in your business: www.web-master.com

✔ **Web Week.** Weekly coverage of Internet- and intranet-related web development issues: www.webweek.com

✔ **Windows NT Magazine.** Monthly in-depth coverage of Windows NT-related issues: www.winntmag.com

✔ **Windows Magazine.** Monthly in-depth coverage of Windows 95- and NT-related issues, networking, and applications: www.winmag.com

Appendix C
What's on the CD?

*I*n this appendix, you find information on the CD-ROM including such programs as:

- ✔ Claris Home Page 2.0 Trial and Adobe PageMill 2.0 Tryout; demos of the popular web page creation programs
- ✔ FirstClass Intranet Client and Server software for Windows
- ✔ WinZip, a popular shareware file compression utility
- ✔ WildCat! Personal Interactive Net Server, a free version of the powerful server program

System Requirements

Make sure that your computer meets the minimum system requirements listed below. If your computer doesn't match up to most of these requirements, you may have problems using the contents of the CD.

- ✔ A PC with a 486 or faster processor
- ✔ Microsoft Windows 95 or Windows NT 4.0 or later
- ✔ At least 16MB of RAM installed on your computer
- ✔ At least 200MB of hard drive space available to install all the software from this CD. (You need less space if you don't install every program.)
- ✔ A CD-ROM drive — double-speed (2x) or faster
- ✔ A sound card
- ✔ A monitor capable of displaying at least 256 colors or grayscale
- ✔ A modem with a speed of at least 14,400 bps (necessary only if you plan to use the software in a typical Internet connection)

If you need more information on the basics, check out *PCs For Dummies,* 5th Edition, by Dan Gookin; *Windows 95 For Dummies,* or *Windows NT For Dummies* by Andy Rathbone (all published by IDG Books Worldwide, Inc.).

How to Use the CD

To install a program from the CD to your hard drive, follow these steps:

1. **Insert the CD into your computer's CD-ROM drive and close the drive door.**

2. **Click Start⇨Run.**

3. **In the dialog box that appears, type the command line provided with the program's description in the "What You'll Find" section in this appendix.**

   The command lines listed with the software descriptions in this appendix assume that your CD-ROM drive is shown as drive D: in the My Computer window. Be sure to type in the correct letter if your drive letter is different.

4. **Press OK to start installation, and follow the on-screen instructions.**

Optionally, if you're handy with My Computer mode or Windows Explorer mode, you can open the program folder on the CD that interests you, and double-click the SETUP or INSTALL icon you find to start installation.

What You'll Find

The programs on the CD can help you evaluate your intranet client and server software needs. Because some of these programs are trial versions, they may not be very useful for long, but at least you get a taste of the cool stuff that's out there. A few of these programs are fully functional and free to use (what a bargain!).

Adobe Acrobat Reader 3.0

The free Acrobat Reader, from Adobe Systems Incorporated, lets you view and print documents created in Portable Document Format (PDF). A PDF document is created with (you guessed it) Adobe Acrobat 3.0, a commercially available program from Adobe. PDF documents retain the formatting and graphics of the original document, and allow for easy distribution over an intranet or the Internet. This feature can be handy when distributing complex charts, publication proofs, and other highly formatted documents that you want to keep in their original form. In fact, the FirstClass and Eudora Light programs on this CD include PDF documents that you can open to see what the fuss is all about. More information about this and other Adobe products can be found at www.adobe.com on the World Wide Web.

To install with the Windows Run command, type

D:\ACROBAT\AR32E30.EXE

Adobe PageMill 2.0 Tryout

Adobe PageMill 2.0 is the premier web page design program for the Mac, and now it's available for Windows 95. This tryout version limits its features or abilities. More details about the program can be found at the Adobe Systems Web site at www.adobe.com.

To install with the Windows Run command, type

D:\PAGEMILL\INSTALL.EXE

Allaire HomeSite 2.5 Trial

If you're comfortable with HTML programming, you may want to try HomeSite, a nifty HTML editor with strong tools to make coding easier. This trial version limits its features or abilities. More details about the program can be found at the Allaire Web site at www.allaire.com.

To install with the Windows Run command, type

D:\HOMESITE\HS25SET.EXE

Claris Home Page 2.0 Trial

Claris Home Page 2.0 is a commercially-available web page design program that makes creating a web site easier, as long as you have a little knowledge of HTML. This trial version is fully functional up to 30 days after you install it. More details about the program can be found at the Claris Corporation Web site at www.claris.com.

To install with the Windows Run command, type

D:\HOMEPAGE\CHPDEMO.EXE

Eudora Light 3.0.2

Eudora Light is the less-powerful sibling to Eudora Pro, the powerful commercially available e-mail program from Qualcomm, Inc. While Eudora Light isn't as powerful, its price is right: free. More information about this program can be found at www.eudora.com on the World Wide Web.

A PDF version of the program's manual for this program is included in the EUDORA folder. You need to install Adobe Acrobat Reader (also included on this CD) on your computer in order to read it.

To install Eudora Light with the Windows Run command, type

D:\EUDORA\EUL302.EXE

FirstClass Intranet Server Demo

FirstClass Intranet Server is a very capable Internet and intranet messaging system that provides a myriad of support and services for Windows and Mac OS systems. This demo version for Windows limits its features or abilities. More details about the program can be found in the ABOUT_FC.PDF document in the FCIS folder (you need to install Acrobat Reader, included with the CD). Or, visit the SoftArc Web site at www.softarc.com.

To install with the Windows Run command, type

D:\FCIS\FCISDEMO.EXE

Microsoft Internet Explorer 3.0.2

Internet Explorer 3.0.2 offers some of the most innovative features available for browsing the Internet Web and your intranet web. This free program also includes an e-mail and newsgroup program, and other nifty additions. More details about the program can be found at the Microsoft Corporation Web site at www.microsoft.com.

To install the version for Windows 95 with the Run command, type

D:\MSIE\IE302M95.EXE

If you use Windows NT, type

D:\MSIE\IE302MNT.EXE

Pegasus Mail

Pegasus Mail, from David Harris, offers strong e-mail services for Windows 95 and Windows NT users. Best of all, it's free. More details and updates to this program can be found at the Pegasus Mail Web site at www.pegasus.usa.com.

To install with the Windows Run command, type

D:\PEGASUS\W32-254.EXE

Wildcat! Interactive Net Server, Personal Edition

Mustang Software's Wildcat! Interactive Net Server (WINS) provides strong Internet and intranet services to users. WINS serves as a Web, FTP, Telnet, and SMTP/POP3 e-mail server, and also gives webmasters and system administrators some powerful capabilities for interactive web content and threaded messaging.

This personal edition of WINS is fully functional and free to use, but allows access to only two users at one time for the messaging, file, chat, and other interactive client systems, and cannot support WINS add-on programs. More details and updates to this program can be found at the Mustang Software Web site at www.mustang.com.

To install with the Windows Run command, type

D:\WILDCAT\WCPERSNL.EXE

WinZip 6.2

Many of the programs mentioned in this book can be downloaded as *zipped archives,* meaning that they are compressed (made smaller) for easy Internet transmission, and need to be uncompressed after you download them. This section provides some information on "unzipping" these Zip archives with WinZip, a shareware program from Nico Mak Computing. WinZip is included on the CD, or you can pick up WinZip and more information about the program from www.winzip.com.

To install WinZip with the Windows Run command, type

D:\WINZIP95.EXE

To extract the contents of a ZIP archive, follow these steps:

1. **Click Start⇨Programs⇨WinZip.**
2. **Click the Open button.**

    A File open dialog appears.

3. **Select the ZIP archive you downloaded.**

4. **Click OK.**

   The WinZip window shows the files that the ZIP archive contains.

5. **Click the Extract button.**

   You are given a choice of directories in which to put your extracted files.

6. **Select or create a directory in which to put your extracted files.**

7. **Click OK.**

   You can now go through the installation steps for the software you downloaded.

If You've Got Problems (Of the CD Kind)

I've tried my best to compile programs that work on most computers with the minimum system requirements. Alas, your computer may differ, and some programs may not work properly for some reason.

The two likeliest problems are that you don't have enough memory (RAM) for the programs you want to use, or you have other programs running that are affecting installation or running of a program. If you get error messages like `Not enough memory` or `Setup cannot continue`, try one or more of these methods and then try using the software again:

- **Temporarily turn off any anti-virus software that you have on your computer.** Installers sometimes mimic virus activity and may make your computer incorrectly believe that it is being infected by a virus.

- **Close all running programs.** The more programs you're running, the less memory is available to other programs. Installers also typically update files and programs, so if you keep other programs running, installation may not work properly.

- **Have your local computer store add more RAM to your computer.** This is, admittedly, a drastic and somewhat expensive step. However, if you have a Windows 95 or NT system, adding more memory can really help the speed of your computer and allow more programs to run at the same time.

If you still have trouble with installing the items from the CD, please call the IDG Books Worldwide Customer Service phone number: 800-762-2974 (outside the U.S.: 317-596-5261).

Index

• *I* •

• *W* •

• X •

• Z •

Notes

Notes

Notes

IDG Books Worldwide, Inc., End-User License Agreement

READ THIS. You should carefully read these terms and conditions before opening the software packet(s) included with this book ("Book"). This is a license agreement ("Agreement") between you and IDG Books Worldwide, Inc. ("IDGB"). By opening the accompanying software packet(s), you acknowledge that you have read and accept the following terms and conditions. If you do not agree and do not want to be bound by such terms and conditions, promptly return the Book and the unopened software packet(s) to the place you obtained them for a full refund.

1. **License Grant.** IDGB grants to you (either an individual or entity) a nonexclusive license to use one copy of the enclosed software program(s) (collectively, the "Software") solely for your own personal or business purposes on a single computer (whether a standard computer or a workstation component of a multiuser network). The Software is in use on a computer when it is loaded into temporary memory (RAM) or installed into permanent memory (hard disk, CD-ROM, or other storage device). IDGB reserves all rights not expressly granted herein.

2. **Ownership.** IDGB is the owner of all right, title, and interest, including copyright, in and to the compilation of the Software recorded on the disk(s) or CD-ROM ("Software Media"). Copyright to the individual programs recorded on the Software Media is owned by the author or other authorized copyright owner of each program. Ownership of the Software and all proprietary rights relating thereto remain with IDGB and its licensers.

3. **Restrictions on Use and Transfer.**

   (a) You may only (i) make one copy of the Software for backup or archival purposes, or (ii) transfer the Software to a single hard disk, provided that you keep the original for backup or archival purposes. You may not (i) rent or lease the Software, (ii) copy or reproduce the Software through a LAN or other network system or through any computer subscriber system or bulletin-board system, or (iii) modify, adapt, or create derivative works based on the Software.

   (b) You may not reverse engineer, decompile, or disassemble the Software. You may transfer the Software and user documentation on a permanent basis, provided that the transferee agrees to accept the terms and conditions of this Agreement and you retain no copies. If the Software is an update or has been updated, any transfer must include the most recent update and all prior versions.

4. **Restrictions on Use of Individual Programs.** You must follow the individual requirements and restrictions detailed for each individual program in the "What's On the CD?" section of this Book. These limitations are also contained in the individual license agreements recorded on the Software Media. These limitations may include a requirement that after using the program for a specified period of time, the user must pay a registration fee or discontinue use. By opening the Software packet(s), you will be agreeing to abide by the licenses and restrictions for these individual programs that are detailed in the "What's On the CD?" section and on the Software Media. None of the material on this Software Media or listed in this Book may ever be redistributed, in original or modified form, for commercial purposes.

5. **Limited Warranty.**

   (a) IDGB warrants that the Software and Software Media are free from defects in materials and workmanship under normal use for a period of sixty (60) days from the date of purchase of this Book. If IDGB receives notification within the warranty period of defects in materials or workmanship, IDGB will replace the defective Software Media.

   (b) **IDGB AND THE AUTHOR OF THE BOOK DISCLAIM ALL OTHER WARRANTIES, EXPRESS OR IMPLIED, INCLUDING WITHOUT LIMITATION IMPLIED WARRANTIES OF MERCHANTABILITY AND FITNESS FOR A PARTICULAR PURPOSE, WITH RESPECT TO THE SOFTWARE, THE PROGRAMS, THE SOURCE CODE CONTAINED THEREIN, AND/OR THE TECHNIQUES DESCRIBED IN THIS BOOK. IDGB DOES NOT WARRANT THAT THE FUNCTIONS CONTAINED IN THE SOFTWARE WILL MEET YOUR REQUIREMENTS OR THAT THE OPERATION OF THE SOFTWARE WILL BE ERROR FREE.**

   (c) This limited warranty gives you specific legal rights, and you may have other rights that vary from jurisdiction to jurisdiction.

6. **Remedies.**

   (a) IDGB's entire liability and your exclusive remedy for defects in materials and workmanship shall be limited to replacement of the Software Media, which may be returned to IDGB with a copy of your receipt at the following address: Software Media Fulfillment Department, Attn.: *Building an Intranet For Dummies*, IDG Books Worldwide, Inc., 7260 Shadeland Station, Ste. 100, Indianapolis, IN 46256, or call 800-762-2974. Please allow three to four weeks for delivery. This Limited Warranty is void if failure of the Software Media has resulted from accident, abuse, or misapplication. Any replacement Software Media will be warranted for the remainder of the original warranty period or thirty (30) days, whichever is longer.

   (b) In no event shall IDGB or the author be liable for any damages whatsoever (including without limitation damages for loss of business profits, business interruption, loss of business information, or any other pecuniary loss) arising from the use of or inability to use the Book or the Software, even if IDGB has been advised of the possibility of such damages.

   (c) Because some jurisdictions do not allow the exclusion or limitation of liability for consequential or incidental damages, the above limitation or exclusion may not apply to you.

7. **U.S. Government Restricted Rights.** Use, duplication, or disclosure of the Software by the U.S. Government is subject to restrictions stated in paragraph (c)(1)(ii) of the Rights in Technical Data and Computer Software clause of DFARS 252.227-7013, and in subparagraphs (a) through (d) of the Commercial Computer–Restricted Rights clause at FAR 52.227-19, and in similar clauses in the NASA FAR supplement, when applicable.

8. **General.** This Agreement constitutes the entire understanding of the parties and revokes and supersedes all prior agreements, oral or written, between them and may not be modified or amended except in a writing signed by both parties hereto that specifically refers to this Agreement. This Agreement shall take precedence over any other documents that may be in conflict herewith. If any one or more provisions contained in this Agreement are held by any court or tribunal to be invalid, illegal, or otherwise unenforceable, each and every other provision shall remain in full force and effect.

Installation Instructions

· ·

For information on installing software from the CD-ROM included with this book, see Appendix C.

IDG BOOKS WORLDWIDE REGISTRATION CARD

Visit our
Web site at
http://www.idgbooks.com

ISBN Number: 0-7645-0276-X

Title of this book: Building an Intranet For Dummies ®

My overall rating of this book: ❑ Very good [1] ❑ Good [2] ❑ Satisfactory [3] ❑ Fair [4] ❑ Poor [5]

How I first heard about this book:

❑ Found in bookstore; name: [6]

❑ Advertisement: [8]

❑ Word of mouth; heard about book from friend, co-worker, etc.: [10]

❑ Book review: [7]

❑ Catalog: [9]

❑ Other: [11]

What I liked most about this book:

What I would change, add, delete, etc., in future editions of this book:

Other comments:

Number of computer books I purchase in a year: ❑ 1 [12] ❑ 2-5 [13] ❑ 6-10 [14] ❑ More than 10 [15]

I would characterize my computer skills as: ❑ Beginner [16] ❑ Intermediate [17] ❑ Advanced [18] ❑ Professional [19]

I use ❑ DOS [20] ❑ Windows [21] ❑ OS/2 [22] ❑ Unix [23] ❑ Macintosh [24] ❑ Other: [25]

(please specify)

I would be interested in new books on the following subjects:

(please check all that apply, and use the spaces provided to identify specific software)

❑ Word processing: [26]

❑ Data bases: [28]

❑ File Utilities: [30]

❑ Networking: [32]

❑ Other: [34]

❑ Spreadsheets: [27]

❑ Desktop publishing: [29]

❑ Money management: [31]

❑ Programming languages: [33]

I use a PC at (please check all that apply): ❑ home [35] ❑ work [36] ❑ school [37] ❑ other: [38]

The disks I prefer to use are ❑ 5.25 [39] ❑ 3.5 [40] ❑ other: [41]

I have a CD ROM: ❑ yes [42] ❑ no [43]

I plan to buy or upgrade computer hardware this year: ❑ yes [44] ❑ no [45]

I plan to buy or upgrade computer software this year: ❑ yes [46] ❑ no [47]

Name: Business title: [48]   Type of Business: [49]

Address (❑ home [50] ❑ work [51]/Company name:

Street/Suite#

City [52]/State [53]/Zip code [54]:   Country [55]

❑ **I liked this book!** You may quote me by name in future
IDG Books Worldwide promotional materials.

My daytime phone number is _____

IDG
BOOKS
WORLDWIDE

THE WORLD OF
COMPUTER
KNOWLEDGE®

❑ # YES!

Please keep me informed about IDG Books Worldwide's World of Computer Knowledge. Send me your latest catalog.

INFO WORLD
TECHNICAL BOOKS

...FOR DUMMIES ™

BESTSELLING BOOK SERIES FROM IDG

...SECRETS®

3-D Visual

Macworld® Books
